RACE AND ETHNICITY IN ARKANSAS

Race and Ethnicity in Arkansas
New Perspectives

Edited by John A. Kirk

Fayetteville
The University of Arkansas Press
2014

Copyright © 2014 by The University of Arkansas Press
All rights reserved
Manufactured in the United States of America
ISBN-10: 1-55728-665-5
ISBN-13: 978-1-55728-665-9

18 17 16 15 14   5 4 3 2 1

Designed by Liz Lester

♾ The paper used in this publication meets the minimum requirements of the American National Standard for Permanence of Paper for Printed Library Materials Z39.48–1984.

LIBRARY OF CONGRESS CONTROL NUMBER: 2014951005

CONTENTS

Acknowledgments — vii

Introduction — xi

Part I: From Slavery to Freedom—New Perspectives on the African American Experience in Arkansas

1. Black and White on Slavery's Frontier:
   The Slave Experience in Arkansas — 3
   KELLY HOUSTON JONES

2. Race and the Struggle for Freedom:
   African American Arkansans after Emancipation — 17
   CARL H. MONEYHON

3. "Send Forth More Laborers into the Vineyard":
   Understanding the African American Exodus
   to Arkansas — 31
   STORY MATKIN-RAWN

Part II: New Perspectives on White Violence

4. Sundown Towns:
   Racial Cleansing in the Arkansas Delta — 49
   GUY LANCASTER

5. Race, History, and Memory in Harrison, Arkansas:
   An Ozarks Town Reckons with Its Past — 61
   JACQUELINE FROELICH

6. The Twenty-One Deaths Caused by the 1959 Fire at the
   Arkansas Negro Boys Industrial School: An Isolated
   Case of "Neglect" or an Instance of Racial Violence? — 71
   GRIF STOCKLEY

Part III: New Perspectives on African American Activism

7. Empowering Families and Communities: African American Home Demonstration Agents in Arkansas, 1913–1965   85
CHERISSE JONES-BRANCH

8. It Should Be More Than Just a Simple Shout: The Life of Elias Camp ("E. C.") Morris   97
CALVIN WHITE

9. Civil Rights Inactivism: Richard Nathaniel Hogan and the "Enemies of Righteousness"   111
BARCLAY KEY

Part IV: From *Braceros* and Refugees to Citizens— New Perspectives on the Latina/o and Asian Experience in Arkansas

10. The Bracero Program: Mexican Workers in the Arkansas Delta, 1948–1964   125
JULIE M. WEISE

11. A Tenuous Welcome for Latinas/os and Asians: States' Rights Discourse in Late Twentieth-Century Arkansas   141
PERLA M. GUERRERO

12. Soy el Jefe: How Hispanic Entrepreneurs Are Changing the Economic Landscape of Northeast Arkansas   153
MELANY BOWMAN

Notes   165

Contributors   197

Index   201

ACKNOWLEDGMENTS

The twelve essays in this collection grew out of the conference Race and Ethnicity: New Perspectives on the African American and Latina/o Experience in Arkansas, sponsored by the University of Arkansas at Little Rock (UALR) History Department, the UALR Center for Arkansas History and Culture (CAHC), the Central Arkansas Library System (CALS), and the Butler Center for Arkansas Studies.

The conference was part of a Rockefeller Centennial Celebration to mark the one-hundredth anniversary of the birth of Gov. Winthrop Rockefeller, Arkansas's first Republican governor since Reconstruction, who served two terms in office from 1967 to 1971. Rockefeller arrived in Arkansas in 1953 with an already established interest in race and ethnicity. The grandson of Standard Oil magnate John D. Rockefeller, Winthrop spent early boyhood holidays at the African American Hampton Institute in Virginia and played an active role on the executive board of the National Urban League while living in New York. In Arkansas, he established a cattle-farming ranch atop Petit Jean Mountain just outside of Morrilton (about sixty miles northwest of the state capital of Little Rock) and put his old friend from New York, African American Jimmy Hudson, in charge as manager. As governor, Rockefeller played an important role in shaping better race relations within Arkansas and promoted a number of African Americans into state offices, including William "Sonny" Walker, the first state director of the Office of Economic Opportunity in the South. In the wake of Martin Luther King Jr.'s assassination in 1968, Rockefeller was the only southern governor to hold a memorial service on the steps of the state capitol in tribute to the slain civil rights leader.

I am grateful to Deborah Baldwin, dean of the UALR College of Arts, Humanities, and Social Sciences and associate provost of CAHC, and to Winthrop Rockefeller Institute's Christy Carpenter, co-chair of the Winthrop Rockefeller Centennial Coalition Executive Committee, for conference funding. I also thank Bobby Roberts, head of CALS, and David Stricklin, head of the Butler Center for Arkansas Studies, for their support. CALS sponsored a conference plenary talk by Douglas Blackmon, author of *Slavery by Another Name: The Re-enslavement of Black Americans from the Civil War to World War II*, through its J. N. Heiskell Distinguished Lecturer series. Blackmon, an Arkansas native, provided the perfect launch for the conference, and I am delighted to acknowledge his contribution to proceedings. Two trusty assistants provided valuable help in coordinating conference logistics: Rebecca (Rivka) Kuperman, from the dean's office, and Andrea Ringer, then a student in UALR's master's program in public history and now a successful graduate.

Four moderators chaired the four conference panels and kept people on time and in order. My thanks for their willingness to participate go to Adjoa Aiyetoro, inaugural director of the UALR Institute on Race and Ethnicity and associate professor of law at the UALR William H. Bowen School of Law; Ranko Shiraki Oliver, associate professor of law at the UALR William H. Bowen School of Law; David Stricklin, head of the Butler Center for Arkansas Studies; and Sherece West-Scantlebury, president and CEO of the Winthrop Rockefeller Foundation. Jay Barth, M. E. and Ima Graves Peace Distinguished Professor of Politics at Hendrix College, provided the conference's closing remarks. I am also thankful to the authors of the essays in this volume for giving up their time to attend the conference, lending their expertise, providing stimulating and convivial company throughout one long day and two evenings of conference activities, and having the staying power to make it through countless emails, suggestions, and queries from the editor as the conference collection came together.

Finally, the UALR Chancellor's Committee on Race and Ethnicity warrants a mention. Since 2006 UALR chancellor Joel Anderson has led weekly Monday afternoon discussions during semesters about issues related to race and ethnicity in Arkansas, the South, and the nation. The voluntarily attended group is made up of faculty, staff, and students and represents an open forum for anyone in the university who wishes to attend. I became part of the committee when I arrived at UALR in 2010, and I have found it a useful and supportive sounding board for my own ideas and a valuable peer group to learn from. In 2011, UALR's Institute on Race and Ethnicity grew out of the committee to provide a more formal structure to, as its mission statement says, "remember and understand the past, inform and engage the present, and shape and define the future" on issues of racial and ethnic justice. Among its projects, the institute has established the Arkansas Civil Rights Heritage Trail in downtown Little Rock to publicly commemorate the many unsung civil rights heroes in the state. All of this is befitting of UALR, whose stated goal is to be "keeper of the flame" on race in the city, whose African American student population is the largest of any higher-education institution in the state, and which is located in a majority nonwhite state capital.

INTRODUCTION

The Little Rock school crisis attracted international headlines in September 1957 and made Arkansas's capital city synonymous with images of racial hatred around the world. Gov. Orval Faubus's use of the Arkansas National Guard to prevent the court-ordered integration of nine black students, who collectively became known as the Little Rock Nine, with two thousand white students at Central High School eventually forced President Dwight D. Eisenhower to act by federalizing state troops and sending in federal soldiers to protect the black students. Quite rightly, the school crisis has attracted a good deal of scholarly and popular attention, but it has also had the unfortunate effect of eclipsing the full richness and diversity of Arkansas's experiences with race and ethnicity. Not until relatively recently have studies begun to emerge that move beyond the school crisis to examine the many other episodes that have shaped the state's racial and ethnic history. Many of those studies have been or are being written by the contributors to this collection. This volume spotlights their research, which is an essential part of the process of uncovering and rethinking racial and ethnic relations in the state and how they continue to shape it today.

The essays in part 1 deal with the experiences of African Americans in Arkansas in three critical periods of state history: slavery, emancipation, and the post-Reconstruction era. Kelly Houston Jones argues that in Arkansas, a state that straddled the slave South and the western frontier, the African American experience of slavery was "fluid and varied." In the northwestern half of the state, bordering Oklahoma and Missouri, some slaves, Jones points out, were armed by their masters for hunting purposes, something that plantation owners in the Arkansas Delta would never have allowed for fear of a slave revolt. Even within the more familiar and limiting experience of slavery in the Arkansas Delta, slaves developed "cultures of resistance" that were manifested in slowdowns, breaks in work when overseers were not looking, "truancy" (that is, brief runaway excursions), and in usurping the authority of white mistresses in running households. Some took more drastic measures, such as running away to freedom across large distances or, more directly, killing their masters. Of course, not all slaves were able to use the frontier experience or to exercise agency to their advantage in all places and at all times. But the possibility of leveraging their circumstances to exercise some control in the overwhelmingly exploitative situations they faced did exist.

Carl H. Moneyhon's essay shows that emancipation posed new issues for freedmen and their former masters. For freedmen, the question was no longer how to resist slavery but how to lay claim to a freedom that they had previously never been permitted to experience. For former masters, the question was how to reconcile the new African American freedom with the same needs that their enforced labor had previously met. Seeking to shape their own destiny, a number of African Americans moved from rural to urban areas in search of new opportunities and safety in numbers. They actively pursued education in an effort to prevent themselves and their children from being swindled out of their newly gained liberty. For those who stayed in the countryside, land ownership as a route to economic independence became a central goal. Meanwhile, whites debated the potential capacities of freedmen. Were former slaves incapable of operating in white society because of their supposed inherent racial inferiority, or was the debilitating historical experience of slavery a shackle that could be undone? Moneyhon determines that the former view triumphed over the latter because of economic and political developments that made continued racism the more expedient choice.

Story Matkin-Rawn expands further on the themes of Arkansas's still frontier-like status and nascent white racism through the post-Reconstruction period. It was, Matkin-Rawn asserts, the promise of higher wages that might (and often did) lead to land ownership that drew African Americans to the state despite the steadily worsening political and civil conditions. The fact that black Arkansans clung onto the gains of Reconstruction longer than those in many other states and that they encountered relatively less open hostility and violence also leant encouragement to new arrivals. Yet the initial hope and optimism soon began to disappear in the 1890s as disfranchisement and Jim Crow laws spread to Arkansas from other southern states. This, added to economic and environmental factors, helped to gradually slow the tide of African American migration.

The essays in part 2 look at various expressions of white violence in twentieth-century Arkansas. Guy Lancaster explores the phenomenon of "sundown towns," those places where whites either ran off existing black populations or refused to allow them to settle there in the first place. Lancaster locates the rise of sundown towns within the wider context of the rise in white vigilantism in turn-of-the-century Arkansas, much of which was aimed at ridding or defending areas from what was now perceived as a surplus of black labor and too much black landownership that provided unwelcome competition for whites. Though historians have often tended to focus on extreme episodes of violence perpetrated against particular individuals, as witnessed in the burgeoning studies of lynching, racial violence manifested itself in a variety of ways with a variety of consequences, all of which, Lancaster argues, warrant attention for their different practices and purposes.

Jacqueline Froelich's essay examines harrowing accounts of racial cleansing in Harrison, Arkansas, in the first decade of the twentieth century, when two outbreaks of violence led to the African American population being expelled. The memory of Harrison's hostility to African Americans still persists today and has attracted white supremacist residents. However, the town's reputation is now causing economic harm since large companies that have located there face difficulties in attracting a diverse workforce and are threatening to leave. The Harrison Race Reconciliation Task Force has been set up to tackle the city's image problem. Within the space of a hundred years, the city that rejected harmonious race relations to get rid of its minority population, and along with it competition for white jobs, has come full circle as it begins to promote harmonious race relations to make it more attractive for minorities to settle there in order to retain the companies that provide white jobs.

Grif Stockley asks that we consider the structural nature of white violence. He tells the story of a fire that broke out at Arkansas Boys Industrial School in 1959, in Wrightsville, twelve miles south of Little Rock, which caused the deaths of twenty-one black boys, and asks, Who is to blame? Outside observers at the time rounded on the "Jim Crow system." White Arkansans insisted that it had "nothing to do with the social and political system that prevailed at the time." To them, it represented an unfortunate incident of benign neglect and individual error. Stockley points out that the black boys were in the school because they had been put there by white judges elected under a racially biased political system; that the school, because of explicitly racial considerations, suffered long-standing neglect of its facilities and was delinquent in its care to its charges; that living conditions were deplorable and corporal punishments severe because of the indifference of a white superintendent and a white state board of education; and that, ultimately, if the facility had been properly staffed, the twenty-one dead boys may well instead have survived.

The essays in part 3 examine varieties of African American activism in Arkansas that all differ from traditional concepts of civil rights activism as popularly imagined in the movement's heyday of the 1950s and 1960s. Cherisse Jones-Branch looks at the work of African American home demonstration agents. Employed by the Agricultural Extension Service (AES), home demonstration agents played a vital role in providing support to rural black families, despite the segregated and underfunded climate they operated in. Husband-and-wife team Harvey C. Ray and Mary McCrary Ray filled the positions as the first US Extension Service agent and first black home demonstration agent, respectively, in Arkansas. Demonstrating the enduring continuities and multifaceted connections of African American activism in Arkansas, Harvey Ray's daughter from a later marriage, Gloria Ray, later became one of the Little Rock Nine students to desegregate Central High School. Home demonstration agents were an early federally funded outlet for African American support and betterment in often-impoverished black families and communities. They also provided centers and networks of mutual help and contact upon which later civil rights activists built.

Calvin White follows the career of Elias Camp "E. C." Morris. At the turn of the twentieth century, when mainstream participation in the civil rights movement by the black church was still many decades away, Morris, according to White, "envisioned black religion aiding in the establishment of black education, business, and even serving as a machine to elect black officials." Morris arrived in Helena, Arkansas, in March 1877. He quickly rose through community ranks and became head of Centennial Baptist Church at the age of twenty-four. In 1880, he was elected as secretary of the black Arkansas Baptist State Convention and, soon after, as its leader. Just a few years later, Morris was elected as president of the National Baptist Convention (NBC). As NBC president, Morris founded a Baptist publishing house, "creating thousands of jobs and generating wealth for the black community." He was also active in politics as a staunch Republican who argued for black voting rights.

Barclay Key focuses on what he terms Church of Christ preacher Richard Nathaniel Hogan's civil rights "inactivism." The Arkansas-born Hogan enjoyed a prominent career in a southern church that was predominantly white, regularly preaching by invitation at black and white churches during the age of Jim Crow. Key asserts that while Hogan was not explicitly concerned with civil rights in the way that we traditionally understand and define that particular brand of activism, nevertheless, his religious message chimed with many of the movement's aims and goals. This dual nature of not attacking Jim Crow head on or voicing explicit support for the civil rights movement, but still attacking the consequences of Jim Crow as un-Christ-like and implicitly supporting the stated aims of the movement, was a mainstay throughout Hogan's career. Key cites Hogan as an important example of the too often overlooked band of African Americans who fought against discrimination not from within the movement but on their own terms and in their own ways—in Hogan's case, through a religious commitment via pulpit and pen.

The essays in part 4 concentrate on the Latina/o and Asian experience in postwar Arkansas. The Latino population has soared in Arkansas in recent years, making it a significant new part of the ongoing dialogue about race and ethnicity in the state. Between 2000 and 2010, Latino numbers in the state doubled; and now at over 186,000, Latinos make up 6.4 percent of Arkansas's population (African Americans account for 15.4 percent of the state population).

Julie M. Weise reminds us that the Latino presence in Arkansas has a long and important history. In the 1940s, 1950s, and 1960s, the United States' Bracero Program brought thousands of Mexican workers into the Arkansas Delta to address labor shortages. Though white landowners welcomed this, Juan Crown and Jim Crow existed side-by-side as Mexican workers suffered from and fought against the prevalent racial and ethnic discrimination of the region. The *bracero* presence in Arkansas challenged that discrimination and the economic exploitation that underpinned it. In this respect, braceros held distinct advantages over the African American population in the delta: they had two governments to appeal to, both in Mexico and in the United States; tactics such as collective bargaining could have a greater impact since braceros could, if they chose to, leave the land and head home (or elsewhere) with greater ease than most black sharecroppers were able to; and as children of the Mexican Revolution, braceros had experienced full citizenship rights for much longer and in different ways than most African American southerners had. One particularly successful bracero-related campaign resulted in the establishment of the first minimum wage for farm workers in the Arkansas Delta, something that had been fiercely resisted in the past and that black and white farmers also benefited from.

Perla M. Guerrero charts the more recent history of Latinas/os and Asians in Arkansas. One entrance point for both groups to the state was Fort Chaffee in Fort Smith, chosen in 1975 as a relocation center for just over two thousand Vietnamese people fleeing their country at the end of the Vietnam War, and then again in 1980 for almost ten times that number of Cubans fleeing Fidel Castro's regime under his "Back Door Policy." Others, mainly Mexican workers, have provided cheap immigrant labor in the chicken factories of northwest Arkansas. Racial and ethnic diversity and economic opportunities for those populations has led to white resentment and resistance. The stigma of the label "illegal immigrants" and how many supposedly reside in the state, Guerrero contends, hovers over all Latino immigrants, illegal or not, and has been used by politicians to make electoral capital out of latent anti-immigrant sentiments in the state. Guerrero points to the long legacy of anti–federal government rhetoric and appeals to states' rights in attempts by Arkansans to control and limit racial and ethnic diversity in the state.

Melany Bowman shifts the focus to Latina/o immigration in northeastern Arkansas, with a specific focus on the university city of Jonesboro and the Latino businesses that are sprouting up there. In this part of the state, jobs in construction and agriculture have been the main draws for Latinos. Some, like the braceros before them, are transitory laborers who come to Arkansas to earn money before returning home. Others have chosen to stay and serve the Latino workforce through businesses such as Mexican restaurants and groceries selling foods and products familiar in Latin America. Phone cards and international money transfer services are likewise popular. Newspapers and magazines that are published in Spanish or directed at a Latino audience are flourishing. These businesses, which form a permanent foundation for a Latino presence, act as points of interaction between members of the Latino community and between the Latino community and the white community, and they provide important conduits in attempts to build better understanding and better community relations.

Collectively, the essays presented here help to broaden and re-contextualize understandings of race and ethnicity in Arkansas. Each essay, like each group of essays, offers its own particular insights. At the same time, dominant and recurrent themes develop across the volume, highlighting how issues of race and ethnicity in the state impact all Arkansans: themes such as land and labor, migration and immigration, freedom and citizenship, civil rights and resistance to civil rights, and the relationship between federal and state authority, to name but a few. In short, the essays demonstrate that the history of race and ethnicity in Arkansas is, in many ways, the history of Arkansas.

PART I

From Slavery to Freedom —New Perspectives on the African American Experience in Arkansas

CHAPTER 1

Black and White on Slavery's Frontier
The Slave Experience in Arkansas

KELLY HOUSTON JONES

VARIATIONS OVER TIME and space are crucial to our understanding of American slavery and have received needed attention in the last decade. Ira Berlin's sweeping treatments, *Many Thousands Gone* and *Generations of Captivity*, provide a bird's-eye view, while works like *Creating an Old South: Middle Florida's Plantation Frontier before the Civil War* by Edward Baptist and *Sold Down the River: Slavery in the Lower Chattahoochee Valley of Alabama and Georgia* by Anthony Gene Carey explore the rapid expansion of slavery in microcosm. But slavery west of the Mississippi River, particularly in Arkansas, remains underrepresented in the historiography. Orville Taylor's *Negro Slavery in Arkansas*, published in 1958, is the only book-length treatment of slavery in Arkansas. Taylor moved away from earlier arguments that slavery was a benign, civilizing institution, but he does not do justice to the negotiation of power between slaves and their masters. While *Negro Slavery in Arkansas* covers slavery's basic development, it all but ignores the point of view of the enslaved and presents the institution as rather static.[1]

The slave point of view has been included, if not specifically targeted for separate study, in recent general histories of Arkansas, such as *Remote and Restless: Arkansas, 1800–1860* and *Arkansas: A Narrative History*, and a few published essays that have also helped to recover some of the story of slaves' agency in Arkansas, but much work is left to do. Focusing mostly on interactions between slaves and whites in the period after statehood and before the Civil War, this essay seeks, first, to present the slave experience in Arkansas as more fluid and varied than in Taylor's portrayal and, second, to emphasize the effect that Arkansas's status as a developing frontier on the southern periphery had on Arkansas's slave society.[2]

Movement was a major part of the frontier slave experience. Slaves undertook an incredible amount of movement, both under coercion and of their own accord. They moved hundreds of miles to, through, and within Arkansas as chattels, pioneers, and fugitives. Slaves found themselves in Arkansas as a result of what historians call the "second middle passage" in the forced migration of hundreds of thousands of slaves west to the fresh cotton lands of the southern interior, a process that has been described as the most formative event in the lives of African American slaves in the nineteenth century. It is estimated that more than 875,000 slaves were removed from the seaboard South to newer cotton states between 1820 and 1860.[3]

As a slave-importing state, Arkansas saw a 136 percent increase in its slave population between 1850 and 1860. By 1860, more than 111,000 slaves resided in Arkansas, owned by more than 11,000 masters.[4] Whites brought their slave property with them or chose from the bodies for sale by slave traders trekking across the Old Southwest. In interviews conducted by the Works Progress Administration (WPA) in the 1930s, many former slaves recall their own and their families' birthplaces east of Arkansas, commonly Virginia, Tennessee, and North Carolina. The second middle passage was not a process limited only to the state's early history of slavery but continued as the major feature of slave life in Arkansas until the demise of the institution.[5]

Historians estimate that around 60 to 70 percent of the forced migration of African American slaves to the cotton frontier took place under the domestic slave trade. New Orleans and Memphis were the two main slave-trading points for Arkansas. Molly Finley's father, for example, was sold in Kentucky to traders and brought to Tennessee, where he was purchased by Baker Jones and taken to Arkansas.[6] But while the majority of the forced migration of African American slaves related to the slave trade, many slaves came to the cotton frontier with white families. In 1837, James Hines Trulock, of a wealthy South Carolina family, moved from southwestern Georgia to Jefferson County, Arkansas. All of Trulock's slaves made the trip except one elderly man, perhaps deemed too weak for the move and work ahead.[7] Bondspeople could also be moved westward when planters expanded their holdings, like seventy-eight slaves who were moved into Chicot County, Arkansas, from Mississippi when elite slaveholder Rice C. Ballard added Wagram Plantation to his extensive westward-growing cotton acreage sometime in the mid-1850s.[8]

Slave migration that took place outside the slave trade per se could mean a greater degree of slave family cohesion but did not guarantee stability. Emma Moore's parents were lucky enough to come from Tennessee to Arkansas together (though it is not known how many loved ones they left behind).[9] The westward migration of whites and their slaves could be prompted by debt, something that was a constant reality for slaveholders. As chattel, enslaved men and women could find themselves whisked away by masters seeking to avoid creditors. In a family financial drama that stretched from the late 1830s into the 1850s, the Holloway family moved from Coosa County, Alabama, to southern Arkansas to avoid creditors, and they took their slaves, including Sam, who was born in Alabama.[10]

William Pond of South Carolina was so terrible with his finances that he sought to protect his wife and children from himself. In 1833, Pond deeded a slave woman named Maria and her children Stephen, Emily, and Harriet in trust for the exclusive use of his wife, Mary Pond, and their children. Possibly at the pleading of his wife, William issued the deed of trust because he sought to protect his family from his cyclical debt problem. "To prevent them from being sold in one of his drinking sprees," Pond issued the deed to a trusted friend. After his wife died, Pond moved hundreds of miles west to Hot Spring County, Arkansas, with his children and Maria. All of her children were able to come along except Stephen, who was left in South Carolina to secure a debt.[11]

Forced relocation to the margins of the South added a greater burden on those who lost connections with family and friends but made the creation of new family and friendship networks that much more important. Slave mobility continued after arrival in Arkansas. Further migration within the state was possible as slaveholders moved, inherited, sold, mortgaged, or gifted slaves. A combination of these forces were at work in 1844, when "old man" John Humphries of Searcy and his sons took a group of slaves down to New Orleans, sold them, brought another group back, and took a man named Bannister north to neighboring Independence County to mortgage for the purchase of a boatload of corn from Morgan Magness. Bannister stayed at Magness's place from February through July.[12]

But slaves sometimes traveled out of their usual neighborhoods in relation to their work. R. C. Ballard routinely moved his carpenters between his plantations in Mississippi and Arkansas as various jobs required their skills.¹³ "Just like a cow would leave a calf," Mary Jane Hardridge bluntly described the necessity of her mother, a domestic worker, to accompany the Scull family on trips away from the plantation. Work in transportation caused slaves to travel for at least short periods. For example, Charles Green Dortch's father (bought in Richmond, Virginia, and taken to Dallas County, Arkansas) may have driven a stage from Arkadelphia to Camden or Princeton. Flan, a slave of George Case (a northern-born merchant in Batesville, Independence County), worked as a cook on the steamboat *Thomas P. Ray* for a couple of weeks in the early 1850s.¹⁴

But whether to escape the work routine, cruel masters, or to reunite with loved ones, slaves engaged in quite a bit of movement on their own accord. Proximity to Indian Territory and geographic isolation provided slaves with chances to run away or to temporarily escape restrictions on their movement to nearby woods or as far away as Canada. While running away usually meant short-term truancy, some slaves went on long journeys in search of freedom. Charles Bolton's work on runaway slaves suggests that Arkansas's slaves may have been more likely to flee long distances because they were generally already well traveled due to the second middle passage. In one of the better-known incidents of long-distance flight, Nelson Hacket (or Hackett) fled a Fayetteville farm owned by Alfred Wallace in the early 1840s. Hacket passed through Kentucky and traveled up the Ohio River into Canada. Because Hacket had taken a horse, a coat, and a gold watch with him, Wallace was able to call for Nelson's extradition for theft. The incident was monitored by the governments of Arkansas, Michigan, the United States, and Canada, as well as by British and American abolitionists. Because Indian Territory was close by for many of Arkansas's slaves, escape to that area outside Arkansas could be an attractive, if dangerous, option for those who wanted to get away for good.¹⁵

Enslaved Arkansans more often ran shorter distances to visit family and friends, to escape work, punishment, or sale, or to simply claim some leisure time, a phenomenon often referred to by historians as truancy.¹⁶ When he realized he was to be sold, a slave owned by partners John A. Harwick and Phillip Costar of Desha County fled Costar's hotel in February 1846. Costar had called the man into the bar of the hotel, where he was looked over by the purchasers, then sent him away while the men settled their accounts. Costar went back and forth over the course of the evening between appeasing his impatient business partners and coaxing the reluctant man to get ready to catch a boat with his new masters. The man resisted because he did not want to leave his wife, and he chose to flee rather than go with the men. Running away permanently would have defeated the man's purpose to stay near his wife. Thus, like many bondspeople, he probably only sought a short-term solution, perhaps hoping his absence would cancel the sale.[17]

Running away could be dangerous, however. Slaves often came back hungry and weakened. Sam, at about twenty-one years old, ran away for several weeks from John A. Lindsay's farm in Powhattan, Lawrence County, in summer 1853 but returned very weak and never fully regained his strength. He eventually died in early fall, a doctor explaining that "excessive fatigue, the exposure undergone by the boy in being out in the woods exposed to the changes and inclemences [sic] of the weather . . . [and] anxiety to which the boy was liable while run away . . . caused the emaciated & debilitated condition" that led to Sam's death.[18]

Sometimes slave flight could fall somewhere in between truancy and total escape. Martha, a domestic servant of R. C. Ballard's, was reportedly "stolen" from Chicot County and turned up in Memphis. After being apprehended, Martha was taken to New Orleans to be sold. While there, Martha reported that her previous "captors" were in the area. She soon disappeared again and was presumed somewhere in Texas with the same white man who had "kidnapped" her before. Martha had alerted whites when another slave in New Orleans named Anthony ran away (perhaps to Natchez) when he was about to be sold to Helena, Arkansas, only to suspiciously disappear herself soon after. Like others, Martha's actions shifted back and forth between resistance and cooperation.[19]

Emphasizing slave mobility widens what Anthony Kaye calls slaves' "terrain of struggle" from immediate neighborhoods outward to reveal a more dynamic slave experience in Arkansas as part of the trans-Mississippi South than Orville Taylor presents. This is not to say that all individual slaves in Arkansas were widely traveled, but that migration and travel, in addition to the fast development of this slave society on the margins of the South, meant that the interplay between slaves and masters took place against a backdrop of shifting landscapes. Mobility touched slave communities as a whole, rather than only those individuals regularly or directly experiencing it. Thus, the communities slaves created for themselves became that much more important.[20]

In addition to movement, masters and slaves in Arkansas interacted and struggled with each other in the arena of work. Slave owners on the frontier expected hard work and efficiency from their labor force in order to make the most out of high cotton prices and fresh land. Plantations that produced much of what was needed on their own grounds made the best profits. On the outskirts of southern society, the opportunity to purchase necessities was not always convenient. Thus, slaveholders tried to make their operations as self-sufficient as possible, "a world within itself," as former slave Henry Turner put it. This meant that there was plenty to do on cotton farms of all sizes and at all times.[21] Plantation journals show very little downtime. Slaveholders were constantly pressing to clear fresh land for cultivation. As soon as any task was ended on the "old ground," it must then begin on the "new ground," after which time newer ground must be cleared to make sure even more acres could be put into cotton next year. And then the cycle would begin again.

Carving out these operations on the cotton frontier and keeping them going, whether large or small, meant hard work in rugged conditions. "Uncle Dock" Wilborn described the work of clearing land for the Wilborn brothers' farms in Phillips County. Whites and blacks camped in tents in the wilderness until log houses could be built. Trees had to be cleared and the resulting logs removed to make way for crops. Molly Finley's father told her about the task of clearing land around the Arkansas River, where slaves "worked in huddles" while overseers stood watch, ready to shoot any "panther, bears, and wildcats" that might make their appearance. The conditions were rugged no matter where in Arkansas whites chose to settle. According to Henry Blake, even Little Rock settlers had to keep fires burning to keep away the wolves and "varmints."[22]

Slaveholders generally assigned tasks and training according to gendered divisions of labor but did not shrink from using any and all labor available when they felt they needed to. In fact, women's resilience under hard labor is a clear source of pride among former slaves interviewed in the 1930s. Although young children and the elderly were unable to perform the most physically demanding work, their tasks were important and there was an expectation that they would be completed in a timely manner.[23] Children would keep needed fires burning, run errands, sweep, gather brush, trash, and rocks from the yard, carry water, feed chickens, milk cows, and carry wood.[24] Older children could also help in the cotton fields by picking or helping to move the sacks or baskets down the rows while adults picked. When old enough, they were assigned a row to pick for themselves. Like children, the elderly were often assigned tasks lighter than fieldwork, although the records show some men over fifty years old doing hard labor. A common and important duty for older women was to watch slave children during the day.[25]

On plantations, generally defined as farms working twenty or more slaves, certain slave women might be designated for housework only. Although these women were kept out of the field, much was demanded of them. In addition, working in the house meant close proximity to whites and could come with a heavier oversight on their activities. Housework meant cooking, sewing, weaving, cleaning, washing clothes, and caring for the white children. Work in kitchens could go on well after 9:00 p.m. In homes without a large enough slave labor force to parse out these tasks, they all fell to the one or two slaves who worked in the home. Molly Hudgens's mother was sold to Judge Allen in North Carolina and brought to Monroe County, Arkansas. Allen's wife had died, and so the responsibilities of Hudgens's mother would have been even greater than in a home with a mistress, though perhaps with less oversight. Molly recalled that her mother's duties included sewing and caring for two other slave children that had been brought into the Allen workforce without their parents. Domestic workers' duties brought them close to whites' lives and bodies. Harriet Daniel, a white woman who had been raised on a plantation in Dallas County, recalled that "we children had never been required to wash our own faces," but that slave women and girls were assigned to do it for them. Planter William Rose would have his cook Mary wash his feet for him.[26] Domestic work did not necessarily mean strictly indoor work, nor did it mean Sundays off. Harriet McFarlin Payne remembered "washday," when a few women would spend the entire day scrubbing clothes to a clean white, possibly gathering the water from a nearby spring. On the Cockrill plantation in Jefferson County, this chore was a Sunday job, to be done every Sunday evening. Hannah Jameson describes the task as taking place well into Sunday nights, by the light of a pine torch, if need be.[27]

For every slave who worked in a white home, scores more toiled in the fields. After their long workdays, which lasted from sunup (or earlier) to sundown (or later), slaves would return to their quarters and fix an evening meal from their weekly rations. But sometimes, after slaves finished their work in the field in the evenings, they set to additional tasks assigned them, such as washing or spinning cloth.[28] Wet or dangerous weather might or might not cause delays. Some slaves were allowed to stop work in the fields in bad weather, though they might have chores to complete under shelter. Lou Fergusson recalled having to work in the fields even in the sleet.[29] While John W. Brown's diary recording the activities of his plantation in Dallas County might record little work done by slaves on some rainy days, other entries revealed hard work in bad weather. In fact, Brown himself complained in 1853 of catching cold while standing watch over slaves at work: "I owe this spell very much to standing out in the new ground all day when the hands were rolling logs and getting my feet cold."[30]

Picking time was crucial on Arkansas's cotton farms and plantations. In 1852, the Brown plantation had harvested about 18,000 pounds of cotton by the end of the second week of October. Brown moved the men from picking to other work in December but kept the women picking well into January 1853.[31] The diary of Maggie Walker Benton of Elmwood, Chicot County, provides a contemporary glimpse into the picking routine. Benton listed the names of slave men and women on a chart that tracked their pounds of cotton picked per day over the course of thirty workdays. In the twenty-nine days that a slave woman named Lithia worked (she was sick one day), she picked 6,752 pounds of cotton, averaging nearly 233 pounds each day. Lithia's numbers were actually a higher total and daily average than those of Bill, who picked the most cotton of all the slave men listed in the record. Bill picked cotton twenty-eight days out of the thirty. He harvested 6,204 pounds total and picked on average 221.5 pounds per workday. This may have been due to Bill's being sent to work other tasks during a couple of the cotton picking days, because his most productive cotton-picking days yielded upwards of 330 pounds, while the least he picked in one day was 140—less than half of what he was capable of. Much of the cotton-picking work must have been shifted to women while men were needed elsewhere on the plantation. Bondspeople knew that they would be at the task until all the cotton was picked and could be driven hard by the whips of masters and overseers.[32]

Masters expected hard work, but bondspeople found ways to alleviate the work routine. These efforts combined to establish a culture of resistance on some places. The slaves on R. C. Ballard's plantation in Chicot County, many of whom were transplanted there from one of his Mississippi operations, seem to have consistently avoided enough work, by faking sickness, running off, or simply sitting down in the shade when he was not looking, that an overseer was fired for his inability to keep them working. In Hempstead County, a neighbor of R. A. Brunson's claimed that an overseer would be justified in asking for more than the usual pay rate on that place because Brunson's slaves were so unruly.[33] Some slaves with special work skills or experience, like blacksmithing or weaving, could receive and capitalize on greater trust or fewer restrictions by whites. At the same time, though, their added value and experience could mean a greater level of attention from masters and overseers. From his letters, we know that Ballard expected detailed reports of the work done by his carpenters and moved them between his plantations that spanned three states as he thought was needed.[34]

Despite forced migration and hard work, slaves sought to carve their own lives and communities out of the slave society on the margins, though some forms of autonomy were harder to come by than others. For example, because population centers were small, few, and far between, it was more difficult, though not impossible, for slaves on the fringes of the cotton frontier to take part in what is known as the slaves' economy. Sources for slavery in Arkansas suggest more limited market activity by slaves than historians have found in other areas of the South.[35] References to the slaves' ability to sell goods of their own production are scarce in the WPA slave narratives of Arkansas. As in many other states, Arkansas law prohibited slaves from buying commodities, especially alcohol, from their masters or from other slaves under any circumstances. The law also barred slaves from hiring out their own time, a practice that would have given slaves disposable income.[36] However, total enforcement of these laws would have been difficult, and they seem not to have been very seriously obeyed most of the time. The few urban areas in Arkansas, such as Little Rock and Fayetteville, provided slaves, and especially those with skills, more access to the market than in places dominated by plantation agriculture. Many slaves in Little Rock were able to use their skills to acquire goods. But only about 3.5 to 4.0 percent of Arkansas's slaves lived in towns.[37] Alcohol was one commodity that slaves seem to have been able to acquire fairly easily in more urban areas, often trading with less affluent whites. The record of indictments against whites for this practice only serves to support the possibility that the practice was widespread. In Pulaski County, fifteen men and women between 1848 and 1863 were charged with selling "ardent spirits" to slaves.[38]

Slave access to commodities like alcohol became a source of contention in western Arkansas, bordering Indian Territory, just before and during the Civil War. In Crawford County, whites kept a closer eye on slaves' handling of cash and liquor. William Powell, a white merchant from the north (born in Ohio), shared a grocery store/dram shop and residence with John Wallace in Van Buren. John, a mulatto slave of Powell's, largely ran the store. John's everyday tasks like bringing water, sweeping, moving stock, and running errands seem not to have been objectionable on their own, although technically illegal, but his unsupervised management of the store and his taking money from customers and assisting them with alcohol purchases were. Powell was charged for employing a slave in a store selling alcohol and forced to pay a fine of seventy-five dollars.[39] Omey, another white northerner (also born in Ohio) living in Crawford County, found himself in quite a bit of trouble for selling two gallons of whiskey to Charles, described as a mulatto owned by wealthy slaveholder Thomas Aldridge of Franklin County. The case, culminating with a final ruling in 1863, like Powell's, might have had more to do with prewar and early wartime tension than with controlling Charles's drinking.[40]

Although life on the southern periphery could limit some autonomy, like access to the market, opportunities for autonomy on the frontier arose in other forms. For example, although allowing slaves to carry weapons would seem to undermine the slave regime, sources show that the carrying of guns by slaves was permitted by those owners who expected their slaves to hunt or to protect themselves, as did Sarah Ridge, owner of thirteen slaves in Benton County (a large holding for that area).[41] Slaves' hunting and fishing supplemented food sources, forged ties in their communities when they shared their bounty, and could endear them to whites who dined on their catches. Betty Brown explained that there was only one slave family on the Nutt farm in Greene County, thus, in addition to other duties, her mother trapped and hunted game.[42] Such tasks must have allowed for some relief for enslaved people, even if that relief was simply getting away from the watchful eyes of whites for a while.

While slaves were known to run away and cause work slowdowns and certainly enjoyed and capitalized on the autonomy that was sometimes a necessary part of life on the southern periphery, they sometimes challenged their masters outright. In the mid-1840s, Mary, a domestic worker for William and Nancy Rose, a planter family of early Chicot County (less than ten years into Arkansas's statehood), became a serious topic in the couple's divorce proceedings due to her disobedience to Nancy. Nancy's legal task was to convince the court that William was a "tyrannical" and unkind husband who disliked her so much that it was impossible for the couple to live together peacefully. As part of her case, Nancy accused her husband of encouraging the slaves, particularly Mary and those who worked in the house, to disobey her. It seems that Mary had been running the Rose house since William moved there in 1839, creating some initial resentment when Nancy arrived in 1841. Mary capitalized on William's disgust with what he saw as the lack of industry in his northern "factory girl for a wife." According to witnesses, William referred to his wife as a "lazy trifling white woman," as opposed to an industrious black woman like Mary. Mary was said to have spoken about poisoning food and would often ignore Nancy's orders, knowing that William would not enforce them. William claimed that Nancy was cruel to the slaves, which, if true, would have only strengthened any resentment harbored by Mary. A witness claimed that Nancy showed bruises on her arm inflicted not by her husband (which surely would have gone further to strengthen Nancy's case) but by Mary. Nancy was afraid that Mary might poison her and sometimes refused to eat her cooking. Mary was able to successfully place herself in supremacy over the mistress of the Rose household, eventually driving Nancy away completely.[43]

Unsurprisingly, in a labor system upheld by physical coercion, sometimes slaves' challenges toward masters turned violent. J. L. Smith, whose father and uncle were enslaved in Monroe County, said his uncle was known to fight so hard that the master's mother took up the task of administering whippings herself because the man was less likely to strike her. With headlines like "Horrible Murder," "Outrageous Murder," or simply "Bad," the stories of masters murdered by slaves were reported with surprise, indignation, and sensationalism by the *Arkansas Gazette*. For example, knowing he would be sold when they arrived, a slave from Benton County killed his master, Anderson, on the way to Fort Smith. Anderson's body (described in gory detail in the *Gazette*) was found in Crawford County, while the slave was sighted back in Fayetteville and chased out of town. To the south, in Lafayette County, two of Thomas Edwards's slaves admitted to killing him and dumping his body in the river.[44]

Clashes between slavery and freedom occurred in more civil ways, too. Enslaved people sometimes took direct steps to free themselves and family members through purchase or legal means. Sometimes this involved a level of trust in whites that was not always rewarded. This was true for Mourning, a Hempstead County bondswoman who risked much in the hope of freeing her child with a white man. Before his death, storeowner James H. Dunn of Hempstead County recognized his paternity of Mourning's daughter Eliza (presumably conceived while she was hired out to him). He apparently made it clear that he wanted to purchase Eliza and manumit her before he died. After Dunn's death, Mourning was living with James Moss and had given him the three hundred dollars that Dunn had entrusted to her to go toward the purchase of Eliza. The money was Mourning's only hope for Eliza's freedom since Dunn's passing, but it was stripped from her as the heirs of Dunn and Moss fought for those estates.[45] Slaves in Arkansas sometimes sued for their freedom when manumitting wills were not upheld by executors of the estates of dead slaveholders or in other circumstances when they thought they had a case.

These suits sometimes exposed the difficulty in legislating concepts of race. In Arkansas and other slave states, if a person was deemed to be black, then he or she was assumed to be a slave unless proven otherwise. A person presumed white was also presumed free. But slaves put these conventions to the test in the courts. A well-known example is the case *Daniel v. Guy*. Sometime in the late 1830s, Abby Guy, born to a mulatto woman named Polly, who died before the journey (and possibly a white father), came from Alabama to Ashley County, Arkansas, with William Daniel and his brother. But around 1844, Abby set up house for herself and her children, Elizabeth Daniel, Mary Daniel, John Guy, and Malissa Arnold, separately from the Daniels. With a light complexion and straight hair, Abby lived as a free white woman, farming along the Bayou Bartholomew. She made her own contracts, paid her own debts, and hired men to do work on her farm. She used her position to board her oldest daughter and pay for her schooling. For some time Abby lived as the wife of a white man with the last name of Guy, though they were not legally married, and he passed some land to her when he died.

Abby and her children moved through their community as white people, socializing and attending church and school as whites with whites. But William Daniel began claiming Abby as a slave after about 1856, causing her to sue for false imprisonment and the freedom of herself and her children in a legal battle that stretched into 1861.

The proceedings of the case demonstrate the difficulty faced by courts when forced to determine a person's race and status, as well as the opportunities that could arise when the frontier offered anonymity. The courts examined Abby's hair, skin color, and nose shape. Abby and her children were even asked to show their bare feet to the jury to be examined for evidence of "blackness." But appearances of whiteness were not the only part of the story. Abby had used her forced relocation to Arkansas to her advantage. She was able to establish her own household, relationship, and social life as a free person and raise her children as free people because her community had never known her as a slave. Her physical features made this possible, to be sure, but the absences of both Abby's slave mother (the main legal indicator of enslaved status) and her master, William's father (James Daniel, who had died years before the move to Arkansas), meant that Abby had room to capitalize on the scattering of the white family in Arkansas. Abby's establishment of herself as a free white woman in her community in Ashley County was so complete that in order to prove Abby's slave origins, the attorneys for Daniel had to call in witnesses who had known Guy and Daniel back in Alabama. Abby eventually won her long legal battle, but she and her children were forced to work as slaves during at least some of the intervening years.[46]

The story of slavery and race in Arkansas is not limited to interactions between slaves and those who claimed ownership of them. Bondspeople socialized, traded, fought, and worked with whites. Slaveholders often made social visits but also stopped by other plantations and farms to check up on the management of crops and slaves on each other's places. Whether they cultivated a record of "good" behavior, armed themselves with an air of toughness, or succeeded in keeping a low profile, slaves were able to build reputations among whites that could be important. One major source of interaction and tension between slaves and whites who were not their masters were the slave patrols, whose ranks were often filled with less-affluent whites. Slaves usually tried to avoid these groups completely but might attempt to foil them. Sometimes slaves fought outright with those who tried to apprehend them. Slaves learned to play whites against each other for gains or to protect themselves.[47] And slaves often had to work their way through disputes between whites in a community (or caused them in the first place). For example, Peter helped his master, Elihu Cornelius, steal neighbors' cows and slaughter them in the middle of the night. But he then cooperated with whites in the neighborhood to catch Cornelius in the act.[48]

Taken together, the interactions between whites and slaves on the move, at work, in social situations, or in court combine to prove that bondspeople on Arkansas's cotton frontier lived in a more bustling and fluid landscape and brokered more power than Orville Taylor presented more than fifty years ago. Whites were largely able to spread and recreate the slave system they knew in older parts of the South, but significant differences were created both by the environment and by the initiative of the enslaved. While slaves on the southern periphery had more limited access to some forms of autonomy more common to longer-settled or more populated areas, they took advantage of what opportunities were available to keep up social ties, make their lives easier, and maintain their dignity. Bringing varying levels of power to each moment of carnage, conflict, compromise, or cooperation, both whites and blacks drew on experiences forged in the older South while adapting to the realities of life on slavery's frontier.

CHAPTER 2

Race and the Struggle for Freedom
African American Arkansans after Emancipation

CARL H. MONEYHON

WHEN THE UNION army invaded Arkansas in 1862, the emancipation of 111,115 slaves began. That process continued throughout the war, ending when the passage of the Thirteenth Amendment abolished slavery forever. The end of slavery, however, did not determine fully what freedom would mean for the former bondsmen. From the beginning, racist opposition to their independence limited that freedom and forced a century-long struggle to define it in its broadest terms. This essay explores the efforts of blacks in Arkansas to gain freedom, a fight that in Arkansas was made all the more difficult by its confrontation with an opposition that was constantly changing in its character, an opposition that suggests the mutability of racism. In this case, at least, changing economic and social conditions transformed racial ideas. In other words, underlying factors produced racist ideas, a possibility that suggests that race problems may be solved only if such factors are addressed. Certainly, the findings indicate that further work on the historical character of racial ideas is essential.

The first slaves in Arkansas found freedom with Union general Samuel Curtis's column that invaded Arkansas in 1862. Thousands joined then, and others fled to expanding Union lines during the rest of the war. They were free, but exactly what freedom signified was unclear. Charles Anderson of Helena recalled much later in life that few African Americans had ever considered precisely what freedom meant while they remained slaves. "Freedom was something mysterious," he remembered. "Colored folks didn't talk it. White folks didn't talk it."[1] From the beginning, however, they found that even their white friends had limiting ideas about what black freedom should be and worked to fasten their definition on them.

The large number of slaves who fled to Union lines during the war forced government authorities to both alleviate their suffering and cope with the problem of thousands of rootless people. Government solutions quickly showed the freedmen that while their liberators may have seen them as free, they did not see them as equal. In 1863, Secretary of War Edwin M. Stanton ordered Gen. Lorenzo Thomas to create a system that would allow the freedmen to "support themselves and to furnish useful service in any capacity to the Government."[2] As implemented, the government's idea of freedom was economic freedom, but that freedmen would labor for someone else: in the army, in support for the army, or on plantations seized and leased to loyal operators. At every turn the freedmen found their path to freedom circumscribed in their efforts at securing this economic freedom by many of the whites they encountered.

The army offered them their greatest opportunity to experience full freedom, even though they faced discrimination in it. As many as five thousand black men enlisted in the five black infantry regiments and one artillery battery raised within the state. There they received less than whites, their pay being ten dollars per month compared to thirteen dollars for white soldiers. White officers also proved reluctant to use blacks in combat, further reflecting white prejudice. Even though black Arkansans proved themselves as capable soldiers, officers relegated their units to garrison duty and foraging for the most part. Still, eventually the government equalized pay. In addition, black soldiers often had an opportunity for some education. At the war's end, many received pensions that helped them in their later lives.

An unknown number of former slaves found themselves working for the Union army in other ways. The military hired them for a variety of jobs supporting the war effort. The growth of the black population in Little Rock reflected this new opportunity. In 1860 the black population there had been 1,818, and by 1864 some 2,650 freedmen lived and worked in the town.[3] Life for many of these workers, however, was difficult, and they faced widespread mistreatment and abuse. One former slave, Josephine Barnett, who had lived near the army camp at DeValls Bluff, remembered that the soldiers "treated them [the freedmen] mean, they didn't like the slaves. They steal from the slaves too." As a result, they hated the Yankees.[4]

In addition to military employment, by the summer of 1864 some 3,561 freedmen were in the fields working on plantations that were seized by the government and leased to loyal planters by the Treasury Department. The army supervised their employment. A few freedmen secured their own leases, but the majority found themselves working for someone else and living lives that differed little from plantation slaves. Plantation lessees put their employees to work in the fields in gangs just as in slave times. The workers often lived in the old slave quarters. The new managers sometimes physically punished their workers to secure better effort. Much of this seemed similar to slavery, although some conditions did differ. In a relationship that foreshadowed farm tenancy, the lessee advanced food, clothing, and even cash to workers, and then deducted the amount from the settlement when the crop was sold. Often, since the lessee kept the books, the worker was simply cheated of his share. The worker usually came out of the year with little to show for his efforts. At the end of the first year of operations an officer assigned to superintend affairs on the leased plantations reported that the freedman "[saw] that the white man ha[d] received his labor and ha[d] paid him with food and clothing—about the same he used to get."[5]

If freedom meant economic independence, then the results by the end of the year were not good. Many freedmen could not save even enough money to take care of themselves. Such conditions produced considerable racial tension. Economic exploitation in particular led blacks to distrust the whites who employed them. One observer concluded that as a result of their ill treatment the freedmen believed that "in all written documents (such as contracts to labor &c.) they [the freedmen] were liable to be swindled by unprincipled white men." One army inspector reported by the war's end, "The rights of blacks . . . have been so long outraged by the whites, that they are exceedingly distrustful." Indeed, blacks had every reason to be distrustful. Many whites, even those who appeared ready to help them, believed that whites could do anything they wished to blacks. An army inspector at Little Rock concluded that blacks suffered to a great extent because the "idea that anything is good enough for a 'nigger' [had] an abiding place still in the midst of not a few connected with the freedmen."[6]

Despite the problems, by the war's end blacks had accepted the idea that economic self-sufficiency was necessary to make them truly free. This realization helps to explain the fact that many freedmen fled the countryside when they had the opportunity and sought economic opportunities in the state's towns, particularly Helena, Pine Bluff, and Little Rock. At least for a time at the war's end the presence of military forces in these communities made them a place that offered employment opportunities. The black population of these towns continued to grow, as in the case of Little Rock, where the number of blacks mushroomed from 2,650 in 1864 to 5,247 by 1870. By the latter year they constituted 43 percent of the population. An observer in Camden summed up the trend, although not the force behind it, when he noted that the freedmen there seemed "'fatuated with town life."[7]

In the city other ideas became a part of the concept of freedom, especially those that helped secure economic independence. Education was particularly important. In the spring of 1865, a combination of groups, including the American Missionary Association, the Quakers, and the Bureau of Refugees, Freedmen, and Abandoned Lands, began to offer blacks educational opportunities to which they responded enthusiastically. Bureau agents reported that by May 1865, some 1,700 blacks attended one of the schools that had been created by the bureau and various religious groups. A representative of the American Missionary Association concluded that at Little Rock the freedmen sought to pattern their lives after their former masters, hoping to secure what whites had, taking pride that they had an "opportunity to educate their children 'like white folks.'" The bureau agent at Little Rock described the demand for schools among blacks as "rapacious." "The desire of the free people for education is unabated," he reported, "and is so strong as to be deemed by some excessive, amounting almost to a passion."[8]

The majority of blacks remained in the countryside, however, and for many of them landownership came to be seen as critical in their achievement of economic self-sufficiency. Land would allow them to control their own destinies by giving them control over the one means of production potentially available to them and a place where they could practice the agricultural skills most of them possessed. The Freedmen's Bureau agent in Arkadelphia saw the desire for land among blacks, reporting that each was "full of the idea of controlling his own time and being a planter."[9] A freedman made his own case in an interview with a military officer at Fort Smith in 1865. Asking for help from the officer, the freedman stated, "I want some land; I am helpless; you do nothing for me but give me freedom." The officer asked if that was not enough, to which the freedman responded, "It is enough for the present; but I cannot help myself unless I get some land, then I can take care of myself and family; otherwise, I cannot do it."[10] Clearly the acquisition of land was seen as another major step toward economic independence.

All of this education and land would be meaningless, however, unless blacks could secure protection of their lives and property in the law. On June 3, 1867, Bishop Jabez P. Campbell of the African Methodist Episcopal Church spoke to a large group of blacks on the grounds of the state house at Little Rock and pointed to this need. He advised his listeners to build schools and to "work hard, save their money, and buy lands." At the same time, he asserted the critical importance of gaining equal rights and protection of those rights before the law. Declaring that he wanted "no one's lands, silver or gold," he insisted that he did want "an equal opportunity of accumulating them for himself."[11]

On November 30, 1865, delegates to the Convention of Colored Citizens in Little Rock, led by black leaders like W. H. Gray of Phillips County, articulated all of these objectives in what may have been the first statement of an African American political agenda in Arkansas. Expressing their hopes for the future, they listed education and land as their goals but emphasized the need for government protection even more. They realized the potential for violence against them and concluded that only if they received legal equality with whites would they be able to protect themselves. They went even further, petitioning Congress to "clothe us with the power of self-protection by giving us our equality before the law and the right of suffrage."[12] If they had a say in government they would be able to ensure that government and the justice system in particular would protect them as they moved toward self-sufficiency.

As black ideas about the requisites for freedom developed, white Arkansans moved through a period of adjusting their own views of their former slaves. They brought with them into the postbellum era a worldview of blacks formulated as a part of the defense of slavery. Contemporary newspapers and politicians had pieced together a complex view of blacks that ascribed to them numerous negative characteristics. In an article typical of that view, William Woodruff, the editor of the *Arkansas Gazette,* detailed the basic argument that blacks could prosper only under slavery. They were intellectually inferior to whites. As a people they were "improvident and careless." In their natural setting they were "savage cannibals."[13]

While whites might agree that blacks possessed these qualities, they did not agree as to their source. They were uncertain as to whether blacks' character derived from their race or their lives as slaves. William Woodruff represented one side of the white argument, concluding that race was the source, pointing to what he called the "anti-progressive" history of the people of Africa. He even insisted that God had created blacks almost as separate beings to serve as slaves. Albert Pike, a prominent antebellum politician, provided an alternative view. In a conference among American Party leaders in 1857, Pike expressed uncertainty about what the future held for blacks. He did not consider the slave simply chattel but "a human being with a soul to be saved," and Pike even considered him to have a "mind to be cultivated and improved until some day he might be permitted to be free." The process might take "long ages," but he believed a "transposition from slavery to freedom would be accomplished by degrees almost insensible." While both justified slavery, their view of the character of former slaves evidences considerable ambiguities.[14]

With slavery gone, whites considered the possibility that a new understanding of blacks as a people might be required. On the pages of the contemporary press some editors began to advance a slightly different view of how blacks should be perceived. In September 1866, William Woodruff, in a seeming change of heart, called upon his readers to adjust to the circumstances created by the end of slavery and the growing likelihood that Congress would force black suffrage on the South. At the heart of his argument were two ideas accepted as truths. Firstly, slavery had left blacks largely ignorant and unable to care for themselves. Secondly, whites needed blacks to secure an economic recovery. He concluded, consequently, that it was the duty of whites to educate the freedmen. They could not be left in ignorance. These "playmates in childhood," "companions in youthful sports," and "nurturing mother[s] in infancy," must be shown that the southern people were their allies and real friends. "Let us discard our old prejudices," he urged, "and bury them in the same grave with slavery." The editor of the *Western Clarion* at Helena also appeared willing to look at blacks differently, although expressing some doubt as to the result. "As they are free," he wrote, "we should all desire to see them advanced as far as they are capable of. Many of us do not think them susceptible of much advancement, *but that must be tried*, and we desire to have it tried." These views were radical ones within the context of antebellum ideas advocated by the same newspapers. It now appeared that slavery, not race, had created the character of freedmen.[15]

All whites did not agree with this conclusion. Replying to a critical editorial in the Little Rock *Pantograph*, Woodruff defended himself by insisting that he had not called for giving blacks a "*collegiate education*," nor had he suggested that whites pay for their educations. What he had suggested, he insisted, was that some plan might be devised to align black and white interests. He admitted, however, that he believed that a freedman could be educated to become a "sensible man" and that he could be changed from an "ignorant barbarian" to an "enlightened creature." Even in defending his position, the *Gazette's* editor accepted a view of the possibilities of blacks in the future that would hardly have been thinkable even two years before.[16] For a brief moment, with slavery at an end, it appeared possible that whites would redefine what they thought it meant to be black. Race, or the white definition of race, seemed flexible.

In the end, the emergence of a more virulent racism blunted any possibility of a change in racial views. Economic factors weighed heavily in this development and produced an almost inevitable result. Agriculture proved highly unstable in the postwar years, and changing crop prices threatened the profits of all who grew the state's great cash crop of cotton. White landowners needed blacks to work their farms, but they also needed a workforce that placed little pressure for wages that would weigh against their profits and one that was fixed as much as possible to the land. True black freedom as defined by freedmen, meaning land, education, equal protection under the law, and political participation, threatened the stability of that labor force. As prices and weather undermined potential profits, whites moved to cut off the avenues that blacks could take to secure their independence. In addition, the aggressive efforts of the national Democratic Party to return to power in the presidential election of 1868 played a major role. All helped produce an environment in which whites visited widespread abuse and outright violence against blacks. A resurrection of racial ideas born in slave times justified white actions. The possibilities of change envisioned by Woodruff failed in their realization.

The rapid reemergence in Arkansas of cotton culture produced the economic forces connected to this process. The return to cotton came in part because while the war seriously harmed the lives and fortunes of many of the state's slave owners, it actually did very little to change the structure of social institutions in Arkansas. The state's surviving elites may have lost their slaves, but they retained the basic means of production and sat atop the state's white society. At the war's end, cotton prices were high and most who had planted cotton before the war returned almost immediately to its cultivation, thinking that they could recoup their wartime losses.

In order for blacks to acquire the land that would give them greater freedom in the state's agricultural society, they had to earn the money needed to buy property in a world where whites owned the land. There were no forty acres and a mule from the government. They would have to work for white landlords. This was made all the more clear by the Freedmen's Bureau, whose commissioners in Arkansas presided over the development of a contract system designed to compel the freedmen to go back to work on the farms and plantations. In his instructions to bureau agents, Gen. John W. Sprague urged them to teach the freedmen to sign labor agreements, to conform to their contracts, and, if the freedmen failed, to enforce the state's vagrancy laws (laws that were firmly on the side of the white landlord). In short, the bureau would ensure that blacks worked and would use the law against those that did not.[17] As the historian of the Arkansas bureau has written, "winning planters' approval clearly became more important [for many agents] than helping blacks gain economic freedom."[18] Most blacks went back to work in the cotton fields, many in the very fields that they had worked as slaves.

Farm tenancy was the system that emerged to play a critical role in postwar race relations. The usual tenant contract saw blacks farming the land of whites for a share of the crop. Blacks actually encouraged the development of this system in an effort to avoid planter efforts to hire them to work in gangs, as on the antebellum plantations. Instead, blacks used a postwar shortage of workers to force the system of sharecropping on the landowners by refusing to sign other types of contracts. The new system placed freedmen on individual farms and gave them some control over their lives, providing at least a sense of autonomy. The Freedmen's Bureau agent in Arkadelphia reported this desire, indicating that the freedmen wished to "become planters by renting land or making crops on shares."[19] There was nothing inherently wrong with such a system if it operated fairly, but considerable potential for trouble was inherent in cropping. Farming on shares required the freedmen to exercise considerable caution. At the end of the year the price of the crop had to cover not only the landowners' share but also any debts that had been run up for the purchase of provisions if they were to have the income necessary to move out on their own. Black success also completely depended upon fair dealings on the part of the landowners.

Trouble emerged on the state's farms and plantations as white landowners confronted falling cotton prices through the postwar years, a collapse that seriously threatened their profits. Cotton prices dropped precipitously after the war, falling from an all-time high of one dollar per pound to thirty-seven cents in 1866, then to seventeen cents in 1867 and down to eleven cents by 1874.[20] In the spring of 1867 the editor of the *Gazette* summed up the situation for the 1866 crop, observing that to restore their lost wealth many planters had "mortgaged their lands and stretched their credit to its utmost." The consequence of their efforts was that "many have sacrificed their all and the experiment has cost them their last dollar."[21] The situation worsened in 1867 when unfavorable spring weather threatened a short crop. Many planters had borrowed, then "failed and involved many merchants in their ruin."[22] Faced with having to repay initial loans, then seeking to ensure their own profits, landowners often protected themselves by defrauding their workers. Bureau agents catalogued the numerous ways that freedmen were cheated. In some cases landowners encouraged their tenants to borrow money, kept the account books, then, inevitably, found at the end of the year that laborers had made enough money only to break even or not even enough to cover their debts. As one bureau agent advised headquarters, the freedmen consequently were "in the *power* of the white man when he keeps a running account against them for a whole year's expenses."[23] The bureau agent at Lewisville complained that part of the debt problem was created by plantation stores that charged "exorbitant" prices for foods.[24]

Anthony Taylor, who worked on shares in Clark County, provided a graphic account of the system. "After he [the landowner] got the cotton all picked and sold, the cotton it would all go to him for what you owed him for furnishing you. You never saw how much cotton was ginned, nor how much he got for it, nor how much it was worth nor nothing. They would just tell you you wasn't due nothing. They did that to hold you for another year. You got nothing to move on so you stayed there and take what he gives you."[25]

Other landowners took more drastic measures. A typical ploy was to drive the workers off the farm, then contend that they had broken their contracts and did not have to be paid. A bureau agent at Lewisville informed headquarters in 1867, "Men in this county have been allowed to whip, swindle, discharge, and fine their employees whenever they saw fit to do so." The Freedmen's Bureau began investigating instances where landowners had been driving their laborers off the land in order to "withhold their arrears of wages, or share in the growing crop." In 1868, the agent at Jacksonport condemned what he called the "barbarous subterfuge" practiced by planters in settling accounts, noting that they were intent on creating a peon class to do their labor. Individuals who protested their treatment or appealed to bureau agents were threatened and, in some cases, murdered. Often lacking an education to check the planter's books themselves, without any guarantee of protection under the law, most blacks did not even bother to appeal their treatment.[26]

Debt was one means of keeping blacks on the farm. Denying them the opportunity for education was another. Education created the possibility of job mobility and escape from the plantation system. Consequently, black schools and their teachers confronted what was often violent white opposition throughout the years following the war. In part, the economic problems of the sharecropper worked against education as families found they needed all family members in the fields. Bob Benford remembered that he never went to school. "If I had a chance to go, I didn't know it," he recalled. Instead he had to help his mother work.[27] Blacks also never went to school simply because no schools were available. Efforts to bring schools to blacks often faced white hostility and violence. Teachers were driven away with threats. Opponents burned black schools. Bureau officials thought that only the continued presence of military force prevented even more widespread violence against black education.[28] In the face of such resistance, the bureau had difficulty in finding teachers and it never created a system adequate to the needs of the free people.

What justified such behavior? Whites readily fell back on the ideas they had used to sustain slavery, using the peculiar definition of race that had served them well prior to the Civil War. Developing the view that blacks were inferior and that whites had the right to do with them as they wished provided the sanction for these actions. A bureau agent explained, "Men who profess to be honest and honorable cannot understand that there is any moral wrong in *robbing and cheating* a negro." One newspaper editor concluded that they deserved such action, concluding that in their labor they were "capricious" and "lazy." They clearly were not like whites, possessing a "want of moral perception," a "want of intelligence," and "brutish instincts." As to education, the bureau agent at Pine Bluff found general hostility in that region to any black schools. "Some think it terrible that the people's money should be wasted for so useless a purpose," he reported, "alleging that the niggers never can be taught anything."[29]

The course of events after the spring of 1867, when Congress intervened in Reconstruction and opened the way for black suffrage, further hardened white attitudes. The presidential election of 1868, the first time blacks could vote in a national election, witnessed the resurgence of the Democratic Party in the South. Northern Democrats, intent on gaining control of the presidency, welcomed this. In Arkansas, as elsewhere in the South, the Democrats chose to secure a majority by urging whites to unify behind their banner on the basis of racial solidarity. Such a campaign, pointing to the need for action to prevent "Negro Supremacy," reinforced the ideas of black racial inferiority born of slave times and reborn in the economic crisis of the immediate postwar years.

As the Democrats organized for the election of 1868, racist rhetoric intensified. William Woodruff, in seemingly yet another change of heart, promised that only in a Democratic victory would it be possible to prevent the "damning evils and expressible horrors of negro [*sic*] supremacy." On December 2, 1867, former leaders of the state's antebellum Democratic Party met at Little Rock to initiate among white people in Arkansas a movement, "in co-operation with the National Democratic Party," to "aid in saving the country from negro supremacy." That extraordinary measures were intended in the campaign was made clear by the *Gazette*, whose editor warned that if blacks did not understand this and yield to southern-born whites they would "fall before the Caucasian like grass before the scythe. The decrees of God are not to be put aside by man's puny hands, nor can the Ethiop possibly change his skin. 'This is a white man's government.'" When Democrats held their state convention at Little Rock on January 28, 1868, their resolutions placed them on record in favor of a "white man's government in a white man's country."[30]

The threat of Negro supremacy, an absurd peril given the overwhelming white majority in Arkansas, had imbedded within it a wide variety of ideas about blacks as political beings. Few contemporary newspapers exist for this era, but, at least in terms of racist rhetoric, William Woodruff's *Gazette* is encyclopedic. In various editorials he and his associates articulated numerous racist views. Blacks were unfit for political life because in such matters "the negro is too ignorant to form any opinion." They could be easily deluded by men who promised to secure "his animal nature longs." "Negro Supremacy" promised the "darkest days in the degeneracy of the nation," placing in power the "race which in the five thousand years of its history has never advanced a step toward civilization." It committed to the rule of the state "savages—whom history has shown have ever, even when fortuitously advanced to a higher civilization and then left to themselves, retrograded to idolatory [sic], fetichism [sic], and even cannibalism."[31]

This represented an even more virulent racism since it no longer justified a labor system but actually encouraged open hostility toward blacks. In some cases it went so far as to totally dehumanize them. Whites had always considered blacks humans, but now some whites came to insist that they were not. An example of this shift may be seen in a pamphlet entitled *The Negro*, sold in Arkansas and excerpted in the *Gazette*. Challenging the antebellum notion that blacks were the descendants of Ham, the author reasoned that they, in fact, must have been created before Adam. This meant, according to the author, "he [the black man] is a *beast*, in God's nomenclature; and being a beast was under Adam's rule and dominion, and, like all other beasts or animals, has no soul." He went on, "The negro is now free. There are but two things on earth, that may be done with him now. . . . You *must send him back to Africa* or *re-enslave him*. The former is the best, *far the best*." In short, blacks were placed on earth to be used by whites for whatever purpose they chose. Further, as beasts they did not need land and education. And they certainly did not need to participate in the political process.[32]

The Democrats did not carry the 1868 election in Arkansas despite clear evidence that they used extraordinary means to achieve that end. Black participation actually helped elect one of the state's more progressive governments. Under Gov. Powell Clayton and a Republican legislature, the state government took steps that might actually have secured for blacks the goals they had put forward in Little Rock only three years before. It created a public school system that enrolled some

19,280 African American pupils by 1870. It also protected the legal and political rights of blacks. Governor Clayton ordered the state militia, in one of the most active uses of force against violence in the South, to suppress the Ku Klux Klan and the violence it leveled at blacks. Republican rule, however, was only a short interlude in the state's history. Democrats continued to appeal to the white majority with racist rhetoric to unite behind them against blacks. In the end, in the state's Brooks-Baxter War of 1874, the Democrats achieved their goal and regained control of the state government. With their return, the state backed away from its efforts to secure the rights of blacks, a retreat continued by Democratic government into the twentieth century.

In the face of such opposition, remarkably, African Americans made progress in their attempts to secure the land and education they considered the underpinnings of true freedom. By 1875 an estimated one out of every two thousand black taxpayers actually had acquired land.[33] The census taken four years later found that about 25 percent of blacks over the age of ten had learned to read and write.[34] Nonetheless, for thousands of the state's African Americans, control over their own lives remained elusive, and the goals set by the men who attended the Convention of Colored Citizens at Little Rock in 1865 remained unfulfilled. The fact that hope had not died, however, was made evident on August 27, 1883, when black political leaders such as Mifflin Gibbs met at Little Rock to discuss the political situation and whether or not they should support the bid for the presidency by Chester A. Arthur. They turned instead to an assessment of the condition of blacks within the state. Although recognizing the gains, they concluded that blacks had made little real progress toward achieving full freedom. In a statement that indicated the course they believed needed to be taken, they returned to that first black agenda advanced eight years earlier. Landownership and education, along with justice and equal protection under the law, remained at the heart of the black vision. This black agenda would remain a focus into the next century.[35]

Despite all their efforts, blacks had confronted forces that blocked their march toward freedom. First freedom was unquestionably limited. For a brief moment it had appeared that whites might accept the aspirations of blacks, but the interplay of the need of the economic system to maintain an immobile and exploitable labor force and the efforts of white Democratic politicians to regain power all worked against Arkansas's black population. Racism served to justify the existing economic system and forge a white political majority. Racist ideas would survive so long as the cotton plantation continued to exist and the heirs of the Reconstruction Democrats held onto the government. Indeed, though once again evolving, these ideas would survive even beyond that.

CHAPTER 3

"Send Forth More Laborers into the Vineyard"
Understanding the African American Exodus to Arkansas

STORY MATKIN-RAWN

AFTER RETURNING FROM a trip to Arkansas in the fall of 1888, Bishop Henry McNeal Turner published a glowing account of his travels. "Arkansas is destined to be the great Negro State of the country," he exclaimed. "The rich lands, the healthy regions, the meagre prejudice compared to some States and opportunities to acquire wealth all conspire to make it inviting to the colored man." The visibility of black elected officials a decade after the end of federal Reconstruction also impressed him: "To see a colored judge, justice of the peace, member of the legislature, clerk of the court, sheriff, policeman and other high functionaries is an ordinary sight." African American in-migration had helped increase the number of black Arkansan officeholders over the 1880s, a pattern that reversed regional trends. Whereas only four African Americans were elected to serve in the Arkansas General Assembly in 1880, ten black men won state legislative seats in the fall of 1888.[1]

Turner's stature, both as a leader in the African Methodist Episcopal Church and as a prominent southern Republican, ensured his comments received a wide audience. Within weeks, the *Indianapolis Freeman* and the *New York Age*, two of the nation's largest black newspapers, reprinted Turner's Arkansas editorial in full.[2] His observations came at a critical moment in a national debate among African Americans over the wisdom of migration to Arkansas as well as to Texas, Oklahoma, and the Mississippi Delta. Between 1870 and 1910, more than one in ten black southerners migrated to another state in the South, often deeper south and nearly always further west.[3] By the time Turner penned his tribute to this small state on the region's wild western edge, Arkansas had for over twenty years led the nation in attracting black settlers. During the 1880s alone, nearly sixty thousand African Americans migrated to Arkansas, twice the number migrating to any other state.[4] Arkansas would continue to lead the nation in drawing African American migrants, adding an additional hundred thousand black settlers by 1910.[5]

Yet migration to Arkansas, like better-known exodus movements to Kansas and Liberia, was always controversial. In a pithy editorial entitled "Why Go to Arkansas?" *New York Age* editor T. Thomas Fortune argued that black southern migration to Arkansas was like "jumping out of the frying pan and into the fire." Why should freedpeople expend precious resources and leave behind friends and family for a state with identical "civil, political, and industrial conditions"?[6] The question of exceptionalism at the heart of both of these positions, whether Arkansas was more racially tolerant than other southern states, played a fairly minor role in most prospective migrants' discussions and decisions. The dream motivating most advocates of migration was not that progressive attitudes in Arkansas (or Texas or Oklahoma) would temper southern white racism. They dreamed that mass black landownership, a feat most believed achievable in the less-settled western South, would provide the necessary leverage to finish the work of Reconstruction, transforming the future of the region, the nation, and their place in it.

By the war's end, mortality and displacement had reduced Arkansas's population by as much as a half. The resulting labor hunger fueled a remarkable surge in wages, roughly double the pay for day labor in the eastern South, and an aggressive recruitment push among Arkansas planters and their representatives.[7] Historian Joel Williamson has estimated that up to 10 percent of South Carolina's African American population left that state during Reconstruction. Nearly all headed to the westerly southern states or to Florida. By spring of 1867, the *Macon Telegraph* lamented that Georgia had lost one-third of its black population since the end of the war. Freedmen's Bureau director O. O. Howard placed that figure at closer to 15 percent. Economic opportunities, specifically higher cash wages, drew these first migrants west.[8]

How did African Americans who considered moving to Arkansas test the claims of labor agents? Early migrants often had the most to gain in terms of increased wages and access to land, but they also faced the greatest difficulty in obtaining information. Slaves' covert networks of communication, a constant problem for slaveholders and a boon for Union army intelligence, persisted after slavery's end. Early southwestern migration, however, often strained this word-of-mouth "grapevine telegraph." Rudimentary railroad infrastructure and burned-out bridges forced migrants to cover zigzag paths of up to a thousand miles on their way west. Jerry Nix, who settled in White County, spent a year walking from Georgia to Arkansas with his seven-year-old son and their two hunting dogs. Nix's story was fairly typical of early settlers. Understandably, few wanted to make such a journey more than once.[9] News did circulate via print and letters, but not to the extent seen by the late 1870s. In the late 1860s, mass literacy was a generation away and southern black print culture was still in its infancy.[10]

One of the few African Americans to comment publicly on migration to the western South during this era was none other than Henry McNeal Turner. At first blush, his 1867 open letter, "To the Colored Citizens of Georgia," published in a white Democratic newspaper, seemed to condemn the "astonishing exodus" of "colored people going West." But the exposition that followed was more nuanced. Turner estimated that over the previous three months, forty-five thousand black Georgians had moved to Mississippi and Arkansas. This exodus had helped local black residents by driving up wages and decreasing rents. But migrants, he warned, would eventually "run into the same dilemma they are trying to run from" when demand for labor in the West slackened. Moreover, torrential outmigration threatened black political organizing in Georgia. Though the Reconstruction Acts were still several weeks away from passage when Turner's letter went to press, his travels to the nation's capital and Republican contacts gave him a keen sense of the major developments, such as black voter registration, temporary military rule, and ratification of the Fourteenth Amendment, that were soon to unfold in the former Confederacy. He encouraged black Georgians to wait and see how conditions might change for the better in their home state and how the migrants who had settled in Arkansas and Mississippi fared. "Surely out of 45,000 Georgians," Turner suggested, "some will come back and show us samples of their great profits."[11]

Political and governmental networks played a leading role in furnishing information and spurring African American migration during the immediate postwar years. The head of Arkansas's Freedmen's Bureau, a federal agency charged with assisting former slaves in the transition to free labor, reported that migrants from Georgia and Alabama typically doubled their wages by relocating. Bureau agents in the eastern South, particularly North Carolina and Georgia, promoted and even subsidized transportation for freedpeople wishing to resettle in southern states with higher wages. Furthermore, in the early 1870s, Arkansas's Republican administration began promoting African American in-migration. In 1870, the State Bureau of Immigration sponsored a junket for black Republican S. M. Walters back to his native Georgia to advertise Arkansas's advantages. Two years later, the governor appointed William H. Grey, arguably the most powerful black Republican in Arkansas, to head the Bureau of Immigration. Though he served only a year, the Democratic *Memphis Appeal* believed that Grey's "toil and genius" sparked a major exodus from Georgia.[12]

In the winters of 1873 and 1874, thousands of black Georgians departed by train and on foot for Arkansas, most from Cotton Belt counties near Macon. Migrants gave not just one reason for their departure to Arkansas. The reasons spilled forth in a chronicle of misery. Low wages, white resistance to black landownership, depleted soil, and limits on livestock grazing, hunting, and fishing impoverished them. Migrants condemned unprosecuted crimes against black victims (ranging from fraud to murder), over-prosecution of freedpeople for petty offenses, failure to secure fair trials, and, above all, unrelieved violence against black voters and their families.[13]

Like subsequent mass movements among black South Carolinians (1881–82) and North Carolinians (1889–90) to homestead in Arkansas, the Georgia exodus generated public exchange on the topic of migration. Conventions in Atlanta and Macon drew black delegates from across the state to discuss emigration to the western South. These gatherings helped prospective settlers to plan and provided a venue for airing black citizens' grievances. The first convention, held on New Year's Day, 1873, established the State Emigration Society, which negotiated contracts with Arkansas employers on behalf of its members. A second convention two weeks later passed a resolution encouraging freedpeople to leave Georgia, where "negroes were defrauded of their rights and denied the protection of the laws," for "Arkansas [where] there were colored judges, and constables, and mixed race juries." A convention the following year focused on creating an all-black town in Texas and colonizing a county in the Mississippi Delta. An 1875 gathering established a society to track positive developments, such as school construction, and negative ones, such as anti-black violence, by county in order to advise prospective migrants on the best locations for settlement.[14]

Efforts to monitor racial terrorism in other states underscore the very real dangers that migrants faced. Andrew Belcher, chair of Georgia's 1875 convention, published a pamphlet entitled "Should the Colored People Leave Georgia?" He entreated black migrants to consider the higher costs of living and higher mortality rates in Mississippi and Arkansas. The Emigration Committee of the Georgia Conference of the African Methodist Episcopal (A.M.E.) Church also weighed in on the "fearful exodus . . . taken place among our people in favor of Arkansas." Committee members (Turner among them) believed the state was too far away for migrants to return "in the event of sickness or disappointment." Proximity was particularly important since poorer migrants often committed to a yearlong contract in exchange for train fare. How would they pay for a return ticket if the situation soured? The committee urged ministers to "exert their influence against this wild and monomaniac form of emigration."[15]

Even skeptics of migration generally accepted claims of higher wages and more fertile soil in Arkansas. That high pay actually increased some black southerners' reservations. Today, many Arkansans and their fellow Americans view the state as the "buckle" of the Bible Belt. However, in the late nineteenth century, most southerners, black and white, saw Arkansas as part of the hell-raising, heathenish West. Church attendance was low and the state had a long-established reputation for moral disorder. According to one antebellum quip, "every man, in coming to Arkansas, left his honesty, and every woman her chastity, on the east bank of the Mississippi."[16] While Arkansas's negative reputation focused on poor whites and their alleged ignorance and immorality, many African Americans also viewed the state as an unruly, uncivilized frontier with a black population in desperate need of missionary activity. When the AME Church transferred Reverend John Collins from Georgia to Forrest City, Arkansas, in 1878, he wrote in "wonder" at how black settlers burned through their earnings. Vain amusements, he sighed, consumed these cash-happy Arkansas brethren. "The country is full of people who emigrated here from the South," Collins observed, "and there is a spirit in people emigrating . . . to feel themselves free, so much so until they are very apt to fall into whatever slothful or sinful habits may prevail around them." For Rev. Isaac Grant, rather than vain amusements, materialism was the problem. Writing from his post in Edgefield County during the South Carolina exodus to Arkansas, Grant chastised migrants for chasing "filthy lucre." "It is not for the glory of God," he wrote, "that this emigration scheme is brought forth. . . . It is to be in possession of wealth." And the desire for wealth, he worried, distracted black South Carolinians from "seeking after the riches of time" through faith.[17]

There were others who marveled at the rapid material gains of black Arkansans. Maryland transplant John Jenifer praised changes he had seen in Little Rock. Just fifteen years after the Civil War, many black families had built sturdy homes, furnished them, and acquired treasured luxuries like musical instruments and books. To Jenifer, these possessions were not the fruit of greed but the fulfillment of prophesies that "every Valley would be exalted." "Young men come South," Jenifer entreated. "The world does move and we are moving with it." Indeed, with respect to home ownership, black Arkansans did not just move, they led. The state boasted one of the highest black home ownership rates in the nation, nearly 30 percent by 1910.[18]

Thus, for many black migrants, wages were a means to an end. And for most, that end was not just a home, but a homestead. Freedpeople across the South considered owning land to be the basis of economic independence and the best guarantee of citizenship rights. By 1870, roughly one in seventeen black Arkansans owned land, double and triple the rate of other Deep South states.[19] These statistics reflected unique local conditions. At the end of the Civil War, nearly 95 percent of Arkansas's land remained undeveloped. In 1866, Congress passed the Southern Homestead Act, opening roughly one-fourth of the state to public settlement. In the mid-1870s, Arkansas's railroads began to sell off millions of acres in federal land grants to subsidize construction and pay off their debts. Though black families still faced financial obstacles, the sheer quantity of land for sale in Arkansas minimized the impact of white hostility toward black property ownership.[20]

The Georgia exodus seemed not so much to end as to diffuse, rippling westward into Alabama and eastern Tennessee.[21] But developments during the 1870s sent mixed messages about the political future for African Americans in Arkansas. In 1874, a bitter factional fight within the Republican Party led to a brief armed conflict known as the Brooks-Baxter War. After the Republicans self-destructed, Democrats quickly won the governor's seat and a majority in the legislature. Yet black men continued to vote with relative freedom after Democrats' accession to power. The desire to increase the supply of labor may well have tempered attitudes among the state's Democrats. New governor Augustus Garland told the *Chicago Tribune* that he considered it his administration's responsibility "to assure the colored voter . . . his rights." Noting the recent influx of African Americans from Georgia and Tennessee, the reporter judged this policy a success: "The labor supply has never been so good."[22]

Elsewhere in the South, white Democrats employed political violence and fraud to cast black Republicans out of office and drive African Americans away from the polls. Determined to live lives free from terrorism and economic exploitation, freedpeople across the South established emigration societies promoting relocation to Liberia and, as that was often unsuccessful, to Kansas. Numerous emigration conventions passed resolutions encouraging black southerners to move where their political and property rights were respected. This movement culminated in 1879 with the Kansas exodus, which generated a congressional investigation and extensive press coverage. Interest in these movements, however, exceeded actual relocation. Between 1870 and 1880, roughly 25,000 African Americans migrated to Kansas. Another 1,200 moved to Liberia.[23]

African American migration to Arkansas also accelerated, though with far less press attention. Over the 1870s, an estimated 36,000 African Americans moved to Arkansas. Yet even as these families arrived, other black Arkansans sought to leave. Former state legislator Anthony Stanford organized some twenty-eight emigration clubs under the banner of the Liberia Exodus Arkansas Colony. Most took root in delta counties afflicted by anti-Republican violence during the 1878 elections. Miller County in southwest Arkansas saw a similar pattern of political repression followed by an exodus movement, in that case, to Kansas. Over 140 black Arkansans migrated to Liberia at the peak of the exodus movement in 1879 and 1880. The number of Arkansas-born black settlers in Kansas actually declined between 1870 and 1880. When voter repression against Republicans in southern and eastern Arkansas eased in the early 1880s, interest in emigration waned. As movements to Kansas and

Liberia declined elsewhere in the South, African American migration to Arkansas surged to an all-time high.²⁴

Did black settlers confer notions of freedom once attached to Africa and the American West onto Arkansas? Historians William Cohen, Nell Irvin Painter, and Steven Hahn have underscored similarities in the logic supporting Kansas and Liberian exodus efforts. Local participation in both movements often corresponded with areas that had seen substantial gains for African Americans during Reconstruction followed by swift, significant reversals, usually resulting from political terrorism. The aims of organizations and individuals advocating emigration to Kansas and Liberia were, therefore, often highly political. Activists in both exodus efforts expressed a desire for self-rule and for the creation of a black settler society that would uplift the status and reputation of people of African descent within the United States and abroad.²⁵

Arkansas also experienced substantial in-migration from regions blighted by anti-black terrorism: Georgians following the violent elections of 1872 and Alabamians after political assassinations and anti-Republican "riots" in 1874.²⁶ Many participants in South Carolina's vibrant Liberian exodus movement who could not afford or chose not to move to Africa refocused their efforts on settling and acquiring land in Arkansas in the early 1880s.²⁷ But rarely did advocates of African American migration to Arkansas express aspirations of building a model, self-governing black society. One exception was an 1881 letter to the editor of the *Christian Recorder* from "Dallas Citizen," proposing a national convention to encourage the migration of four million African Americans to Louisiana, Mississippi, Florida, and Arkansas. By "centralizing" the black population and creating political majorities, Dallas Citizen believed, "we would be able to build up for our race, a reputation that would be as lasting as the government."²⁸

Though few proposed a vision as large, complex, or symbolic as that of Dallas Citizen, many black migrants to Arkansas did demonstrate through their actions a "desire for social separatism" and community autonomy. When the Georgia exodus first drew the nation's attention, a *New York Times* article noted that black migrants made use of the vast "undeveloped wilderness" of Arkansas to "establish their independence by accumulating such property as a mule, a gun, a cabin, and an acre of land." "They seem tired of the white man and his complaints and fears concerning them," the report continued, "and when they do form communities, form them by themselves, shunning, to a certain extent, contact with the Caucasian." A correspondent for *Scribners* concurred: "They [black migrants] show [in Arkansas] as indeed, almost everywhere in the Mississippi Valley, a tendency to get into communities by themselves, and seem to have no desire to force their way into the company of a white man."[29]

Rev. James Sisson, who transferred from Georgia to an A.M.E. circuit in the Arkansas River Valley, had a slightly different take on black migrants' desire for separation. Referring to his years in Georgia, Sisson recalled "whites unwilling to deed lands to our people," "our people shot down like 'varmints,'" the impossibility of securing "lands for school and church purposes," and "odious" laws stipulating that "not a mess of vegetables for a family dinner could be sold [by a sharecropper] without an order from the white owner of the land." Clearly, the desire for autonomy meant more than avoiding white complaints and fears. Autonomy allowed for the creation of community institutions and improved physical safety. Sisson urged migrants to Arkansas to "settle as compactly as it is wise for farmers to locate" in order to build good schools and strong churches and "place such men into office as you can trust to rule and govern well." "There are ample lands in Arkansas," he encouraged, "for you to make your own communities, and control them."[30]

The desire to build black farm settlements and community institutions over which residents exercised control was certainly akin to the separatist, sometimes utopian visions fueling emigration movements to Kansas and Liberia. But there were also important differences. For one, Arkansas was a majority-white state, nearly 75 percent white in 1880. And unlike Kansas, it had no prominent heritage of anti-slavery activism. Thus, African American settlers in Arkansas, more so than prospective emigrants to the Midwest and Africa, retained some hope regarding their status as citizens of the United States living in the South. Transplants to Arkansas tended to stress economic opportunity, landownership in particular, as the foundation of their future political and social advancement.[31]

Indeed, if supporters of African American migration idealized any aspect of Arkansas, it was the land itself. The path by which most black settlers arrived, westward from Memphis, all but ensured a dramatic impression of Arkansas's landscape. Trains and steamships first drew migrants through flooded canebrakes, then the deeply shadowed cypress swamps of the delta. In as little as an hour, travelers burst upon gently rolling plains, the state's Grand Prairie, "covered over with grass and flowers" in spring and summer. Cattle roamed around small cottages surrounded by fields of grain and hay. Those traveling west of Little Rock, a river bluff city at the center of the state, wound upward through Ozark highlands heading north or the Ouachitas Mountains further south. Here many black settlers, like their white neighbors, embraced hunting and subsistence farming, staking a milk cow behind their cabin, running hogs in the bottoms, and growing corn, fruit trees, and cane for molasses. Wherever migrants traveled, fields of cotton stretched along fertile river bottoms. For farmers accustomed to the worn-out soil of the southeast, the sight of cotton six feet and taller, untouched by commercial fertilizers, was never forgotten.[32]

The land could also be terrifying. Trees along streams and rivers bore flood marks anywhere from three to twenty-five feet above the ground. The abundant wildlife, so attractive to hunters, seemed more menacing at night when settlers woke to the sounds of bears and mountain lions crashing through the underbrush. More dangerous still were the "miasmas" that brought deadly fevers, shakes, and chills. At the turn of the century, scientists confirmed that mosquitoes transmitted diseases like malaria and yellow fever. Until then, southerners believed these illnesses were spread by unhealthy "vapors." Thus, even humidity, the defining trait of summer in Arkansas, signified danger for black settlers.[33]

Despite these challenges, many advocates of migration saw the environment as their ally. Migrants emphasized the fertility of the soil, repeatedly describing Arkansas's lands as "new," "rich," "flourishing," and "productive."[34] Vincent Henry Bulkley, a black Methodist minister from South Carolina investigating the condition of African American migrants in the Arkansas River Valley, expressed astonishment that an acre of land produced a bale of cotton or fifty bushels of corn without the use of fertilizer. Rev. Andrews of Greenville toured western Arkansas seeking land for a colony of South Carolinians. He reported "cheap land for sale all over the State and a better cotton-growing State I don't think can be found. . . . [G]rain grows in abundance there. The land is heavily timbered; good springs of water and good streams." Half a century later, when the Works Progress Administration interviewed former slaves about their migration experiences, Arkansas's land seemed to be the one attraction that had disappointed no one.[35]

What of political and social conditions in Arkansas? Prospective black settlers showed few signs of real concern about whether white Arkansans were less racist than other white southerners. Indeed, contrary to the tone set by Bishop Henry McNeal Turner's proclamation that Arkansas, the "great Negro state," was a land of "meagre prejudice," even passionate advocates of resettlement in Arkansas usually made modest claims about its political or social advantages. Sisson thought African Americans "suffer[ed] less from outrages of whites." Vincent Bulkley believed that black men were "richer in Arkansas than in any other place." "It is said by many that they are freer there than in any other State," he added, "but I cannot say this is strictly true." Booster Charles Zigler called Arkansas "the mecca for the colored man," asserting that his home county, Crittenden, could "boast of many intelligent colored men engaged in every conceivable position in life." Yet the following year, in 1888, armed white Democrats ran nineteen of those "intelligent colored men," including the county judge, a prominent physician, and the editor of the county's only newspaper, out of the state and threatened their lives should they ever return.[36]

For most migrants, Arkansas's political climate was an improvement on what they had left behind. But voter suppression, unpunished tenant fraud, and unequal treatment in the courts remained serious problems. In the 1880s, black Arkansans gained political strength through their increasing numbers and the rise of third-party agrarian movements. The excited editor of the *Southwestern Christian Advocate* exclaimed that it was "almost impossible to resist the conclusion that a great change politically will be wrought out by the changing conditions and new elements of population." But most black settlers had already witnessed the collapse of interracial government once, back in their home states, and with it their status as citizens. They arrived wary that what had happened before could happen again. If their political status were to improve, that change would spring from a meaningful expansion of their economic options. Arkansas, they believed, was their best hope of ensuring that their children need not labor as "hewers of wood and drawers of water," their frequent reference to Joshua's decree of generational slavery in the Old Testament.[37]

In this regard, two temporary opportunities continued to play in their favor. By the 1880s, migration advocates hoped that Arkansas's labor shortage would do more than raise wages. They hoped that it would raise the status of the workers themselves. Newspaper editor Marshal Taylor speculated that labor hunger in the Mississippi River

Valley produced beneficial competition between planters, merchants, and land speculators for the labor and trade of black workers. "The interest of each of these is so distinct from that of the others it is impossible for them to unite in any common policy looking to the oppression of the laborer, upon whom they are mutually dependent for success," he wrote.[38] An association of Georgia planters opposed to the Arkansas exodus bemoaned how migration divided elite white men. "Men to the manor born, our pretend friends and neighbors," engaged in bidding wars for the labor of black men and women, a situation they found intolerable. The *Christian Recorder,* national organ of the A.M.E. Church, "applauded" the South Carolina exodus to Arkansas for similar reasons: "South Carolina has too many laborers," proclaimed the editor. "Whenever that is the case, capital becomes domineering." Migrants believed that needs shaped human nature, including prejudice, and hoped that need was, at least for a time, on their side.[39]

Migrants' second advantage during the 1880s was the flood of still more land into a saturated market as railroad construction accelerated. Proponents of emigration urged black men and women to take advantage of a short window of opportunity to buy land before the best acreage was developed. Given their literacy and local leadership roles, ministers were often at the forefront of this movement. "Our people ought to buy land in one county in Arkansas," wrote a Mississippi Methodist transplanted to Arkansas. "Come now or never," wrote a Louisiana minister who urged all "Suffering People" to move to South Arkansas. "If you don't come now the opportunities will close." Even Rev. John M. Collins, who seven years earlier had expressed astonishment at the "slothful and sinful habits" of black Arkansans, by 1885 had found a new source of wonder: "With thousands of acres of government land in Arkansas, where a man can get a home for almost nothing, . . . [i]t is very strange why the negro remains in Georgia among the basest set of white hypocrites and vile demons that this world has ever heard of."[40]

Black political leaders also offered their aid to migrants seeking land. S. H. Holland, a prominent Chicot County Republican, wrote the *Arkansas Mansion* asking that representatives scouting out homesteads for black families "be directed to this section . . . as we would like to have them reap the advantages to be derived from securing homes ere the land grabbers get ahead of them." Mifflin Wistar Gibbs, a former municipal judge and registrar at the United States Land Office at Little Rock, urged

African American migrants "to endeavor by all possible means to secure homes," either on public land or along the recently surveyed Little Rock and Choctaw railroad. "Here is a chance for good homes at a very small cost, with no grasping landlord to turn you out from year to year . . . confiscating your crop under a mortgage. Colored friends think of this." Evidently they did. By 1890, one in four black Arkansan families owned land, ahead of the South's average of one in five and far higher than other Deep South states.[41]

It is difficult to overstress the degree of consensus concerning the aims of landownership and community autonomy. Individual landownership was rich with possibilities: bond for a political officeholder, collateral for credit, acreage for a school or church, and a place to reunite family. Above all, landownership could expand opportunities for the children and grandchildren of black pioneers.[42] Arkansas's vast public acreage and railroad land made it easier for African Americans to buy and settle in large groups. Settlers pursued this goal in nearly every corner of the state: Tiny Tollette in the southwest, Liberia City in the rich soil of the delta, Bookman in the pine hills of central Arkansas, Immanuel on the edge of the state's Grand Prairie region, Menifee at the foothills of the Ozarks. Here and in dozens of other black communities, settlers could build and control their own churches, schools, and community institutions.[43]

The last and largest coordinated, independent mass movement of African Americans to Arkansas, the North Carolina exodus, took place in 1889. Frustrated with poor crop yields and new laws undermining black laborers at the ballot box, in contracts, and even in grazing livestock, approximately fifteen thousand black North Carolinians left for Arkansas, Mississippi, and Texas. Unlike the Georgia Emigration Association of fifteen years earlier, which invited delegates from across the state to its annual meetings, the North Carolina Emigration Association actively organized local emigration bureaus, setting up branches in as many as forty-three counties.[44]

Yet even as black North Carolinians met, saved their money, and sent representatives to meet with land agents and employers, Arkansas was convulsed by political terrorism. As if to make up for time lost during the 1870s and 1880s, when they had focused on compromise while their compatriots in Louisiana and Mississippi turned to murder, during the 1888 and 1890 elections, Democratic Party operatives exploded into violence against black voters, and the growing ranks of disaffected whites allied with the new Union Labor Party. While temporarily staving off threats to their political dominance through fraud, intimidation, and bloodshed, Arkansas Democrats passed the state's first segregation and disfranchising laws in 1891, the formal beginning of the Jim Crow Era. Thus ended a remarkable period of possibility in Arkansas's history.[45]

Nevertheless, migrants continued to arrive. Though their numbers fell by nearly one-third, in the 1890s Arkansas still maintained one of the highest black in-migration rates in the nation. Soil exhaustion, boll weevil infestation, and obstacles to property ownership elsewhere contributed to a steady inflow of migrants from the Deep South through the 1910s.[46] However, 1890 still marked a turning point, both in migrants' movements and in public debate. For the first time, black Arkansans began to emigrate in sizeable numbers. In the 1890s, at least 5,000 black Arkansans left for Oklahoma. Another 3,700 moved to Texas. Arkansas's rates of out-migration began to approach regional averages after decades of running far below the rest of the South.[47]

The 1890s also saw greater focus among African Americans debating southern interstate migration: who should move, under what circumstances, and to which parts of Arkansas. Given the increasingly depressed market for cotton, both opponents and supporters of emigration feared that destitute families would sell themselves for passage westward. At its worst, the southwestern exodus had grown to resemble a resurrected slave trade based on raw coercion and exploitation and cloaked by the respectability of a contract. North Carolina minister Isaac Aldridge worried that he was witnessing "a speculation in human beings, carried on by the cattle planters, railroads and agents of Arkansas." Yet even Aldridge saw migration to Arkansas as a useful strategy as long as it was "independent." In Louisiana, D. J. Manley, an ardent supporter of emigration to South Arkansas, warned, "Agents both in Mississippi, Louisiana and Arkansas are doing only speculation in our people—selling them for a price, receiving from $2 to $5 per head." As in the interstate slave trade of thirty years before, some migrants were "held and guarded in certain towns till the buyers [came]." Manley urged collaborative migration of a kind long employed by southwestern migrants: "First organize . . . into clubs from twenty-five to fifty families in a club, appoint committees, buy the return tickets and send them the right to contract and bring out the families of their clubs." "If your committees were here now," he urged, "it would not take long before they could raise money to bring out several families."[48]

The attitude of early migrants helps us to understand the arrival of these later settlers. Whatever the state's boosters and critics might say, migrants did not expect an egalitarian paradise. They chose Arkansas because it offered resources. As one Arkansas migration supporter wrote, "My prayer is that God would send forth more laborers into the vineyard." Most migrants seemed to believe that migration would provide the possibility of actively building a new freedom rather than finding a ready-made paradise on earth.[49]

PART II

New Perspectives on White Violence

CHAPTER 4

Sundown Towns
Racial Cleansing in the Arkansas Delta

GUY LANCASTER

JAMES LOEWEN'S 2005 book, *Sundown Towns: A Hidden Dimension of American Racism*, was one of the first to bring national awareness to the phenomenon of the "sundown town," a community or neighborhood whose white residents have driven African Americans away at some point in the past, usually violently, and/or work to keep African Americans from settling there, often through a campaign of organized harassment. These sundown towns did not occur, for the most part, in the "traditional South," the South of lowland cotton agriculture, where African slaves lived and worked before the Civil War and where many African Americans continued to live even after the war and emancipation. Instead, they predominated in the "nontraditional South," such as the Ozark Mountains in Arkansas, which Loewen singles out as a region particularly emblematic of the sundown impulse in the state, exemplified by the 1905 and 1909 Harrison race riots in Boone County and the 1906 expulsion of African Americans from Cotter in Baxter County.[1]

Though Loewen does make note of Arkansas sundown towns that occurred outside the highland regions of the Ozark and Ouachita Mountains, such as the northeastern Arkansas city of Paragould, he does not provide an explanation for why such communities seemed to be following the patterns of upland areas nor how such communities may have themselves represented the nontraditional South. Neither does he explicitly link the emergence of sundown towns to the much broader phenomenon of whitecapping or nightriding, which was manifest in both those regions that went sundown and those that did not. Following in long-established traditions of vigilante violence, whitecappers or nightriders were "bands of armed white men who engaged in what they viewed as community 'regulation' and retaliation, moving against those who violated norms, transgressed boundaries, or threatened livelihoods." In many areas, as the economy in the late nineteenth century soured, whitecappers expanded their targets beyond cotton merchants and revenue agents and began attacking African Americans, specifically, those who "rented farms, owned land, or otherwise worked for merchants or large planters," as well as those who had found "alternative employment in newly opened railroads, lumber camps, and sawmills."[2] The attempt to drive off black laborers, especially in those areas where such workers constituted the majority of any black population, would certainly seem to be related to the emergence of sundown towns, which occurred during a period when whitecapper violence was particularly ubiquitous.

This essay surveys several late nineteenth- and early twentieth-century incidents of racial violence and intimidation in the Arkansas Delta, incidents which fall under the rubric of racial cleansing or white-capping, in order to determine what connections might exist between the two phenomena. While this survey focuses upon the northern part of the delta region, where known sundown towns were concentrated, instances of whitecapper violence in and around other communities, such as Pine Bluff, are also examined.

This survey begins at the northernmost point of the Arkansas Delta in Clay County. In 1880, there were only forty-three African Americans listed as Clay County residents according to the US Census. Certain locals were determined to keep the number of black residents low, even to the point of preventing the temporary workforce laying the railroad through Clay County from employing any African Americans inside its borders. Two different versions of the story exist. According to one, after the construction crew moved its black laborers over to the Arkansas side of the St. Francis River, to the settlement named St. Francis, "a group of white men, with lighted lanterns, marched single file past these tents, opened the tent flaps, passed their lanterns inside, just looked around and passed on."[3] The result was that the black laborers, understanding the implied threat, moved back over to the Missouri side and refused to enter Clay County. Another story holds that Bill Waddle, who was supervising a black labor force on the Missouri side of the river (and who was a member of the local Ku Klux Klan), recruited some local people and "led a shot gun parade" to the Missouri line, where he "told the bosses and Negroes, who were doing the work, that was where the Negroes stopped and the whites would take over."[4]

In October 1887, a "party of masked men" raided black tenant houses in the Lawrence County town of Clover Bend, informing the farmers that "they must leave the country." The F. W. Tucker and Company, which had been employing African Americans since Reconstruction, contacted the county sheriff, as well as Gov. Simon P. Hughes, who wrote to the sheriff with the message, "Citizens everywhere must be protected against lawlessness and violence."[5] Nothing much seems to have arisen from this event, but something similar occurred the following decade in the Lawrence County town of Black Rock, situated where the Arkansas Delta meets the Ozark Mountains. On the night of Friday, January 12, 1894, a group of whitecappers posted in a public place in town a notice that read: "All negroes must leave this town inside of ten days or take what follows, and all who have houses rented to them must fire them or we will fire the houses inside of ten days. Negroes, don't let this slip your mind." Subsequent verbal and written notices were issued to major employers, the mills and the factories, warning owners that their property would be burned should they fail to discharge their black laborers. According to reports, African Americans had been run off from neighboring towns (the *New York Times* reported that they had been ordered out of the county, as well as the town), and, as the *Arkansas Gazette* noted, "if driven from Black Rock [they] will be without friends and money in an inhospitable country." Gov. William Meade Fishback took a personal interest in the case and was in contact with the manager of a folding-bed company, as well as with T. D. Compton, editor of the *Lawrence County Democrat*, and was reportedly willing to take action "necessary to the protection of life and property." Despite this elite support, the largest firm in the town did dismiss "all its colored labor rather than take the risks of losing its property," and one-third of the black population, estimated then at three hundred, reportedly fled.[6] The *New York Times* reported two days later that Black Rock had settled into an armed quiet and that "no overt acts have been committed by the persons who have attempted to drive the negroes from town," though whitecappers had by then published three notices.[7]

Paragould in Greene County is probably the most notorious sundown town of the Arkansas Delta. A letter printed in the April 21, 1888, issue of the *Arkansas Gazette* reported: "We are but a few colored people here in Paragould, and the white people are very cruel to all. They are now coming every night shooting upon houses and throwing rocks upon our houses every night, and I write this to you for information, because I don't know what it is best to do, but please give some information what to do. We are got [*sic*] land. We cannot stay upon it to save our lives. They burn our houses down and church down, and in fact we can't have no peace here."[8] In late October 1892, "twenty-five or thirty men went to the houses and residences of the most of the colored population" of Paragould "and notified them to leave within three days and nights."[9] By the time the event was reported in the *Gazette*, a number had apparently left or were planning to leave.

Marauders, "believed to be the lowest element of the white population," again attacked local African Americans in August 1899, leading to an exodus from Paragould that the *Gazette* reported under the headline "Negroes Are Leaving Paragould by Hundreds." According to the article, a "self-appointed vigilance committee visited the negro citizens of Paragould" on the night of Thursday, August 3, to deliver notice to them "to leave the city of Paragould, bag and baggage, on or before next Saturday night, and never return again, for any purpose whatsoever, or suffer the consequences of staying." The African American population applied to the mayor for protection, but he declined. Through the weekend, "cabins where the remaining negroes reside were stoned," the Stancill Hotel "was stoned and window lights knocked out," and "a notice was left on the door of Charles Wyse, a wealthy colored barber, ordering him and his assistants to leave," despite the fact that Wyse had lived in Paragould all his life and was determined, according to the report, to defend his property, even at the expense of his life. Though an August 5 meeting of "many of the best citizens in the town" did pass resolutions opposing the violence, they also opposed the importation of "negro labor for any purpose whatever at this time" and requested that "the lumber companies or the corporations in our midst employing labor to refrain from giving employment to any others than those who are residents of our community."[10] Labor issues rose again on October 19, 1903, when unknown arsonists burned down the Paragould Cotton Compress; the owners of the facility linked the incendiary act to their employment of African Americans and planned to rebuild in Forrest City, further south in St. Francis County, the following year.[11] On April 9, 1908, the *Gazette* reported that a band of nightriders styling itself the "Dirty Dozen" attacked the home of some African Americans and ordered them to leave town on pain of death. By that time, according to newspaper accounts, there were no more than forty African Americans living in Paragould.[12]

In 1909 and 1910, archaeologist Clarence B. Moore, who was conducting research in northeastern Arkansas along the St. Francis, White, and Black Rivers, reported that the people along the Little River above Lepanto in Poinsett County were known for their "hostility against negroes" and, in fact, maintained "a negro dead-line, permitting no colored person to go among them." His company of men included several African Americans, and as local "race prejudice has resulted in the murder of a number of negroes, we did not deem it fair to expose to slaughter men who had served us faithfully for years."[13] A 1987 publication about Buffalo Island Drainage District No. 16 reports: "Historical research shows that an ironclad but unwritten rule of exclusion existed and was enforced from about the year 1900. From that date until after World War II, black Americans were forbidden to live on Buffalo Island or even to spend the night on Buffalo Island. Blacks who visited the Island, being fearful of being mistreated, each day left the Island before sundown."[14]

According to a 1961 folklore report by L. A. "Buddy" Diebold Jr., the white residents of Hickory Ridge in Cross County, located on the western side of Crowley's Ridge, expelled local African Americans around the year 1910. Diebold's informants reported that groups of whites took to "catching young buck niggers up town, day or night, and whipping them in gangs—then taking them into the 'holler', tying them to what they called the 'hanging tree', and bull-whipping them in front of everyone." After this, reportedly, a young black man whistled at a white girl and was subsequently wrapped with log chains and thrown into the bayou, while another black man committed an act of murder in revenge for his son's whipping and was subsequently burned to death. However, "the crowning blow came when a group of nigger boys raped and killed a white girl. The white men of the town started dynamiting the houses in the 'holler' at night, not caring how many or who they killed and hurt. This caused the niggers to give up the battle and move out. Every last one of them was harassed by the dynamiters until they were forced to leave." Afterwards, there were no African Americans living in Hickory Ridge, which quickly gained a reputation for possessing an "unwritten law that they [blacks] must be out of town before sun-down." Diebold does record some instances of harassment, of which he had personal knowledge, directed against African Americans who ended up briefly working for rice farmers in the town, noting, "It is a common thing for the younger boys to inform any nigger passing through and happens to stop, that all niggers are either out of town by sundown or they'll be 'ridden out on a rail.'"[15]

In mid-August 1908, there spread fear of a possible race war in the Poinsett County town of Trumann, southeast of Jonesboro, after the Springfield Lumber Company brought in African American workers to help clear the land for farm use. "This action is said to have aroused the sentiment of some of the white men employed at the mill," reported the *Arkansas Gazette*, leading one of them, identified as J. B. Briggs, to attempt to run off the black workers with a shotgun.[16] Briggs was actually arrested, sent to the jail in Jonesboro, and eventually fined five dollars for his role in the affair, while the superintendent of the company made a request to the governor for troops in order to ward off possible violence. However, the following day, the newspaper reported that the black workers "have scattered in every direction and all fears of a race riot . . . have vanished with them," adding that "there may be further trouble, but it is not believed that any negroes will come here, as the community has never been inclined kindly toward them."[17]

Just a few years later, in 1912, the Poinsett Lumber and Manufacturing Company, later taken over by the Singer Manufacturing Company of Chicago, Illinois, was established in the town.[18] Singer employed many African Americans, who inhabited company-built shotgun houses along what was called "Three Row," near the plant.[19] According to an informant of folklorist Richard Burns, who has studied those shotgun houses, white residents in the 1920s one day roused the black inhabitants, "rounded them up, put them on the railroad track, and stayed behind them until they got out of town."[20] Some black workers continued to remain employed at the Singer plant, though they commuted to town daily by train from nearby Marked Tree.[21]

In April 1912, notices signed "Kit Karson and Band" were posted in Walnut Ridge in Lawrence County, ordering local African Americans to leave the city. A committee of white citizens responded to this threat by posting their own warnings to the band in question, asserting, "We will protect our help and prosecute you to the limit of the law. Furthermore, the white people will arm their servants with instructions to shoot the first intruders who disturb them."²² Despite this warning, on the night of April 19, a "crowd of unidentified white men" dynamited one black-owned home, fired upon the house of another, and "terrorized the entire [black] section of the city for several hours," ceasing only "when practically all of the negroes had fled from the district," according to the *Jonesboro Evening Sun*.²³

Several "prominent citizens" of Walnut Ridge communicated with Gov. George Washington Donaghey that night, expressing "fears that bloodshed would result if immediate action was not taken," in response to which the governor called out the local militia, stationed at Black Rock, to restore order. As in other cases, the vigilantes also threatened specific employers; in Walnut Ridge, the black employees of the Phoenix Cotton Oil Company were driven from the business and ordered out of the county.²⁴ Half of an estimated black population of four hundred at the time was reported to have fled the city by the time the militia arrived.²⁵

It was not only the northern Arkansas Delta that saw attempts to drive off African Americans. In early 1898, a representative of the Brinkley Stave and Heading Company wrote Gov. Daniel W. Jones to complain about notices threatening the company's black tenant workers southeast of Brinkley in Monroe County, notices warning these tenants to leave within ten days or be killed.²⁶ In April 1908, unknown assailants shot into the cabins of black laborers located on plantations in the Lonoke area of Lonoke County, apparently in an attempt to drive them off.²⁷ As historian Jeannie Whayne notes, for many lower-class whites, tenant farming could be the first rung on the ladder to actual landownership, and so the "presence of lower-paid black sharecroppers simply worked against their economic interests."²⁸

Even historic delta cities with established black communities were occasionally subject to this kind of violence, as exemplified by the headline "Negroes Warned to Leave Pine Bluff" from the March 15, 1915, *Arkansas Gazette*. Far from being an example of vigilante overreach, the story actually entails an attempt to remove African Americans from a part of the Jefferson County city dubbed Hoboken. Two weeks prior to the report, unknown individuals posted notices warning black residents to leave: "Negroes, beware. We want your jobs. You are given two weeks to leave the city or suffer the penalty of death."²⁹ After the deadline, more notices were posted, and a fire broke out in a black-owned house, spreading to consume four houses eventually; locals connected the fire with the warnings, pouring into the streets and shooting at suspected nightriders, a situation that led to one instance of black-on-black manslaughter during the confusion.[30] Authorities managed to restore order, but no one was ever charged for either the night-riding or the apparent arson.[31] In fact, the only person ever held in the affair was Monroe Flowers, an African American accused of stealing a neighbor's shotgun during the confusion.[32]

In Mississippi County, in early March 1915, notices were posted warning African Americans to leave the area around O'Donnell Bend, northeast of Osceola and near the Mississippi River. In addition, one white man received a warning that any continued employment of black labor would be met with his house and property being burned. A search by the deputy sheriff and a marshal netted five people; a later search brought in two more suspects, while others reportedly escaped to Tennessee after burning a "negro tenant house" on the plantation of one J. C. Spann. Of the seven suspects brought in, the grand jury laid indictments against three: Mark Rogers, Jesse Swafford, and Giles Simpson. In his instructions to the grand jury, Judge W. J. Driver emphasized the heinousness of the crime and added that "if anyone ever loses his life while engaged in night riding, the man who kills him in defense of his home shall never go to jail for the act so long as the court has the power to set aside the verdict of guilty."[33] Swafford quickly turned state's evidence against his co-conspirators, thus securing for the prosecution the conviction of all three men. Rogers, the alleged ringleader of the group, was sentenced to almost eight years in the state penitentiary, while Simpson, convicted on two counts, received a four-year sentence, and Swafford, convicted on one count, received one year.[34]

What do these stories of racial cleansing in Arkansas tell us?

Firstly, one cannot assume any easy regional divisions in the distribution of sundown towns in Arkansas, assigning such places to one side of the line separating the Ozark Mountains and the Arkansas Delta. Rather, one needs to take into account the temporal divisions that separate new communities, especially those tied to specific industries emerging during the late nineteenth and early twentieth centuries, from other, longer-established towns and cities. St. Francis, Black Rock, Paragould, Hickory Ridge, Trumann, and Walnut Ridge were all communities that coalesced around railroad developments, along with attendant timber industries, in the late nineteenth century. In these places, African Americans were not well established and could be easily marginalized, being new arrivals to an area that had been but sparsely settled. Of course, most whites were new arrivals too, although no one complained about companies importing white workers. By contrast, in such cities as Pine Bluff and Osceola, African Americans were longstanding residents and an important part of the local economy. Here, massive flight did not occur, in part due to the successful intervention of local authorities. State and local authorities also intervened in Black Rock and Walnut Ridge, but African Americans there either understood their position to be more precarious than their counterparts in more established black communities or were more willing to leave, being part of a largely transitory labor force.

Secondly, racial cleansing should be understood as a complex and nuanced practice. A few of the places examined here became what we today acknowledge as sundown towns, such as Black Rock, Paragould, the various towns on Buffalo Island, and Hickory Ridge. Clay County is sometimes called a "sundown county," never having had a black population higher than ten for the first six decades of the twentieth century and then dropping to zero in 1970. The other communities, however, continue to represent the legacy of past hostilities, even if they are not explicitly labeled as sundown towns. Trumann, for example, has a black population of just over 4 percent as of 2010, significantly lower than the county black population, at 7.2 percent. Poinsett County, in which Trumann is located, deviates from its immediate neighbors in being entirely surrounded by counties where the black population ranges from 13.1 percent to 51.2 percent. While Walnut Ridge is also generally not labeled as a sundown town, its black population is only about 1.8 percent, meaning that it mimics to a greater extent nearby sundown towns than it does other regional cities.

Thus, the precise dividing line between what is labeled as a sundown town and a non-sundown town is unclear. Indeed, while the term "sundown town" can be useful in confronting present-day institutional racism, framing the phenomenon exclusively in terms of the resulting community, rather than in historic acts of racial cleansing, covers over the varied motivations underlying white exclusionary violence against African Americans. In short, it lumps together as a single phenomenon what are actually a multiplicity of agendas and motivations. Sometimes what white vigilantes wanted, such as land and jobs, was just as important a factor in the violence they perpetrated as what they did not want, that is, the presence of African Americans.

Thirdly, understanding racial cleansings as more complex and nuanced episodes means that understanding white-capping is just as important as studying lynching in the history of racial violence in the South, although the publications about lynching currently far outweigh those that examine other forms of racial violence. Scholars have, perhaps understandably, been drawn toward those manifestations of white supremacist violence that have the direst consequences.[35] Whitecapping, as has been outlined here, however, did not always produce such extreme results as lynching. In Walnut Ridge, for example, not a single African American was actually murdered during those many hours of shooting and dynamiting, albeit that half of the estimated black population was reported to have fled the city. In some acknowledged sundown towns, such as Paragould, white-capping violence did not result in as complete and dramatic an exodus of African Americans as did certain racial cleansing events in the Ozarks. Nonetheless, this violence did have an impact that can be read on the map in changing the racial demographics of those communities, and it deserves to be studied both by those researching racial cleansing and those researching better-known forms of southern violence.

Finally, analyzing racial cleansing and whitecapping together presents opportunities to move beyond the distancing of typical historical practice. As the Swedish novelist and historian Vilhelm Moberg once wrote, "Obviously, men are indistinguishable from the age in which they live, and must not be considered outside its context. But I do not judge our history's men of violence—and they appear in great numbers—*only* as products of the spirit of their age and environment. I call their evil deeds by their proper name. After all, many good and peaceable individuals, living at the same time, resisted the spirit of their age and environment, and refused to let it set its stamp on them. For me, a murder committed in the 14th century is still murder."[36]

Indeed, the 1915 trial of whitecappers in Osceola demonstrates that it was within the scope of the white power structure of this era to bring wrongdoers to justice; and historians have noted that whitecappers, unlike participants in lynch mobs, occasionally faced arrest, had their identities revealed, and were convicted, if only due to the fact that their actions threatened the profits of white plantation and mill owners.[37]

Therefore, the failure to arrest or prosecute whitecappers (or those comprising lynch mobs, for that matter) was a deliberate choice, for clearly local governments, in most cases, had the resources needed to track down the perpetrators. Historians have regularly been loath to appear to judge those in the past by the standards of today, but if we can take heart in the just conviction of whitecappers in Osceola in 1915, then surely we can let ourselves feel a righteous dismay that such an event stands as the exception to the rule.

CHAPTER 5

Race, History, and Memory in Harrison, Arkansas

An Ozarks Town Reckons with Its Past

JACQUELINE FROELICH

AN AGITATED THRONG of angry white residents, armed with guns and knives, attacked their African American neighbors in the isolated Ozarks lumber town of Harrison, Arkansas, in the autumn of 1905.[1] Men, women, and children were tied to trees and whipped, others were roped together and tossed into nearby Crooked Creek. Homes were torched, windows shot out. All were ordered to leave town immediately.[2] The *Harrison Daily Times* newspaper records of the period have long been missing, but an anonymous reporter covering the riot for the *Arkansas Gazette* wrote a story the following day headlined "Negro Residents in Panic, Expected to Cause Exodus of Blacks."[3]

One hundred and fifteen of Harrison's fifteen hundred residents were African American, and some had lived there for decades.[4] They had their own church, the Union African Methodist Episcopal, and a school. Some operated businesses; most worked as laborers and housekeepers. And by all accounts, blacks and whites got along.[5]

But mix up Harrison's reputation for chronic street brawls with shrill racist propaganda, a plague of lynchings, and sanctioned segregation, and race violence was bound to rise.[6] Adding to tensions was the failure of the newly constructed Missouri and North Arkansas Railroad, in which some locals had invested. Facing bankruptcy, and the relocation of its terminus from Little Rock to Helena, the venture was doomed.[7]

What sparked the riot was a break-in by a homeless black railroad laborer who was subsequently jailed with another black prisoner.[8] The mob stormed the jail, violently dispatched the men, and set its sights upon the black district, wreaking violence door-to-door and banishing entire families. Once those properties were purged of their black residents, white residents would eventually take adverse possession of them.[9]

Local law enforcement took no measures to arrest the race rioters, but Western District judge John Henry Rogers happened to be in town during the unrest. In his charge to a grand jury already scheduled for impaneling, Rogers reportedly called "special attention to the reported whipping and intimidating of Negroes in Harrison recently by mobs." He said that every participant in the affair should be punished to the full extent of the law without regard to his or her standing in the community.[10] The case was heard in Western District Federal Court in Fort Smith, but no victims were willing to come forward to testify. Participants in the mob violence were never indicted.[11]

The black families driven out of Harrison fled north to Springfield, Missouri, where they would, a year later, face another race revolt with a macabre ending. A lynch mob grabbed three young black youths on their way home from work, wrongfully accused them of raping a white woman, and hanged them on the town square, incinerating their dead bodies over a blazing bonfire on Easter eve. The event was celebrated with the striking of a commemorative bronze coin. One side read, "Easter Offering," the other, "Souvenir of the hanging of Three Niggers, Springfield, Missouri, April 14, 1906."[12] Other Harrison refugees traveled to established black districts in Muskogee and Tulsa in Oklahoma. But fifteen years later in Tulsa, they too would bear witness to yet another a racial conflagration. A mob six thousand strong destroyed a thirty-five-city-block area of the black-owned Greenwood District, again triggered by fabricated black-on-white rape hysteria. An estimated three hundred blacks were killed and eight thousand left homeless.[13]

Some fortunate Harrison refugees escaped to the resort village of Eureka Springs, forty-five miles west. Among them was Alice Fancher (nee Sewell), her son Richard Banks, and sister Mattie Fancher (nee Rollan).[14] At the time, Eureka Springs was the fourth largest city in Arkansas, with a small but established African American community concentrated north of downtown along a steep mountainside. Like everyone else, blacks found plenty of work in the resort economy, working as farriers, stone masons, porters, and maids, operating laundries, and serving as bathhouse attendants. Some managed boardinghouses. Eliza Richards, along with her friend Cora Richardson, acquired a dozen parcels and homes in the black district. African Americans also enjoyed visiting Eureka Springs as tourists, staying at the Congress, a black-owned hotel built in a spring-fed hollow across from the town library.[15]

In Eureka Springs, the Fancher family and other race violence refugees from Harrison found safe haven in a place historically known for its racial tolerance. Of the town's nearly fifty springs, centrally located Basin Spring first attracted the most attention. In his 1881 guidebook, *The Healing Fountain*, Professor L. J. Kalklosch, a teacher at the Normal School in Harrison, marveled at the diversity of the health seekers:

> People of all classes could be assembled at Basin Spring. Here could be seen an amusing spectacle. No other place upon the continent ever was made up of a conglomerate, heterogeneous mass of humanity, as was this. It seemed as if a cyclone had passed through all the natives and landed them at the health resort. We see the Northern man, and the Southern man, the Eastern and the Western man, the Negro and the Red man, the Mexican and the Canadian—in short, men, women, and children of all persuasions of color. Religious, politics, nor any previous condition is recognized in the social circles. The Yankee and the Johnnie are fast friends. The Baptist Elder and the Methodist Deacon drink out of the same fraternal jug and feel glad.

For decades afterwards, visitors continued to congregate around popular cold-water springs seeking rejuvenation.[16] African Americans would especially gather at Harding Spring, which locals referred to as the "Negro Spring," after church on Sunday, where they were heard singing spirituals and worshiping.[17] All attended Pilgrim's Chapel, the African American Episcopal Church in Eureka Springs, and the children had their own segregated school. Yet no blacks ever gained a permanent economic stake, and as a segregated population they could never freely enjoy the resort. The collapse of the spa industry and the Great Depression eventually caused most of Eureka Springs's blacks to join the great migration North. Hattie and Mattie Fancher, along with Richard Banks, were the only ones who stayed. Today, their remains rest in Eureka Springs' cemetery.[18]

"If there was any place where there were good race relations, it was here in Eureka Springs," claimed John Cross, a native and local banker. Yet he and certain other natives continue to refer to historic black residents as "niggers." Cross claims that the term isn't racist. "Fred was called 'Nigger Fred' and Alice was called 'Nigger Alice,'" he said. "No one thought anything about it. It wasn't oppression. They were happy!"[19] Pat Matsukis, a Chicago native who purchased a home in the Eureka Springs old black district in the 1980s, moved her arm in a wide arc and said, "This all used to be known as—and this is the term they still use—'niggertown.'"[20]

For decades, rumors had persisted in Eureka Springs that all the African American residents had been purged: "The blacks were a problem," said Bernadine Miller, who moved to Eureka Springs in the 1920s. "So the Ku Klux Klan came in and burned them all out."[21] It's likely that the story of Harrison's race conflict, intentionally covered up for almost century, had somehow become sublimated and transposed onto Eureka Springs history.

Back in Harrison, after the 1905 riot, a few black residents managed to stay, likely protected by white families. Four years later, they too would be driven out. It began when a black teenager, Charley Stinnett, a resident of Yellville who had been staying in town with relatives, was arrested and jailed for robbing a sixty-year-old woman for whom he had been chopping firewood. He would have been lynched from his cell had he not been transferred to another town jail. At first he confessed to the crime, but later, likely under coercion, he admitted to an assault charge (a euphemism for rape) and was hastily tried, found guilty, and sentenced to hang.[22]

Charley's mother, Lettie Stinnett, a resident of Muskogee, Oklahoma, attempted to save her son by circulating a petition to commute his sentence to life imprisonment. Nearly one thousand residents signed the document. She then sent the request on to Arkansas governor George W. Donaghey, who granted a thirty-day stay of execution to investigate.[23] Nothing came of the investigation, and Charley was hanged from a scaffold hidden by a canvas-covered enclosure to prevent public viewing and, likely, more vexation.[24]

Charley Stinnett's two-hundred-pound body was hastily crammed into a small, rough coffin, his head and arms twisted to fit. The casket was shipped that day to Muskogee for burial, where his distraught parents received it, still dripping with blood.[25] The horrific story was picked up and carried by regional newspapers, including the *San Antonio Light*.[26]

Harrison's last remaining black residents, fearing for their lives, hurriedly left town after Charley Stinnett's sentencing, fearing more mob violence.[27] A century later, Hugh Cotton, the only contemporary resident willing to recount events after the history came to light, talked about how his grandfather, George H. Cotton, aided one of the victims:

> Grandad used to have an abstract office and a saloon on the south side of the square, and Nigger George done all the cleanin', washing out the shot glasses and sweepin' and all. And when they had all the trouble, they run 'em out. They hung one and gave the rest of 'em 24 hours—all ten, eleven, twelve [of them]—to leave. Then they got hot and heavy after Nigger George because him and one old lady was still in Harrison. They threatened to lynch him, so Granddad put him in the buggy one night at midnight and took him to Eureka Springs. All the rest of the night and the next day at noon, it took him, twelve hours to drive him from here to Eureka Springs. And I think he lived there until he died.[28]

Fifty years after the race riots, the stench of Harrison's half-buried race riot history and the region's lily-white populace attracted an array of modern bigots. Among them was Gerald L. K. Smith, who built his anti-Semitic Great Passion Play in 1964 in Carroll County. Thom Robb, national director of the Knights Party U.S.A., a faction of the Ku Klux Klan, moved to the tiny town of Zinc, east of Harrison. White separatist militia camps sprouted to the north and west like toxic mushrooms across the Ozarks landscape. Just south of Harrison, white supremacist Mike Hallimore established his secretive Kingdom Identity Ministries compound.[29] African American Arkansans avoided driving through Harrison for fear of being harassed or worse.[30]

Even after accounts of Harrison's historic race riots were published and broadcast in the late 1990s, residents remained silent.[31] But emotions finally broke loose on Halloween night in 2002, when several black junior high school football players from Fayetteville were harassed by local white boys wearing sheets. That winter, George Holcomb, a cub reporter for the *Harrison Daily Times* and a newcomer to Harrison, wrote a series of stories finally wrenching open the town's racist history. The articles created a firestorm of opinion. Some said the history was sheer fiction, while others were deeply ashamed such a thing had occurred in their town.[32]

It was an itinerant preacher who took the first step toward reconciliation. "Ninety-eight years is a long time to be silent," said Pastor Wayne Kelly in a KUAF Public Radio interview. "Silence is what allowed

Harrison's stigma to persist. So now we are speaking up against those things."[33] Kelly was pastor at New Hearts Church, a charismatic southern Baptist denomination. His storefront church was just off the town square along Crooked Creek, close to where, a century earlier, black residents had been terrorized and banished. Kelly said those who committed the race crimes were dead, but descendants and local churches remained accountable for their ancestors' actions. "By our silence we condone sinful racist attitudes," Kelly said.[34]

To rid the town of its racist reputation, Pastor Kelly, along with an ecumenical group of ministers, at the request of the town mayor, formed the Harrison Community Task Force on Race Relations in 2003. On May 1 of that year, several hundred men, women, and children congregated on Harrison's town square to pray and apologize for committing violent acts of racism nearly a century earlier.[35] Within six months, over eight hundred Harrison residents, including then town mayor Bob Reynolds, signed documents, filed at city hall, personally affirming and welcoming people of all races into their community.[36]

Emerging from his compound south of Harrison, Mike Hallimore proclaimed his disgust. "Race reconciliation," he said, "should be called racial agitation."[37] Hallimore, who for years had proselytized via shortwave radio and webcasts, insisted the United States needed a nationwide ethnic cleansing.[38] Referring to himself not as a white supremacist or separatist, but rather as a Christian "racialist," he claimed many people in Boone County shared his beliefs that women are inferior, that the offspring of interracial marriages are mongrels, that Jews are the spawn of Satan, and that homosexuals are an abomination and so should be put to death. "Therefore," he said, "Harrison's racist stigma serves a purpose."[39]

To blunt race reconciliation, Hallimore mass mailed over twelve thousand flyers four months after the town square ceremony, claiming that Harrison had been a peaceful white community and that inviting blacks and Mexicans to settle in the area would cause a surge in violent crime.[40] The *Harrison Daily Times* printed Hallimore's literature. When queried as to why he would print racist propaganda, publisher Jeff Christenson said it was his first amendment right to print whatever jobs he wished.[41] In retaliation to Hallimore's mailing, the city council passed a special resolution declaring Harrison to be a "warm and welcoming community, inclusive of all races."[42]

In January 2006 a public declaration, signed by more than twelve hundred residents, was published in the Sunday edition of the *Harrison Daily Times*, proclaiming: "We the undersigned citizens of Harrison, Arkansas, and surrounding areas do hereby denounce the blatant racism and bigotry of a very small minority in our community. We stand for respect, harmony and acceptance of all people. We do not want the fine city of Harrison, and its citizens to continue to be known worldwide as tolerant of hatred, racism and bigotry. By signing, we declare that we will remain SILENT NO MORE on this issue and will continue to speak out and change this perception of our town."[43]

The traveling preacher who was responsible for bringing Harrison to its knees in repentance has since moved on. Yet membership in the task force continues to grow to include local and regional political, education, religious, and business leaders. The city is becoming increasingly diverse, due in part to the ongoing work of the Harrison Community Task Force on Race Relations. Members have assembled a mobile exhibit on their black history, facilitated diversity trainings for both schoolchildren and the public, established a local community college scholarship for minority students, and early on struck up a sister relationship with an African Methodist Episcopal Church in Helena, a delta town that was once linked to Harrison by the old railroad.[44]

Task force members also sought to substantiate and expand on Harrison's black history. Resident Carolyn Cline continues to lead that effort.[45] A sixth-generation Ozarks native, Cline said she had no idea the black population had been driven out a century earlier. "What is shown in the record was a stable, literate, Christian community, with the Union African Methodist Episcopalian Church as their center of their lives. And property maps indicate that black and white people lived very close to each other, so apparently were getting along just fine," she said. "But that leaves many questions as to why a community would attack it's own."[46]

Patty Methvin, president and CEO of the Harrison Chamber of Commerce and an original member of the task force, said that the group is reframing Harrison as a welcoming place. "Over the years we've taken every opportunity to show that Harrison is a wonderful and safe community for all people."[47] Methvin said that numerous businesses with multicultural staff have set up operations in Harrison and national business development conferences are commonplace, indicating that Harrison's reputation must be improving.[48] Cline, Methvin, and Layne

Ragsdale, another founding member, also participated in the Clinton School of Public Service at the University of Arkansas "Pathways to Racial Healing and Equity in the American South" summit in 2011 to share their story for the first time and to learn from other community organizers. "It was an exceptional opportunity to talk about Harrison," Methvin said.[49]

In the winter of 2012, the task force co-hosted an Arkansas Martin Luther King Jr. Commission Nonviolence Youth Summit at North Arkansas Community College in Harrison. "It's our responsibility to quell rumors that continue to stigmatize the town," said Ragsdale. "And we are reaching out for guidance to Arkansas's African Americans."[50] Aiding their effort is the withering of self-promoting hate mongers like Thom Robb and Mike Hallimore, mere caricatures of a once-powerful American white separatist movement.[51]

Word of Harrison's historic race riot first spread after it was featured in the documentary film *Banished: American Ethnic Cleansings*, produced in collaboration with the Center for Investigative Reporting and Two Tone Productions, airing on PBS's Independent Lens series. The film examined how early twentieth-century black communities were systematically purged by white residents across the mid-South.[52] In the film, a spotlight was shone on Harrison's race reconciliation task force.

Still, some Harrison natives will go to their graves denying their violent racist past.[53] In the spring of 2012, a *Wikipedia* entry on Harrison stated that the documented black history was "mostly false and misleading at best."[54] By then, Harrison was also beginning to attract national media attention after Associated Press reporter Jeannie Nuss wrote a story in March 2012 characterizing the town's attempt to rebrand its image as disingenuous.[55] The article also linked Harrison to a virulent faction of the Ku Klux Klan. Yet what the reporter failed to note was that the self-described KKK "grand dragon," Thom Robb, has an insular following comprised mostly of family members surviving on sales of cheap racist novelty items.[56] In the days following Nuss's wire story, an article published in the *Harrison Daily Times* quoted local city and task force leaders claiming that her story was sensationalized.[57]

Today, of Harrison's thirteen thousand residents, three dozen are African American, one hundred are Asian, and almost three hundred are of Hispanic or Latino origin.[58] And while they are free to live wherever they wish, early twentieth-century black residents were mostly concentrated on the eastern side of town, a region now illustrated and mapped by the Harrison Race Reconciliation Task Force on a self-guided history tour.

Even after Harrison's African American district stood empty by 1909, only one woman chose to stay—likely protected by a white family with whom she lived—until her death in 1916.[59] Referred to by locals as "Aunt Vine," she preferred her given name of Alecta Caledonia Melvina Smith. According to a rare Boone County black history record, she said she was proud to be the last of her race in the town, proclaiming herself "the best niggah evah bawn, cuz all de rest was run off."[60]

Efforts to trace descendants of Harrison's historic black community failed until an amateur genealogist made contact. Joyce Coker was working to resolve disturbing questions regarding her family tree. She discovered that she was related to executed Harrison teenager Charley Stinnett. "He was my first cousin twice removed, my grandfather's first cousin," Coker said.[61] The retired telecom worker, who lives in New Jersey, learned she had family roots in Yellville, Arkansas, which was Charley Stinnett's hometown, as well as in Muskogee and Joplin. "I found a small article about a Charley Stinnett being hanged in Harrison in 1909 and wondered if this was my Charley," she said. "I thought about how his mom felt trying to get his execution changed to a life sentence, and how she felt receiving her son that way," referring to articles she had found on Charley's body being crushed into coffin for shipment out of state.[62] Coker hopes to someday travel to the Ozarks, to meet her long-lost family, to pay her respects at her ancestors' graves, and, if she can draw up the courage, to visit Harrison. On the town square Coker will see a lawn studded with historical monuments.[63] But no monument stands to commemorate Harrison's destroyed black district. Reconciliation has occurred in Harrison, but reparation, that is, compensating victims' descendants for blood and treasure lost, may take another century.

On October 15, 2013, a racist billboard was erected on a major thoroughfare in Harrison, Arkansas, by an anonymous individual; it reads, "Anti-Racist is a Code Word for Anti-White." Members of the community staged a protest to illustrate that the offensive billboard message did not speak for the town. The Harrison Community Task Force on Race Relations, which now counts two African American members, paid to erect a countervailing billboard a few months later; it stated, "Love your neighbor," featuring a quote by Martin Luther King Jr.: "Hate cannot drive out hate; only love can do that."

Five months after the billboard incident, on April 1, 2014, the task force hosted a Unity Arts Celebration at the Lyric Theater in downtown Harrison to coincide with an Arkansas Martin Luther King Jr. Commission youth summit titled "Life after Hate." Of the more than four hundred who attended, half were African American youth. After the arts celebration, a contingent of task force members, city officials, and summit participants marched from the Lyric Theater to city hall, where a symbolic grave had been dug. Together they lowered an empty infant-sized wooden casket. The burial site will remain forever marked as the end of hate and racism in Harrison.[64]

CHAPTER 6

The Twenty-One Deaths Caused by the 1959 Fire at the Arkansas Negro Boys Industrial School
An Isolated Case of "Neglect" or an Instance of Racial Violence?

GRIF STOCKLEY

IN THE PAPERS of Gov. Orval E. Faubus, housed in the Special Collections archives at the University of Arkansas at Fayetteville, there are twenty-eight letters and telegrams from out of state addressed to Faubus (including one from Great Britain) in early March of 1959 condemning the deaths of twenty-one boys in a fire at Arkansas Negro Boys Industrial School. Frazier Peters of New York wrote, "Dear Sir: The more I read about your state the less I am interested in keeping it in the Union. Archaic and barbarous." Luville Milton of San Mateo, California, added, "My dear Governor Faubus, Each time I see in the newspaper a by-line 'Little Rock, Arkansas,' I shudder because I know it means yet another atrocity against the Negroes. . . . With all my heart and soul, with the full strength of my being, I utterly condemn the treatment of Negroes by the government and people of the state of Arkansas." A telegram from a labor union in Detroit reads, in part, "We hold you and the Jim Crow system of the South just as responsible for the burning of the Negro children in Little Rock as if you had struck the match. We pledge to fight until you and the subhuman racialism you represent are thrown into the garbage dump of history."[1]

The words "archaic," "barbarous," and "atrocity" would suggest to most people that a lynching or even a massacre had once again taken place in Arkansas. But these were people outraged by wire service accounts that reported sixty-nine boys had been locked inside a dormitory at the

Arkansas Negro Boys Industrial School, twelve miles south of Little Rock in the mostly all-black community of Wrightsville, while a fire had raged through the property. Forty-eight escaped burning to death only by knocking out two of the windows in the dormitory. Another twenty-one, unable to escape, had burned to death. By their responses, the individuals writing to the governor interpreted the deaths of the boys as an all-too-familiar example of racial violence by white southerners.

Yet just as clearly, the white Arkansans who responded publicly to the news of the early morning fire and the deaths of the boys saw things very differently. To be sure, they agreed, it was a terrible tragedy. As K. August Engel, publisher of the *Arkansas Democrat*, editorialized that evening, it was "on the conscience of Arkansas." But in the view of whites it had nothing to do with the social and political system that prevailed at the time. According to publisher Engel, the institution at Wrightsville suffered from "a long history of neglect." In fact, Engel, who served on the state social services board, acknowledged that "almost all the physical plant was allowed to deteriorate." The problem was, according to him, that "in the competition of state agencies for funds, the Negro Boys Industrial School never fared well."[2]

The boys, aged thirteen to seventeen years old, who died in the fire had been committed to Wrightsville by Arkansas County judges who had broad jurisdiction over matters involving juveniles.[3] The offenses were generally minor. Superintendent Lester Gaines told a reporter that "one of the boys we lost was sent here when he got picked up soaping windows on Halloween, I understand."[4] For the minors in the "older boys' dormitory," Wrightsville, in some respects, was still more of a prison work farm than an educational institution, eerily mimicking some of the worst features of adult male prisons and county farms in the South, including institutions like the Cummins and Tucker state prisons.

First built in 1923, eighteen years after the initial legislation creating the state's first reform school, the Negro Boys Industrial School in Pine Bluff was underfunded from the beginning. Yet superintendent T. W. Coggs received high marks for his initiative in running the school on a shoestring budget. An African American who received a two-year degree from Hampton Institute in Virginia and taught carpentry at Branch Normal in Pine Bluff, Tandy Coggs was considered the ideal superintendent. In the words of social worker and historian Erle Chambers, "Mr. Coggs' service to the State has long justified the board's choice of a superintendent. He is representative of the best type of negro. A college graduate skilled in the manual arts and child psychology, he has brought to his task the peculiar gift it needs. His indomitable determination to 'carry on' and the morale of his institution at once impress the visitor. There is a distinct *spirit de corps*."

Despite the usual condescending language, such as the "best type of negro," clearly the board (then all-white) had made an inspired choice; but it wasn't just the cheerful personality of the superintendent that was noticed:

> He raises good food crops so that his charges may be fed a varied diet; strawberries are grown and eaten as well as sold. The place is clean and well kept. Under the merit system the boy works his way out. Salaries for officers and teachers seem too meager for good work, yet half the officers are high school or college graduates with teaching experience. And yet two farms seventeen miles apart must be administered, and buildings on neither are adequate to house decently the inmates. There is no money for medical service, books, for any of the things that go to make a school. And yet thus "making bricks without straw," the management can point with pride to the school's achievement. As of December 1, 1926, 217 boys had been committed; eighty-four had been paroled or discharged, and only six had escaped. Of the entire number paroled or discharged, but six had been returned to any kind of correctional institution. Besides agriculture, the boys engage in dairying, poultry raising, carpentry, shoe repairing, laundry work and household tasks.[5]

Coggs remained as superintendent for fourteen years, until he was abruptly replaced by a white former Mississippi County sheriff in 1937, whose job it was to run the black institution as a 2,300-acre penal work farm. Reports from and about the white and black institutions for boys during the 1930s and 1940s indicate that from 1937 through 1952 the Negro Boys Industrial School, which had been relocated to Wrightsville in Pulaski County, twelve miles outside of Little Rock, was virtually ignored by the state government except for what its adolescent farm labor could produce and sell.[6]

During much of this same period, boys at the white school in Pine Bluff were trained in "carpentry and joining work, cabinet work, glazing, painting, cement work, bricklaying, wood and metal-lathe operation, blacksmithing, acetylene welding, plastering, tailoring and shoe mending." The only mention of the Negro Boys Industrial School is in a 1940 report that acknowledges the boys at Wrightsville were the recipients of 156 mattresses made at the white school.[7]

With the Arkansas economy growing again after the Great Depression, significant improvements at the white boys' school in Pine Bluff were reported in the mid-1940s, even as the institution remained a political football under different administrations. Significantly, it was reported, "Considerable equipment for vocational training has been added at the school . . . [and] an entire new water system has been installed, and with adequate piping. Six fire hydrants and 900 feet of hose have been placed on the grounds. Hydrants and fire hose are of standard thread. An entire new gas heating system, including gas in the kitchen and cannery, has been installed. The abandoned trade school building has been entirely reconditioned, also the inside of the laundry." The article went on to note that the boys now had a "library and a reading room and a new motion picture machine purchased with screen." Moreover, the American Legion was "taking active interest in the school, especially in providing Christmas parties."[8] No mention was made of the Wrightsville institution.

In September of 1947, an editorial in the black-owned *Arkansas State Press* noted that "new courses were planned at the [white] Boys' Industrial School at Pine Bluff." Sarcastically, the article applauded the addition, stating, "That is fine, we want the boys in the Pine Bluff school for white boys to have everything necessary to make them better citizens. That may help keep them from lynching Negroes." S. S. Taylor, assistant editor at the *Arkansas State Press*, published by civil rights leaders L. C. and Daisy Bates, pointedly noted that the black school "need[ed] not new courses but *some* [emphasis added] courses."[9]

Though Gov. Sid McMath's two terms (1949–53) as chief executive of the state provided a much better tone in race relations (for example, he welcomed blacks into the Arkansas Democratic Party), unfortunately he did virtually nothing for the Negro Boys Industrial School except promote a black employee into the role of superintendent. On March 26, 1952, a five-person "committee for Study of State Training Schools" from various departments of state government visited the institution and its "newly appointed" superintendent, John Rawlings. In that group was veteran Department of Education employee Ed McCuistion, who made the following observation: "I found myself somewhat depressed after returning home and thinking, here are 60 young boys, many of them with as much promise as the average youth in the homes and communities over the state. I actually felt that in some cases these boys are worse off in the institution than they might be back home where organized community enterprises might give them better opportunities to reconstruct their lives and re-fit themselves for better citizenship. I certainly feel that Arkansas should take steps as soon as possible to improve the experiences these 60 boys are having while wards of the state."[10]

What the committee found on this brief visit was that forty-six of the boys were receiving no education at all: "This is a large farm and requires a great deal of labor, much of which is done by the boys." The wife of the superintendent taught the fourteen youngest boys. McCuistion noted, "Interviewing the boys I found a keen desire of boys in bricklaying, agriculture, mechanics, bus drivers, and guidance." The committee, which also included a physician and the head of the Welfare Department, commented on "the great shortage in personnel in handling boys in the dormitories." No number of employees was given. The committee reported that there was "no regular organized recreation program. Have a picture machine and a work shop but no teacher." The report noted that "feeding [was] good on allowances available. Clothing woefully short and dirty. Laundry services seemingly limited [in fact, there was no laundry equipment].... There were few sheets or pillowcases. The mattresses appeared to be worn and soiled. No spreads other than army blankets were on beds." The committee found that "the great need is more staff for better training and supervision of the boys." There were two different views of the "newly appointed" superintendent. "He is evidently a little unsure of himself and is feeling his way," ran one account, while another report described Rawlings as "well prepared with good reputation. Needs some administrative assistance."[11]

Superintendent Rawlings needed more than administrative assistance but never received it. After the McMath administration foundered on charges of corruption in a highway scandal, Gov. Francis Cherry replaced Rawlings when pressure began to be exerted from a number of quarters, including African Americans themselves, who had long been interested in the welfare of the boys. An all-black inspection team headed by Little Rock community activist and politician Charles Bussey had revealed appalling conditions at Wrightsville. In a letter to the governor that was also circulated to members of the legislature, Bussey's committee found that in the storeroom

> meat was being eaten by rats; dirty bed mattresses were being stacked around the meat, which was very unsanitary. . . . [W]e went to the boys' dormitory no. 1. This building was as filthy as any place we had ever seen. . . . [T]he pillows were black and greasy. . . . The entire building was a disgrace to the human eye. Boys' dormitory no. 2, for smaller boys, was in the same condition as no. 1, except that the boys had soiled their beds. There had been a fire in this building the night before; and the superintendent stated that the boys were locked in this trap. . . . [There are] no recreational facilities. . . . One large boy was in charge of the smaller ones in the class room. . . . Forty boys, not one clean one in the building, had on clothes too dirty for any human to wear. . . . Finally we visited the laundry. . . . To our astonishment there were no laundry facilities whatsoever. The boys were beating the clothes, putting them into old pots. . . . All in all, as for management, we found the boys' Industrial School at Wrightsville, Arkansas, to be in a deplorable condition.[12]

The outrage expressed in the report over the physical appearance and living conditions of the boys simmered beneath the surface of polite interracial discourse in 1953, but the wholesale lack of human dignity was clearly a severe affront to the pride of the black Arkansans on the committee that day. On the last page of the report, along with the name of Charles Bussey, were the names of five other committee members. Two bear particular mention. One was Earl Davy, who over the years worked off and on as a photographer for L. C. Bates and the *Arkansas State Press*. The other was Lester Gaines. On February 11, Bussey followed up the January report with a letter to Governor Cherry recommending that the "State Education Commissioner . . . give L. R. Gaines a years [*sic*] leave of absence to head the institution and perfect those parts of the rehabilitation program that are needed at the school."[13]

Before the session ended that winter, the legislature also passed Act 511 of 1953, which increased the total number of teachers at the school to five, including an "Industrial Art" teacher.[14] It was the first indication that white lawmakers saw the school as anything but a prison farm whose mission was to remain as self-sufficient as possible. And yet, by 1956, Wrightsville was going nowhere.

African American University of Arkansas sociology professor Gordon Morgan, who did fieldwork for his master's thesis during the winter of 1955–1956 at Wrightsville, provided a comprehensive summary of the conditions. He noted that "vocational education suffers greatly at the School. There is no adequate shop only a few old tools which can't be used. Some agriculture and wood-working is taught but most of the training is in the form of practical work." By this he primarily meant picking and chopping cotton. "Many boys go for days with only rags for clothes. . . . Each boy was provided a single sheet for use that was supposed to last for most of the entire winter. . . . [It is] not uncommon to see youths going for weeks without bathing or changing clothes."[15] For infractions of the rules, the boys were brutally whipped with a leather strap.[16]

The conditions at Wrightsville were no secret. When asked at his press conference the morning of the fire if the fire could be as similarly devastating at other state facilities, Governor Faubus, who had inspected the facility a year earlier, answered, "No, this was perhaps the worst facility of them and it would not have happened here if adequate precautions had been taken." Nearing the end of a regular legislative session whose main focus was measures to stop or prevent integration of public schools, Faubus, then on his third term as governor, added that no deaths would have occurred if someone had been at the dorm to unlock the door. He announced that he would "conduct his own inquiry to find the guilty in the tragedy as well as to absolve the innocent."[17]

How the governor tried to accomplish this and absolve himself of all responsibility is a different story, but suffice it to say here that he succeeded in having four individuals fired. His effort to have someone, namely, superintendent Lester Gaines, criminally prosecuted failed when the Pulaski County Grand Jury concluded its work without a single indictment. The report read in part: "The blame can be placed on lots of shoulders for the tragedy: the Board of Directors to a certain extent, who might have pointed out through newspaper and other publicity the extreme hazard and plight of the school; the Superintendent and his staff, who perhaps continued to do the best they could in a resigned fashion when they had nothing to do with; the State Administration, one right after another through the past years, who allowed the conditions to remain so disreputable; the General Assembly of the State of Arkansas, who should have been so ashamed of conditions that they would have previously allowed sufficient money to have these conditions corrected; and finally on the people of Arkansas, who did nothing about it."[18]

In fact, it was not merely a matter of disreputable conditions at Wrightsville. At the white boys' school in Pine Bluff, the boys were not locked in at night. There were two house parents on duty, while at Wrightsville there was only one, and he was in the hospital. Not only was the school short staffed, the older boys' dormitory was an admitted firetrap with rotting floors and frayed wiring.[19]

What or who was culpable for the tragedy at the Arkansas Negro Boys Industrial School? Was it segregation or individual responsibility on the part of an employee or employees, the governor, or, more generally, as the grand jury report suggests, a kind of collective negligence on the part of individuals, government, and "the people of Arkansas"? Or was it something else? It appears that most white Arkansans publicly shared the view that the worst fire in terms of loss of life in Arkansas history at that time was a long-running and highly embarrassing but isolated case of negligence at a black institution.

Certainly, there is overwhelming evidence that in 1959 most white and black Arkansans of this era expressed the view that both social and political realities had everything to do with segregation by law and by custom and the pace and conditions of its dismantling. And this view has often been accepted at face value by writers (including the author) who have characterized white Arkansans during this period variously as "southern Moderates," "Neo-Bourbons," "segregationists," "radical segregationists," "liberals," and "conservatives" in an effort to give meaning to the differences among them.[20]

Though books and articles on that era continue to pour forth analyzing the behavior of white Arkansans from this perspective, this nomenclature, while relevant in a different context, can obscure rather than clarify what has been most important in Arkansas's racial past. In fact, racial segregation by law and custom was only one of numerous tools of implementing white supremacy.[21] It was the intention to maintain white supremacy that united white Arkansans during the era of the Negro Boys Industrial School in Arkansas, a period that encompasses and overlaps the period of the 1957 Little Rock Central High crisis.

The paramount issue in that era of pushback by the federal government and African Americans themselves that often divided white Arkansans was how to perpetuate white supremacy, how to manage it, not whether to abolish it.²² Politically and culturally since the days of slavery, white Arkansans, to one degree or another, were, for all practical purposes, white supremacists. Whatever the differences among the white community, there was little question about who would remain in control politically and set the context for interaction between whites and blacks. Before and during the history of the Arkansas Negro Boys Industrial School, the states that once composed the "Old Confederacy" operated not as representative democracies but rather as one-party states ruled by white males (the "solid South") whose most important order of business, privately and publicly, was very often to control and manage the black populations within their jurisdictions.

Indeed, Harry Ashmore, editor of the *Arkansas Gazette*, commented in an editorial, "The South—mistakenly we believe—has tended in the past to make all of its political decisions in terms of the single issue of race."²³ It was in this political context that the fire occurred. Arkansas's commitment to white supremacy had made undesirable a two-party system and free elections. But it was not just the political system that guided the state's commitment to white supremacy. As had the rest of the Old South more than a century earlier, Arkansas whites "recast" their cultural institutions and previously held values, such as free speech, religious beliefs, and concepts of justice, in order to facilitate the continuation of white supremacy in the form of slavery. As put none too delicately by the *Encyclopedia of Religion in the South*, "The adaptation of religious values to racial needs had a long history in the region."²⁴ The willingness to put "racial needs" ahead of traditional political, economic, ethical, and religious values would continue throughout the era of the fire and would have disastrous and unintended consequences for the state's development.

It has only been roughly in the last thirty years that Arkansas historians have begun to rigorously document that white supremacy in Arkansas was implemented variously by slavery, murder, rape, terror, lynching, massacres, peonage, disfranchisement, segregation, intimidation, humiliation, discrimination, termination from employment, a massive theft of resources lawfully intended for black citizens, and racial cleansing of black communities. The official and unofficial writing of Arkansas's racial history has often resembled propaganda more than history.²⁵

Focusing only on the past denial of resources to the African American community on a statewide basis, one still learns a great deal about how white supremacy was implemented. There were major disparities in all the other so-called separate-but-equal institutions in Arkansas, often with shocking consequences.

It was not by coincidence that education was the major topic on the agenda for the 1949 Arkansas Social Work Conference held at the Hotel Marion in Little Rock on April 4 and 5. The keynote speaker was Gov. Sidney McMath's new commissioner of education, A. B. Bonds, whom McMath had persuaded to give up a prestigious job at the Atomic Energy Commission and come home to help his native state. Clearly, the conference was a highly orchestrated event to try to build support for the state of Arkansas taking responsibility for equalizing funding for its black schools. As chairman of the conference, Ed McCuistion, who was director of Negro education in the Department of Education, presided and made the case with Bonds that money for black schools was being "diverted" to white schools on the local level. At one point McCuistion even "interrupted" his boss to say that the "diversion amounted to $4,250,000 last year," which in 2012 would be equivalent to $40,962,857.[26]

Giving the keynote address at the conference, Bonds explained that this "diversion" of funds was not occurring at the top. The Department of Education was distributing money on an equal basis for black and white schools, and "diversion occurs on the local level," meaning that elected boards in each school district, which doled out money to the schools in their geographical area, were shortchanging black schools to the tune of millions of dollars each year.

The words "theft" or "stealing" would have more accurately described what was taking place. But whites in 1949 Arkansas were not of a mind to accuse each other of stealing money from blacks, nor is there any evidence that whites were willing to think of their actions as stealing. Had they been willing to do so, it would have opened up for scrutiny the state's entire racial history.

Prophetically, nothing came from the education conference. Within days, the State Board of Education rejected Ed McCuistion's proposal, "which would have required all schools in a district, Negro and white, to meet accrediting standards before anyone could be accredited." As in the past the State Board responded by doing nothing more than to direct the Department of Education to send a letter to "all school district officials urging serious and immediate efforts at equalization," a solution, as noted by McCuistion, that had accomplished nothing in the past and would accomplish little in the future.[27] Diversion of funds from black schools had been going on for decades and would not completely end until the Supreme Court required unitary school systems in the early 1970s, and then it would be black teachers and administrators who would lose their jobs, another part of the legacy of white supremacy.

While it is useful and necessary for an accurate portrayal of the history of the Wrightsville fire to determine what responsibility specific individuals had for the deaths of the boys, whether it was the employees at Wrightsville or Governor Faubus or both, the history of the Negro Boys Industrial School and the fire that took the lives of twenty-one boys must be evaluated in the context of the political and social system of white supremacy. What happened at Wrightsville was far more than a long-running case of negligence, but rather a consequence of racial inequality that was typical in every situation involving black institutions in Arkansas.

What does the fire at the Negro Boys Industrial School have to do with racial violence? As suggested at the outset, typically, racial violence is associated with discrete events, such as lynching or race massacres or riots, that were intentional acts resulting in harm or damage to African Americans. Perhaps, if one is willing to think of white supremacy as a political and cultural system underpinned by violence that took many forms, we can begin to acknowledge and evaluate its wide-ranging, far-reaching, and ultimately devastating consequences for all of the people of Arkansas.

PART III

New Perspectives on African American Activism

CHAPTER 7

Empowering Families and Communities
African American Home Demonstration Agents in Arkansas, 1913–1965

CHERISSE JONES-BRANCH

THIS ESSAY TRACES the work of African American home demonstration agents in Arkansas from 1913 to 1965. Throughout the South, home demonstration agents were trained and employed by the Agricultural Extension Service (AES) to share their domestic science expertise with people in rural communities. They sought to modernize rural homes by teaching wives and mothers to be better homemakers or, more appropriately, to behave like their middle-class counterparts. The story, however, was more complex for African American home demonstration agents. Like black agents around the South, they had to navigate deeply entrenched racism and segregation as they helped African Americans in rural Arkansas improve their quality of life by imparting farm and home management techniques as tools for self-sufficiency. Black home demonstration agents were often hampered by African Americans' endemic poverty, malnutrition, and unsanitary and unsafe living conditions. Unequal funding of extension services circumscribed their efforts. Yet despite the constraints of racism, segregation, and severe privation, agents utilized the Arkansas Agricultural Extension Service's agenda to meet the needs of rural black communities.

Home demonstration work in Arkansas and nationwide was buttressed by the passage of the Smith-Lever Act in 1914, which created the US Department of Agriculture (USDA) Cooperative Extension Service.[1] Named for US representative Asbury F. Lever of South Carolina and US senator Hoke Smith of Georgia, and informed by progressive era concern for southern rural reform and development, the act, using federal, state, and local funds, supported the establishment of an AES at state land grant colleges and universities. Impacted by the advances in and the efficacy of scientific agricultural education, the AES was established in Arkansas shortly after the passage of the Smith-Lever Act and was headquartered at the University of Arkansas in Fayetteville for whites and at Arkansas Agricultural, Mechanical, and Normal College in Pine Bluff (Arkansas AM & N) for African Americans.[2]

AES policies perpetuated traditional gender divisions of the early twentieth century. It hired and supervised farm agents, who were almost exclusively male, that advised farmers on such practices as crop rotation and livestock breeding.[3] The AES also employed female home demonstration agents who worked with farmwomen and taught them how to improve their homes and the lives of their families.[4] In 1915, Harvey C. Ray, also known as H. C., became the first federally appointed African American US Agricultural Extension Service agent in Arkansas. In 1916, his wife, Mary McCrary Ray, a home economist, was appointed the state's first black home demonstration agent. She was later promoted to district agent, a position she held until her death in 1934.[5]

The AES reinforced Jim Crow laws mandating racial segregation. Because it was socially and politically unthinkable for white women to even consider entering black people's homes, employing black home demonstration agents was the only logical choice to avoid transgressing racial and social norms.[6] Black demonstration agents reported to white supervisors and worked within almost impenetrable community racial boundaries. In Arkansas, they were perceived as a threat because of their educational backgrounds. White landowners were often initially suspicious of black agents because they feared they might encourage tenant farmers and sharecroppers to challenge the carefully crafted social and economic control they held over them. Most agents had attended college and some had earned degrees. Others had done some graduate work and had even taught at a university.[7] Mary Ray, for example, had been head of the Home Economics Department at Langston University, a predominantly African American institution in Oklahoma.[8] Many had also grown up in rural environments themselves and sought to inculcate the farmwomen with the most current home management techniques.

In Arkansas, and particularly in the delta, black and white agents were reluctant to sacrifice their programs by challenging white supremacy.[9] H. C. and Mary Ray, for example, traveled throughout Arkansas demonstrating farming, canning, and home improvement techniques.

As they did so, however, they carefully cultivated the goodwill of planters and county officials. This allowed them to maintain a force of farm and home demonstration agents in areas with a large concentration of blacks who desperately needed their services, but it also exposed whites to the economic, health, and sanitation issues plaguing African American communities.[10]

Even before the passage of the Smith-Lever Act, farm and home demonstration work could be found in rural communities throughout Arkansas, particularly after the boll weevil devastated cotton crops in the southern part of the state in the early twentieth century.[11] African American home demonstration agents had been working in Arkansas since 1913.[12] But America's involvement in World War I increased the need for their services around the state. Home demonstration agents were concerned about cash-strapped homemakers who were often unable to prepare nutritious meals for their families. Because cotton remained a primary crop for many farm families, they were often unable to grow vegetables to supplement their meager diets during the winter months. Throughout the war years farm and home demonstration agents encouraged black Arkansans to increase food production and conservation by planting gardens and canning produce.[13] Mary Ray, for example, taught farm families how to turn canning tomatoes into a community project. Using the facilities of a local black school or church, they constructed a cannery made of zinc tubs, with a foundation, top, and the joints of two stovepipes. This crudely made but efficient contraption allowed them to can five hundred quarts of tomatoes daily.[14]

Although local funds were limited during and after World War I, white landowners who feared the outmigration of the black labor upon which they depended supported agents. In particular, they encouraged the work of the AES as a means to help overcome what one agent called "the poverty, dissatisfaction, and unrest among Negro farmers."[15] This suggests that African Americans did not passively accept their conditions. They questioned and contested the economic and political structures that held them captive. And, when all else failed, they simply left the state. Increasingly, then, rather than perceiving educated black home and farm demonstration agents as a challenge to the plantation system, white landowners decided it was in their best interests to cooperate with the Arkansas AES reform efforts.[16]

In the 1920s, it became even more important for home demonstration agents to impress the importance of food preservation upon rural women, particularly as the nation began sinking into an economic depression. In Arkansas, in 1924, black women and girl members of home demonstration clubs showcased clothing, poultry, and fruit and vegetable preserves for which they won prizes at the Pulaski County State Fair.[17] Although a food shortage would certainly affect poor, rural black families in the years leading up to the Great Depression, many were first devastated by the Mississippi flood of 1927. Black home demonstration agents' skills helped destitute but proud African Americans survive the storm. Relief worker Lula Toler, a home demonstration agent from Pine Bluff, recalled the suffering she encountered: "My first day's work with the sufferers were ones long to be remembered. The scene was most pitiful and shall even haunt me while life lasts. The screams of the people and the lowing of cattle could be heard in the distance." St. Francis County agent Lugenia Bell Christmas, employed by the AES since 1917, assisted those who had waded through floodwater for miles in search of food and shelter for their families.[18] Home demonstration agents also helped find lost loved ones, organized soup kitchens, conducted sanitation and hygiene demonstrations, and, along with male farm agents, led agricultural demonstrations and provided landless and displaced victims in Arkansas Red Cross emergency relief camps with much-needed psychological support as they rebuilt their homes and lives.[19]

In particular, home demonstration agents wanted to reach African Americans who lived in rural areas to ensure that they were trained in the most current farming and home management techniques and to also perpetuate the message of rural uplift. That is, one of their objectives was to extol the virtues of Booker T. Washington's philosophy of black self-sufficiency and determination, which would allow African Americans to move up from the bottom of America's social, economic, and political hierarchy. To this end, in 1928, the Arkansas AES established the "Movable Demonstration School for Negro Farm Folks."[20] Movable Schools, developed by George Washington Carver and Booker T. Washington in the early twentieth century, were agricultural schools on wheels that were moved by farm and demonstration agents from one community to another. By traveling almost to the doorsteps of the most isolated rural black farm families, agents were able to demonstrate the latest agriculture, home management, and public health innovations.[21] C. C. Haraway and Jennie Lou Woodward, who had been trained at

Tuskegee Institute, served as Movable School agents in Arkansas in the 1920s.[22] They traveled around the state in a one-and-a-half-ton Ford truck and performed demonstrations in approximately twenty-eight to thirty counties in the first year of the Movable Schools' existence.[23]

As the demand for home demonstration agents grew across Arkansas, so too did the need for a statewide organization of home demonstration clubs to unite rural women and coordinate their activities. Home demonstration clubs served many purposes in rural communities. They provided rural women with a forum to ask questions and to discuss health and child care concerns. Home demonstration clubs also combined educational programs with the AES agenda. They allowed agents to educate rural women, and the agents expected them to share their newfound knowledge with others.[24] And because farming families often lived far from their neighbors, home demonstration clubs also provided opportunities for women to socialize.[25]

In 1929, white demonstration agents organized the Arkansas Council of Home Demonstration Clubs.[26] As was typical of the Jim Crow restrictions of the time and the policies of the AES, its membership excluded black women. But because black women served the most impoverished communities around the state and often had to do so with fewer resources, they understood the importance of coordinating their efforts into a state organization of their own. In 1936, two home demonstration agents, African American Cassa L. Hamilton and white Connie J. Bonslagel, helped establish the predominantly black State Council of Home Demonstration Clubs at a farmers' conference at Arkansas AM & N. Like the Arkansas Council, the State Council created a network of county clubs in rural black communities around the state. Most of the members of the State Council also had long tenures with the state Agricultural Extension Service program.[27] Fannie Mae Boone, for example, the parliamentarian of the new organization, had worked for the AES since 1929. Born in Alpine, Georgia, and trained at the Kansas Industrial and Educational Institute (also known as the Western Tuskegee and, later, as Tuskegee), Boone became the supervisor of black home demonstration agents in Arkansas in 1942 and remained in this position until her retirement in 1958.[28]

Although the State Council of Home Demonstration Clubs had been founded in the 1930s, most local black home demonstration clubs in Arkansas had been around since the mid-1920s. Two factors quite likely account for the growth of home demonstration agents and clubs during the Great Depression years. The impoverished conditions in which many rural blacks found themselves made it imperative for agents to teach them new farming and home techniques. These, in turn, would allow them to improve agricultural production and generate much-needed cash income.[29] Community improvement and self-sufficiency held great import for home demonstration and farm agents and Arkansas black leaders throughout the 1930s. In 1932, home demonstration agents met at the African American Fargo Agricultural School in Monroe County, where they outlined plans to assist black farmers throughout Arkansas who were devastated by the Depression.[30]

Concerns about ways to improve black farm life informed agents' rural uplift agenda.[31] In Osceola, Arkansas, in 1938, the local home demonstration council and the county farmers' association held a meeting where home demonstration agent Mary M. Banks gave a talk entitled "Home Improvement" and where attendees discussed plans for the first annual Colored Farmers' Cured Meats show.[32]

In the 1940s, African American agents increased their activism in rural black communities. Despite the nationwide mobilization for the war effort, blacks still suffered disproportionately from the economic privation of the Depression years. Black home demonstration agents focused on teaching farmwomen to improve their homes, families, and communities by doing more with less. In 1940 in Pine Bluff, local home demonstration agents sponsored a "Cotton Dress Revue" as part of a weeklong community-wide "Better Homes" campaign that included a showcase of home improvement activities.[33] The Lee County Home Demonstration Council encouraged rural homemakers to make bed mattresses stuffed with cotton as part of a program initiated by the USDA. Because many poor blacks and whites often slept on bundle of rags or "ticks" (a bag of made of cloth) stuffed with pine needles, home demonstration agents saw the mattress program as a way to modernize rural homes.[34] In keeping with the patriotic theme of the war years, rural black women also constructed "Victory Garments" from flour sacks in addition to their home improvement efforts, which included exhibiting pride in their homes and their country by planting shrubbery.[35]

Home demonstration agents also utilized the democratic sentiment of the war years to encourage black farmers to help the USDA meet food production goals. In 1942, black home demonstration and extension agents, ministers, educators, and farmers met in Little Rock, Forrest City, and El Dorado to discuss how farmers could use the features of Agricultural Adjustment Act, a New Deal program, to implement the objectives of the USDA "Food for Freedom" program.[36] The program's plenary sessions stressed galvanizing rural black communities' support for the war effort by increasing food production and preservation. But the underlying theme was improved race relations and civil rights that would emanate from the democratic rhetoric of those years. In attendance was home demonstration agent Fannie Boone, who implicitly underscored this feeling with a talk entitled "Cooking for Freedom."[37]

African American home demonstration agents also continued their quest to improve nutrition among blacks in rural Arkansas during World War II. Fannie Boone's 1942 talk, "Cooking for Freedom," for example, also included the more practical imperative of encouraging rural blacks to cook nutritional meals and to preserve food because of the shortage of rationed goods during the war years.[38] This initiative had a statewide impact. In 1944, for example, a Poinsett County home demonstration agent, Lena H. Eddington, helped black families improve their nutrition by implementing dietary plans and instructing them in food production techniques. She also linked good nutrition and health to national wartime goals when she asserted that "Health on the Home Front" equaled "Victory on the War Front."[39]

Eddington, a graduate of Arkansas AM & N and the University of Minnesota, in Minneapolis, had begun her career as a home demonstration agent in 1941. She supported the "Live-At-Home" program that was established in Arkansas in 1931 and supported by politicians, the AES, and state and local government agencies. The "Live-At-Home" program promoted crop diversification and self-sufficiency among farming families in poverty-stricken rural areas.[40] For black Arkansans the campaign served additional purposes. Not only were they able to improve their standard of living by becoming self-supporting, but home demonstration agents also used the program to dissuade African Americans from leaving rural areas and migrating north.[41] Their efforts were facilitated by the Memphis *Commercial Appeal* and the Memphis Chamber of Commerce Agricultural Committee, which began sponsoring a "Live-At-Home Competition" in Tennessee, Arkansas, and Mississippi in 1937 in an effort to keep black laborers in the region. In 1941 and 1944, two farm families from Crittenden County won the prize, which included a $250 award. County home demonstration agents Corrie J. Jarrett and Clara M. Howard were awarded trophies for selecting the winners. This was quite likely done as an incentive to continue encouraging rural blacks to remain in the tri-state area.[42] African American agents were also rewarded for procuring farm families to participate in the program.[43]

African American home demonstration agents most often found themselves performing dual roles in rural Arkansas. They had to tread lightly as the longevity of their programs in black communities was largely dependent upon cooperation with white landowners and officials. Agents taught farmwomen home management techniques. But many of them also advocated Booker T. Washington's rural uplift philosophy. Home improvement was tantamount to racial uplift in rural black communities, and black women often promoted their work as such.[44] Home demonstration agents, however, were mindful of the racial environment in which they existed.[45]

In Arkansas, black home demonstration agents and their work were no less affected by the undercurrents of the burgeoning freedom movement as they worked under the auspices of the AES to uplift poor rural black communities. Local home demonstration clubs continued to focus on home and community improvement and food preservation. At a February 1950 meeting in Woodruff County, club members discussed strategies for "Better Rural Living," a campaign that encompassed all of the work black agents performed in local communities.[46] In March 1950, Faulkner County assistant demonstration agent Maude B. Davis showed black women how to store home-cured meats and preserve eggs so that they could increase their food supply. To modernize their homes, members of the "Lucky Twenty" home demonstration club in Lake Village, Chicot County, learned to make cypress knee lamps.[47] In 1956, in Dermott, also in Chicot County, black women learned how to use a "dial telephone."[48] Black agents also guided farm families who owned their land, as they learned how to diversify their crops and increase livestock to improve their income. By doing so, they believed rural black Arkansans were well on the way to "lifting themselves to better living by their own bootstraps."[49] Such efforts continued to underscore agents' longstanding goal to encourage blacks to become self-sufficient producers.

Increasingly, however, throughout the 1950s and 1960s, State Home Demonstration Council meetings included themes with such implicit political messages as "Working Together for World Understanding,"

"The Homemakers' Responsibilities in Changing Times," or "Symbols of the Sixties—Alert Homemakers," which reflected black agents understanding of the interconnectedness of their work to the changes occurring around the nation.[50]

African American home demonstration agents acknowledged the historical transformations in black life as the civil rights movement gained momentum. Yet, they still faced rampant discrimination throughout Arkansas. In 1956, home demonstration agents in Poinsett County protested when the AES decided to eliminate the county Negro home demonstration agent position. This was particularly alarming for African Americans because the white home demonstration agent position was not eliminated. The associate director of the AES, C. A. Vines, argued that this was due to the decrease in Poinsett County's rural black population. However, Elveria Heard, president of the county home demonstration council, who led a petition to maintain the position, saw it as a "great loss to the Negro Homemakers and Negro 4-H boys and girls of this county." Couching her response in carefully chosen but politically loaded terms, Heard asserted, "In view of the past achievements that have been accomplished through Extension Work in the County, State, Tri-State and National activities, we feel that this will deprive these citizens of equal opportunities with other citizens of the State. We petition that you find a way to maintain the Home Demonstration and 4-H work in this county for all citizens."[51] It is unclear whether or not Heard and Poinsett County blacks were able to retain a home demonstration agent. But what is evident is that blacks in rural Arkansas communities relied heavily upon the services of black home demonstration agents. When faced with the loss of this most important resource, they had few qualms about organizing, petitioning, and challenging the authority of the AES.

African Americans were adamant about retaining agents in their counties because they not only provided them with home management techniques, but also often brought much-needed health information to rural black communities. In 1960, home demonstration agent Mrs. Clothilde M. Shivers and the Ouachita County Rural Development Advisory Board worked with the residents of Amy, Arkansas, a small black settlement near Camden, in their efforts to improve their community. Shivers, the county agent since 1952, taught rural black women to conserve food so that they would have ample supplies to feed their families. She conducted a cooking school where she taught them how to create nutritional meals.[52] At a time when many African Americans only had access to inferior medical care and could not afford the necessary inoculations to avoid communicable diseases like tuberculosis, Shivers and the rural development committee also employed a county nurse who held immunization clinics.[53] Agents further combated the myriad health issues that plagued rural black communities by demonstrating treatments for mastitis and by discussing the importance of mental and dental health care.[54]

Although they worked for the Arkansas AES, black home demonstration agents were not welcome as members of the all-white state council of home demonstration agents. Nor were they permitted to become members of the all-white National Home Demonstration Agents' Association (NHDAA), which had been had been established in 1933.[55] In 1957, twenty-four years after the founding of the NHDAA, black home demonstration agents met in Jackson, Mississippi, and organized the Negro National Home Demonstration Agents Association (NNHDAA).

Black home demonstration agents from Arkansas assumed prominent roles in the founding of the NNHDAA. Women from El Dorado, Forrest City, Texarkana, and Lake Village were among its founders and first elected officials. In 1958, the NNHDAA held its first annual meeting at Arkansas AM & N. Twenty-five of the fifty-six home demonstration agents attending the gathering were from Arkansas.[56] Because they were subject to the control of white officials who ran the Agricultural Extension Service in Arkansas and throughout the South, agents had to be very careful about advancing any political positions. This was particularly true in Arkansas, where a tense racial atmosphere prevailed after the desegregation of Little Rock's Central High School in 1957 and when Gloria Ray, the daughter of H. C. and a later wife, Julia (Miller) Ray, became one of the Little Rock Nine students caught in the international news headlines that surrounded the event. They did, however, implicitly tie their concerns to the overarching theme of farm and home improvement by encouraging all agents to "readjust their teaching methods to changing conditions as a means of more effectively helping farm people achieve a higher standard of living."[57] Black home demonstration agents could then turn their political agenda into terms that were acceptable to white supervisors and Agricultural Extension Service administrators. After the passage of the Civil Rights Act of 1964, which prohibited discrimination based on race, color, religion, or national origin and denied federal funds to organizations that failed to integrate, the NNHDAA held its last annual conference in Hot Springs, Arkansas, in 1965. It was subsequently absorbed into the NHDAA.[58]

Because they were employed by the Arkansas AES that received federal dollars, the impact of the Civil Rights Act of 1964 also gained traction among home demonstration agents throughout the state. In 1965, the Arkansas Council of Home Demonstration Clubs merged with the State Home Demonstration Council. Throughout the state, black and white county councils combined to form a single organization to serve the needs of all of their rural citizens. In 1966, the new and inclusive state body changed its name to the Arkansas Extension Homemakers Council in order to align itself with the newly integrated National Extension Homemakers Council that had changed its name two years earlier.[59]

Despite the victories of the civil rights movement and end of segregation in home demonstration clubs at the state and local level, most rural blacks in Arkansas were still poor and marginalized throughout the 1960s. As a consequence, black home demonstration agents remained primarily concerned about helping them improve their farms, homes, and communities. The philosophy of self-help and community uplift remained an integral part of their work. Home demonstration agents understood the social and racial complexities of the environment in which they operated and the realities of the lives of the poor blacks they encountered. Yet working under the auspices of the Agricultural Extension Service and utilizing the network of black women created by the State Council of Home Demonstration Clubs, they often managed to subvert those circumstances to exact the most change possible for rural blacks in Arkansas.

CHAPTER 8

It Should Be More Than Just a Simple Shout
The Life of Elias Camp ("E. C.") Morris

CALVIN WHITE

LOCATED ON THE corner of York and Columbia Street, Centennial Baptist Church stands in need of serious repair. Erected in 1905 in the Gothic Revival style of architecture, the building at the time of its completion in many ways reflected the rising status of African Americans. The structure boasted two Gothic towers and double-hung windows, and its stately appearance gave blacks a sense of profound pride as no more were the days of secretly worshipping in brush harbors. Blacks in Helena, Arkansas, now worshipped in a grand building that symbolized their racial advancements. Centennial Baptist Church embodied blacks' efforts of thrift, uplift, and progress in education, and no one personified those traits more than the gentleman who occupied its pulpit, the Reverend Elias Camp Morris.[1]

Described in 1897 as a man who "possessed the best qualities of a Negro" and being of the highest moral fabric, E. C. Morris understood that perception meant everything. From his pulpit in Helena, he also became aware that the church could be used as a vehicle to produce a refined, educated clergy and professional class of African Americans. Morris envisioned black religion aiding in the establishment of black education and business and even serving as a machine to elect black officials. The pastor of Centennial Baptist understood that religious influence could extend beyond the pulpit into the public sphere to produce social change, which contributed to racial uplift.[2]

The eighth child of slaves James and Cora Morris, Elias was born in Murray County, Georgia, in 1855. Due to their bondage, his parents lived apart on two adjacent plantations, but James's master granted him approval to visit Cora and his children two nights a week. Evidence supports the fact that the Morris's owners treated the family with benevolence. In an 1897 letter to his former owners, E. C. Morris wrote, "God bless your father, he was one of the best men that ever lived. . . . I can't tell you how near I feel towards you and all those who are left in the family. My father and mother used to talk about you all so much before they died." Although we cannot determine the sincerity of Morris's words, their masters seemed to have respected James and Cora's relationship, as the two would have ten children before the start of the Civil War.[3]

At the conclusion of the conflict, Elias's parents, like so many other slaves, began to move once they received their freedom. The family eventually settled in Stenson, Alabama, where James worked as a blacksmith. Their economic situation placed an emphasis upon work, and, therefore, young Elias received little to no formal education. On the other hand, James, who had been a literate slave, taught his children to read and write. However, in the turbulent aftermath of the Civil War, tragedy struck when both James and Cora died within months of one another. Left in the care of his older sister and her husband, the Reverend Robert Caver, Elias would form a bond with his brother-in-law that would shape the rest of his life. Known to be a taskmaster and a stern man, Caver not only served as a minister but also became a shoemaker. Having to earn his way, Morris worked as Caver's apprentice and learned the craft of repairing shoes. Unlike Elias's father, Caver understood the importance of a formal education and demanded that Morris acquire one.[4]

During the era of Reconstruction, blacks sought out education wherever they could find it. Although still in its infancy, black education remained confined to dilapidated, poorly equipped buildings. Yet blacks still overcrowded these structures in search of instruction. Tolerating similar conditions, Morris received his first formal education at Stenson Institute, but for unknown reasons he later moved to Nashville, Tennessee, where he enrolled at the Nashville Normal Theological Institute. Morris studied for a year at that institute and later enrolled in Roger Williams University, also in Nashville, one of four institutes that had been founded in 1864 with the mission of educating African American Baptist ministers. The first classes met in the basement of the First Colored Baptist Mission Church, where instructors taught ex-slave preachers basic skills of literacy and introduced them to the concept of theological respectability, which stressed a refined liturgy in which the clergy delivered rational sermons rooted in reason. Teachers also encouraged students to move away from sermons that were designed to arouse and excite congregants, causing services to descend into frenzies characterized by shouting and dancing. The lessons learned in Nashville clearly shaped Morris's worldview of religion, as he later implemented his own brand of theological respectability in Arkansas.[5]

A drifter by nature, Morris decided not to make Nashville his home. Faced with the entrenchment of Jim Crow and the peonage system of sharecropping, which severely hampered blacks economically, thousands began to move in search of better living conditions. Benjamin "Pap" Singleton, one of the leading promoters of this migration, argued that blacks should move west in search of land instead of suffering from the exploitative measures of sharecropping. Seeking his fortunes, Morris moved westward, but on his way to the "promised land" he would make a stop in Helena, Arkansas, in March 1877, where he found the place he would call home.[6]

Located in eastern Arkansas, Phillips County and the town of Helena were rather unique. Sylvanus Phillips, a migrant from North Carolina, first settled in the region in 1797. When the residents incorporated the small settlement into a town in 1820, they named it after Phillips's daughter, Helen. Blacks in the region viewed Helena, part of the black belt of Arkansas, as a modern new southern city and the jewel of the Arkansas Delta. The city thrived commercially due to its close proximity to the Mississippi River, giving rise to a small black middle class. Blacks also enjoyed the majority they held in the population, which gave way to meaningful political participation. In 1880, the black population stood at 74 percent. Census files reveal that in 1870 the illiteracy rate among blacks over the age of ten was at 39 percent, indicating that blacks in the county had not made many strides in the economic or educational realms as the white minority owned the majority of the land and blacks' primary occupation remained that of farm laborers.[7]

Due to his educational training, Morris quickly came to the attention of local black residents. While a small, black middle class existed, black educational facilities remained poor and inadequate. Although young, the educational skills he had acquired in Tennessee gave Morris the opportunity to assume a leadership role within the community. He began to worship at the Centennial Missionary Baptist Church, and three years later, at the age of twenty-four, local Baptist leaders ordained him. Shortly after his ordination, members elected him to lead the congregation.⁸

Morris's rise to a position of leadership coincided with a general trend occurring across the nation. With the end of Reconstruction in 1877, which left African Americans at the mercy of whites, blacks were reliant on self-help for racial uplift. Clergymen "now not only looked after the spiritual needs of their congregations, but also stressed the usefulness of the church as a means of challenging segregation."⁹ Even famed black intellectual W.E.B. DuBois commented that preachers should serve as "leaders, politicians, and idealists" as they used their pulpits to better the race. Following the national trend, Morris, with lessons learned in Tennessee, would begin a campaign within Arkansas to uplift the race and bring forth a more refined and educated clergy and a fuller religious experience.¹⁰

In an effort to bring a better organizational structure to independent black Baptist congregations, black Baptists after the Civil War began to form their own state conventions. Baptist leaders throughout Arkansas also felt it necessary to establish their own convention. Although not popularly supported, the leadership of the Arkansas Baptist State Convention (ABC) continued to gather yearly. Morris, as a newly elected pastor, first attended the organization's convention in 1880. To his surprise, delegates elected him to serve as the organization's acting secretary. Working as an administrator gave him the opportunity to make a name for himself throughout the state. Two years later, at their annual convention in Marianna, Arkansas, representatives elected Morris as president of the Arkansas Baptist State Convention. As president, Morris designed his platform around the concept of serving the spiritual needs of blacks throughout the state while also acting as a practical self-help organization.¹¹

The pursuit of a formal education became blacks' number one priority and was deemed the most important aspect of racial uplift. With the success of the Hampton Institute in Virginia and the Tuskegee Institute in Alabama, and Morris's own experiences at the Nashville Institute and Roger Williams University in Tennessee, as president of the convention he envisioned the creation of a similar institute in Arkansas. Witnessing the conditions blacks endured in Phillips County strengthened his devotion to promoting black education. This resolve can be seen in an 1894 sermon when he stated, "When darkness was looming upon the face of the great deep and in order to remove the confusion and establish order, He said, 'let there be light.'" Morris reasoned that many African Americans languished still in darkness and the light that would bring order would be education.[12] Therefore, at the insistence of Morris, the Arkansas Baptist Convention in November 1884 created the Ministers' Institute in the basement of Mt. Zion Missionary Baptist Church in Little Rock, Arkansas's state capital. The school's existence would be short-lived due to a lack of financial support, and it closed its doors in April 1885. Refusing to allow their endeavor to fail, the Arkansas Baptist Convention, at a meeting in Brinkley, Arkansas, committed to funding the school. Delegates renamed the institute Arkansas Baptist College, and in September 1885 the school reopened, becoming "the flagship for black Baptist education within the state."[13]

Controversy, however, soon erupted at Arkansas Baptist College due to the conservative reaction of some preachers who responded negatively to the growing authority of the Arkansas Baptist Convention. They rejected the convention's assertion that only educated ministers who had received instruction at Arkansas Baptist College and delivered sermons in a rational manner could be licensed to preach. Known as conservers, these clergy also rejected the notion of moving away from a charismatic religious liturgy that remained closely associated with the traditions of slave religion, which Morris and other members of the Arkansas Baptist Convention now viewed as being outdated and embarrassing to the rising efforts of the race.[14]

Conservers also subscribed to the theological theory of sanctification, which asserts that Christians could live a sin-free life while here on earth. Sanctification drew large numbers of African Americans into its ranks because sanctified Christians continued to practice an emotional liturgy that reminded them of the religious practices of their slave ancestors. The theory of sanctification grew so strong within the state that Morris and the Arkansas Baptist Convention were forced to address the issue. Morris argued that those who followed the doctrine of sanctification had in fact misunderstood its true meaning. He further asserted that followers had honest convictions but had been misinformed by ill-prepared teachers. To Morris, sanctification (or to sanctify) simply meant "to set apart, or appoint to service." Or, simply put, "a call to service, a getting ready for a meeting in which to worship God; a laying aside of secular matters, that for the time, the whole being may be devoted to the service of God, and thereby turn back the calamity which was about to come upon the nation." In conclusion, Morris believed, "A call to sanctification . . . does not imply that the individuals are entirely purged from sin" or could live a Christ-like life while here on earth.[15]

The theological misunderstanding of sanctification troubled Morris, but equally as important, he understood how the theory affected the efforts of racial uplift. Morris worried that those who continued to worship using a charismatic liturgy indirectly propagated stereotypes of black inferiority. Furthermore, Morris understood that black Baptist clergymen had traditionally been ridiculed, and the denomination's ministers had been dubbed as the most ignorant of the race because of their manner of worship. In an effort to quell the doctrine of sanctification, Morris and the Arkansas Baptist Convention directed instructors at Arkansas Baptist College to find theological evidence that attacked the notion of a sinless, perfect life.[16]

Morris and instructors used the night before Jesus's crucifixion as an example that even righteous men could not live free of sin. The disciples who had followed Jesus for three years and were fully dedicated to the Son of God displayed imperfection and were not sinless. For example, one would betray him and yet another would deny him. Thomas even argued that "he would not believe him risen except he could put his finger in the nail prints and thrust his hand into the wounded side of the Redeemer." These men were with the Son of God and were his most trusted companions, yet they did not live perfect lives; Peter became so disillusioned that after the Crucifixion he and the other disciples returned to their old occupation of fishing. But Morris instructed, "The Son of God met them on the bank early one morning asking, 'Children, have ye any meat?' and they responded 'No.' He instructed the disciples on the proper place to cast their net in order to catch fish that morning, illustrating their imperfection of faith, which placed them in need of divine intervention."[17]

Although progressives worked to stamp out the theory of sanctification, the belief proved to be a formidable foe. Propagators of the idea, such as Charles Harrison Mason and Charles Price Jones, two Baptist ministers and one-time students at Arkansas Baptist, would continue their quest to spread the controversial teaching. Mason and Jones also fought against what they believed to be a surge in denominationalism, which removed power from local congregations and placed it in the hands of a supervisory board such as the Arkansas Baptist Convention. They also argued against administrative panels that set licensing and educational standards for preachers. For a brief while Arkansas Baptist College and the school's newspaper, *The Arkansas Baptist Vanguard*, became their battleground.[18]

In the end, the fight resulted in a formal schism within the Baptist denomination. After the break, Mason, Jones, and their followers formed a holiness association named the Churches of God in Christ. Congregations within their association continued to worship in the tradition of their slave ancestors. Nevertheless, the charismatic liturgy continued to serve as a source of embarrassment and a perceived threat to racial uplift for progressives such as Morris who believed that one's religion should serve a larger purpose other than to excite parishioners, resulting in a simple shout.

Morris proved more successful in other aspects of using the Baptist denomination as a vehicle for racial uplift. In 1885, national delegates elected him president of the National Baptist Convention. This was quite an honor as members organized the convention to act as a national advisory board for black Baptist associations in the country. By 1900, all black Baptists, with the exception of the New England Baptists, answered to the National Baptist Convention. At annual meetings, delegates not only tended to the business of the denomination, but also made statements designed to show the loyalty of African Americans and to draw attention to issues affecting the race. For instance, as president of the national convention, Morris argued, "Our race for many years in this country was held as slaves and not able to enjoy the full protection of the flag." But he challenged the audience to find a more faithful and loyal group of people than African Americans, arguing that blacks believed that the American Revolution would bring a better day. Even after America's war of independence, slaves followed the flag into the Civil War without hope of reward and helped to save it from the dishonor of the Confederacy. In more recent days, Morris pointed out, blacks had followed the flag into Santiago.[19]

Morris's words indicate that he was aware of the importance of African Americans' loyalty to the country. More importantly, he used his position as president of the National Baptist Convention to speak to larger secular issues concerning the race, such as blacks' participation in US military campaigns. Invoking the notion of black patriotism that stemmed back to the American Revolution and continued through the Civil War and, most recently, the Spanish-American War, he made the argument that blacks' participation in these conflicts made them deserving of the same equality as whites. Some eighteen years before W.E.B. DuBois made the call as the editor of the *Crisis* in an emphatic plea to African Americans to close their ranks during World War I, Morris used his national pulpit to make a similar argument with the hope of gaining equality.

As president of the National Baptist Convention, Morris also envisioned the creation of a national publishing house that would highlight the intellect of the race. Officials of the convention recognized that a press would also employ hundreds of blacks and spur black-owned subsidiaries such as print, paper, and ink companies. Black self-determination also remained a major motivating factor, as Morris did not want the National Baptist Convention beholden to the white-owned American Baptist Publication Society, which published all religious literature for the black Baptists. In the past, black ministers pleaded to have their articles published, but the influence of white Baptists had always proved an obstacle. Morris's thoughts were thus: "Some of the ablest scholars of the race have been forced to occupy very menial positions because there is such little organization among our people that they are not willing to place their genius and learning at our command." Until blacks controlled their own modes of publishing, their scholarship would continue to be at the mercy of white publishers.[20]

In order to circumvent white obstruction, Morris argued that it was now time for the creation of a black-owned publishing house. This "would show that while it cost nothing materially to become a Baptist, it is worth something materially to be a Baptist." Closer examination of these words shows that Morris understood that the Baptist denomination should offer its members something more than just salvation and that adherents should be able take advantage of the services the denomination provided. For instance, with the creation of a press, black intellects could see the benefit of Baptist membership, while others could profit from gaining bookmaking, clerkship, and management skills designed to produce a black labor force that could be employed by the publishing house. In sum, Morris understood the potential of black religion to promote scholarly criticism, but, more importantly, business opportunities for its people.[21]

In 1897, the National Baptist Convention passed a resolution for the creation of a Baptist publishing house. Delegates appointed Richard Boyd, a businessman and fellow Baptist, to lead the new enterprise. Boyd secured property in Nashville, Tennessee, and the National Baptist Convention raised funds for the construction of a building to house the press. The convention incorporated the publishing house the next year, and although a dispute arose over the leadership of the business, the press began to publish materials for black Baptists. Over the years, the press became the jewel of the black Baptist denomination, creating thousands of jobs and generating wealth for the black community. It also provided black intellectuals and clergymen with the opportunity to construct their own religious and intellectual discourse, which in turn fostered educational advancement, making the National Baptist Publishing House an extension of black self-help due to Morris and the National Baptist Convention.

Recognizing the importance of creating black-owned businesses, Morris became one of the foremost supporters of the National Negro Business League. John Hope, a professor at Atlanta University, first began the discussion of black-owned businesses designed to create jobs and to provide services to the African American community. Booker T. Washington, also a promoter of black enterprise, in 1900 invited four hundred black businessmen to Boston, Massachusetts, for the purpose of establishing a national program to promote black-owned businesses. Their efforts resulted in the creation of the National Negro Business League, and their organizational platform expressed the belief that "taxpaying African Americans of intelligence and high character almost were always treated with respect by whites and urged shiftless, idle, and useless African Americans to be transformed into valuable law abiding citizens."[22]

Delegates elected Washington their first president, and with his help by 1907 the organization possessed over three hundred branches throughout the United States. Morris became interested in establishing chapters in Arkansas as they were seen as an extension of racial uplift. During Reconstruction, he witnessed black victimization due to black codes such as vagrancy laws that forced freedmen back into the service of planters. In Helena, things were not much better, as the black population, although in the majority, remained economically dependent upon the white minority.[23] In 1902, businessmen asked Morris to serve as the executive director of the Arkansas Negro State Business League. He also worked tirelessly to establish a chapter in Phillips County, where he served as president. Although an opponent of segregation, Morris realized that Jim Crow provided blacks an opportunity to benefit financially. Due to whites' refusal to provide services to blacks, it afforded the black community the opportunity to create businesses such as barbershops, funeral homes, restaurants, boardinghouses, and insurance agencies. In the opinion of Morris, "it provided Negroes with the opportunity to train their own leaders and to become economically independent of whites."[24]

A devoutly religious man, Morris also remained an astute businessman. He owned a small farm in rural Phillips County, and he and his wife owned and managed several properties throughout the county. Even in death, Morris proved to be a savvy entrepreneur. His will listed "six insurance policies, [and] ownership of stocks in an Arkansas bank and an insurance company." Though he never became wealthy, Morris's business sense allowed him to amass a considerable estate for someone born into slavery and a victim of Jim Crow his entire life. Morris learned the value of independence from his father, who worked as a blacksmith, and his brother-in-law, who earned a living as shoemaker; this kept both men from the exploitative measures of sharecropping and made them economically independent from whites. As an adult, Morris received his pay from his black congregants and as a landowner. As president of the National Baptist Convention he continued to preach black independence and self-determination. An argument can be made that Morris never truly cared about accruing a fortune in the capitalistic sense but rather that he recognized the value of independence, which allowed not only his family but the entire race to prosper, resulting in racial uplift.

Morris's sense of self-determination and position as president of the National Baptist Convention naturally led him into the political arena. Phillips County had always been a hotbed of black political participation and a stronghold for the Grand Old Party. A staunch Republican supporter, Morris attended every Republican state convention, arguing for black political participation. He would even become active on the national stage, serving as a delegate to the GOP general convention in 1884, 1888, and 1904. In 1897, however, Morris made his only known bid for public office when he submitted an application for recorder of deeds for the District of Columbia.[25]

The White House was inundated with letters of support from across the nation in support of Morris's application. The correspondence spoke to Morris's natural ability as a leader. For example, David Abner Jr., a delegate to the National Republican Convention from St. Louis, described Morris as "the ablest man of our race in this country." He continued, "In the first place, he is a scholar and well informed. Second, he has splendid executive ability. This is observed more pointedly when it is remembered that he is the president of the greatest religious organization in this country, numbering over one and a half million members as well as president of the greatest religious body in his own state of Arkansas." Morris's supporter concluded, "He is strictly honest, sound in morals, and a polished gentleman all round. His appointment would be hailed with universal satisfaction by his own people, regardless of religious sect or creed, and by the Republican Party, whose cause he has so earnestly espoused these years, especially in the recent election."[26]

In the end, President McKinley failed to appoint Morris to the position of recorder of deeds. But due to his work in the Republican Party, in 1908 President Theodore Roosevelt did select him to serve as part of a special envoy to the Belgian Congo. Morris and his wife visited the African country on what has been called a humanitarian mission. Although Morris never sought another political office, he remained politically connected for the remainder of his life. He defended his political affiliation by coupling it with the larger issue of the day, racial uplift, arguing, "The people of the Gospel should participate in political affairs to help the Negro race." As a result of his political activity, the Helena preacher became well respected in the eyes of blacks and whites throughout Arkansas. This admiration would be tested in 1919 when race riots occurred in his home county.[27]

During the summer of 1919, the country witnessed a wave of racial violence that engulfed most major cities. The conflicts occurred so frequently that black writer James Weldon Johnson dubbed the period the "Red Summer." The catalyst was returning African American soldiers who demanded respect and equality due to their service in the war. Black veterans argued that they had aided in the preservation of democracy in France and that they now wanted their country to extend to them the same rights that they had fought for in Europe.[28] Violence first occurred in Texas, quickly spreading to Chicago, Illinois, and on to Washington, D.C., and Rosewood, Florida. By the end of the summer, the United States seemed to be a racial powder keg. The next eruption of violence occurred in Phillips County, in the small town of Elaine, Arkansas, not far from Morris's hometown of Helena. Although this time black soldiers were not directly involved, the violence in Elaine coincided with the national push for black equality. In an effort to negotiate better wages, black sharecroppers attempted to unionize. As a hundred or so farmers met at a church in nearby Hoop Spur, Arkansas, violence erupted when county officials tried unsuccessfully to disband the meeting. The ensuing fracas left A. D. Adkins, a railroad detective, dead, and a sheriff critically injured. County officials quickly gathered a posse, and instead of a peaceable surrender, blacks joined their national counterparts and chose to fight back.[29]

The violence lasted for three days as whites from neighboring locales descended upon the county. White newspaper headlines referred to the episode as a "Negro Uprising" and called on the governor to send help. Things grew even worse when authorities arrested O. S. Bratton, a white man and suspected socialist, who, according to the *New York Times*, "had been preaching social equality among the Negroes."[30] Although no one knows how Morris first became involved in the incident, most believe it was due to the death of Dr. D. A. Johnson, a black dentist and resident of Helena who was arrested for his alleged involvement in the riots. Accounts claim that upon his apprehension, Johnson wrestled a gun away from O. R. Lilly, a businessman and alderman of Helena, killing him in the process. In response, law enforcement shot Johnson on the spot, resulting in his death. In an effort to regain control, state officials sent five hundred troops from Little Rock's Camp Pike to restore order and begged for black leaders of the county to appeal for peace.[31]

Morris pleaded for peace and argued against the mob violence, insisting, "The taking of human life without judge or jury are held up as an excuse for the mob's shameful work." He asserted, "There seems to be an unholy alliance between some of the officers of the law and the mob to overturn the foundation on which our government rests. . . . [A]nd men who gather for no other purpose than to empty their revolver into the body of helpless criminals, are themselves guilty of a crime."[32] Morris also spoke out against the rape and abuse black women suffered at the hands of soldiers during the riots. The father of three daughters, Morris understood the perils black women faced in Jim Crow America. Even in times of peace, black women were often sexually assaulted at the hands of whites. Although no confirmed reports exist on the number of such attacks during the riot, Morris's words testify that they did occur. He called rape the most "heinous of all crimes." He begged his fellow citizens to pray that peace be restored and reminded them that the Lord had exclaimed, "Vengeance shall be mine."[33]

It is hard to ascertain exactly how big of a role Morris played in restoring peace and order after the Elaine race riot, but we do know that due to his position within the community whites turned to him. Morris again used his position as a man of the cloth to bring about calm. More importantly, during the riots he used his pulpit to speak out against lynching and the rape of black women in similar ways that secular organizations were doing. Again, Morris seized the moment to render a service to his people by calling attention to lynching, which threatened the liberty of blacks across the nation. In the end, twelve black sharecroppers were handed death sentences, and the courts handed sixty-seven others long prison terms for their role in the race riot. The courts later commuted the sentences of the twelve men given the death sentence.[34]

A man with a cause, Morris worked tirelessly to uplift his race. Whether arguing for the creation of Arkansas Baptist College, a Negro Business League chapter in Helena, the National Baptist Publishing House, or running for public office, Morris personified the qualities of an African American who understood the power of religion and the influence of the pulpit. Always aware of the conditions of blacks, Morris worked to uplift the race until the very end. Morris died on September 5, 1922, after suffering from an unknown illness for much of the year. To honor his contribution to black education, his body was placed in the chapel of Arkansas Baptist College, the intuition he founded, where it lay in state before being shipped to Helena for burial. On September 12, 1922, to honor Morris, black and white business owners closed their doors as friends interned his body at the Starkey-Dixon Cemetery. In honor of his contributions to the Baptist denomination and his efforts of racial uplift, delegates erected a grandiose monument befitting the man who spent his life working to better his race in Arkansas and beyond.[35]

CHAPTER 9

Civil Rights Inactivism
Richard Nathaniel Hogan and the "Enemies of Righteousness"

BARCLAY KEY

WITH GOOD REASON, traditional narratives of the postbellum South and the long civil rights movement emphasize that the organizations blacks created frequently built upon relationships and networks that predated the Civil War.[1] Independent of white control, these organizations provide historians with clues to the needs and priorities of blacks in the wake of emancipation and amid the chaotic and often violent turmoil of the early twentieth century. The same was generally true for religious affiliations. Throwing off the burden of white control and oversight, blacks, for example, formed the Christian Methodist Episcopal Church in 1870 and the National Baptist Convention in 1895.[2]

One notable exception to this trend involved the Disciples of Christ and their southern offspring, Churches of Christ, an unlikely development given their characterization as "the spirited offspring of the religious rednecks of the post bellum South."[3] Churches of Christ had perhaps the highest percentage of blacks in a predominantly white denomination, at approximately 10 percent. This sizable black presence within a mostly white denomination raises numerous questions about racial and religious identities, especially as conflicts over civil rights unfolded in the twentieth century. Why would blacks associate with a predominantly white denomination when independent black churches proliferated? How did blacks and whites within the denomination navigate racial customs and the restraints of Jim Crow laws? Answers to such questions are obviously complex, but clues can be found in the life of a native Arkansan, Richard Nathaniel Hogan (1902–1997), a prominent black preacher within Churches of Christ.

Hogan is notable for two reasons. First, he was popular among black and white members of the church. He accepted invitations to preach from and regularly corresponded with blacks and whites. As an author of religious literature, Hogan's readership included both blacks and whites. Second, Hogan warrants scrutiny because he was not a civil rights activist. As this essay will show, Hogan frequently displayed contempt for racial segregation, but this disposition did not propel him to civil rights activism in any traditional sense. His life is instructive for understanding how blacks outside of traditional activist circles were nevertheless emboldened by the changes unfolding in the long civil rights movement. Hogan even criticized black preachers for becoming preoccupied with civil rights activism as he became an outspoken critic of racial segregation within Churches of Christ.

Although he spent much of his life in California, Hogan was imbued with religious zeal from an early age. His father died when he was only three years old, and when Hogan was eight his mother sent him to a Christian boarding school in remote Silver Point, Tennessee, about sixty miles east of Nashville. She entrusted her son to George Phillip Bowser, a black educator and preacher of considerable renown within Churches of Christ who undoubtedly had a profound impact on Hogan. Bowser was born in 1874 and received a remarkable education for his time at Walden University in Nashville, where he studied Greek, Hebrew, Latin, French, and German. Bowser became an iconic preacher who reportedly memorized almost all of the New Testament. At the age of twenty-three, he joined Churches of Christ and soon committed himself to providing educational opportunities and religious literature to blacks in the denomination. To this end, in 1902 he founded the *Christian Echo*, a periodical published primarily for black church members. With financial backing from whites, Bowser helped start a Christian school for blacks in 1907. This was the context in which Hogan first encountered Bowser in 1910.[4]

The relationships between Bowser and whites in the denomination must have affected Hogan. A "spiritual and financial paternalism" characterized numerous white denominations, and Churches of Christ were no exception. But Bowser was a proud, educated man, who finessed the South's race relations to meet his objectives. He accepted white assistance out of a sense of shared purpose: blacks and whites believed that evangelism was imperative and that Christian education was beneficial to all. And while he exercised caution around potentially violent whites, Bowser was certainly not deferential. The best example of his disposition around whites occurred in 1920, when he became the principal of a Christian school in Nashville, where Hogan followed him as a student. To curry favor with potential white patrons, a white preacher was named superintendent of the school and he insisted that blacks use the building's back door. Bowser was appalled. He refused to comply and within a week he resigned in protest. Some blacks within the denomination wanted to abide by the customary back door entrance. Challenging the South's social customs was not a priority for them and the educational opportunities were too valuable in a political climate that treated black education as an afterthought at best. But Bowser was no civil rights crusader. He simply refused to suffer the indignity of entering the back door or allowing his students to endure the same and the school soon faltered without his presence or support.[5]

Bowser also had positive experiences with whites in the denomination, as evidenced by an account he shared in the *Christian Echo*. Bowser was invited to conduct a revival for a white church in Jonesboro, Arkansas. "I seldom meet a body of white disciples to cooperate more freely," he wrote, before describing the white preacher in Jonesboro as "a genuine Christian worker. Through him a piece of property was bought for the colored worship. Several were baptized." The *Christian Echo* is replete with examples of black and white cooperation in evangelistic endeavors, including several in Arkansas. A lady from tiny Wabbaseka wrote to the *Christian Echo* about "several white friends" who attended a revival there in 1941, and Bowser reported from Blytheville in 1947, where a revival drew about one thousand people and occurred with the help of a local white preacher, "one of the greatest CHRISTIAN WORKERS we have ever met." Bowser struck a remarkable balance between pursuing what he perceived to be the best course for black churches and maintaining his personal dignity, a lesson that Hogan learned and implemented in his own career.[6]

Like his mentor, Hogan became a well-respected and popular preacher among both blacks and whites in Churches of Christ. In 1938, for example, white churches in Oklahoma City sponsored a revival that featured Hogan and was intended to establish a new church for blacks. Within two years, a vibrant congregation of over one hundred people was meeting regularly. But the white churches who initiated the revival seemed to have chosen the preacher, a black man named Walter Weathers, and arranged for a white preacher to assist him. Yet these decisions apparently received Hogan's approval because he praised the white churches for sacrificing "one of their best . . . to help with the Colored work." About the white family hired to assist Weathers, Hogan said, "This is one of the finest Christian couples that I ever had the privilege of meeting." Hogan periodically supported this church by holding revivals there in subsequent years, and according to one new member, "The white disciples manifested great interest by attending in large numbers."[7]

Historians of the South have long grappled with how to interpret the religious sentiments of blacks and whites. Competing racial ideologies easily infused otherwise benevolent endeavors. Some whites undoubtedly perceived black preachers as entertainers, curiosities to witness, or sources of humor. Other whites shared the passion for evangelism that characterized Bowser and Hogan and supported preachers, black and white, whose sermons resulted in baptisms or spiritual renewal. Marshall Keeble, the most renowned black preacher among Churches of Christ, discovered that whites might even fit both of those characterizations. "In my work many white people come to hear me and are converted," he wrote in 1929. They "come to hear me to get something to laugh at, and they get caught in the gospel net." Two years later, he estimated that he had converted at least eight hundred whites.[8]

Regardless of how one perceives Hogan's seemingly benign popularity, it clearly rankled some whites and did not go unchallenged. In 1941, a prominent white preacher and writer named Foy Wallace, known for his "swashbuckling, fighting style," clearly felt jealous of Hogan's popularity despite insisting otherwise. Wallace published an essay in his periodical, the *Bible Banner*, that questioned the "manner in which the brethren in some quarters are going in for the negro meetings [leading] one to wonder whether they are trying to make white folks out of the negroes or negroes out of the white folks." Wallace specifically mentioned reports of "white women . . . becoming so animated over a certain colored preacher as to go up to him after a sermon and shake hands with him *holding his hand in both of theirs*." He called these actions "pitiable" and was furious over the thought of a white woman who would "forget her dignity" and "lower herself" in this manner. Wallace further complained about a black couple that operated a home for orphans and espoused "social equality" and about whites that were "apparently encouraging them." He lamented a visit to a white church where the black janitor would frequently attend services and shake hands with members as they exited the building. "When I insisted that it be discontinued some of the white brethren were offended," Wallace wrote. Unapologetic for his staunch segregationist disposition, Wallace recoiled at the increasingly common sight of blacks and whites attending revivals together. These events were typically segregated, but mingling inevitably occurred. "I am very much in favor of negro meetings for the negroes," he explained, "but I am just as much opposed to negro meetings for white people, and I am against white brethren taking the meetings away from the negroes and the general mixing that has become entirely too much of a practice in these negro meetings."[9]

Wallace may have had Hogan or Keeble in mind when he bemoaned handshakes between black men and white women, but he called Hogan by name in describing an instance when Hogan and a white preacher briefly traveled together and shared the same boarding room. Wallace was absolutely appalled, calling it "an infringement on the Jim Crow law . . . a violation of Christianity itself, and of all common decency." In his estimation, Hogan had "been too much inclined to mix with the white people and to favor, in attitude, a social equality" and "cannot be expected to have any too much sense about anything." Wallace went on to suggest that Keeble, who never openly advocated racial equality, "teach these negro preachers better."[10]

Keeble attempted to placate Wallace in a subsequent issue of the *Bible Banner*. His most recent biographer explained, "Keeble without doubt detested Wallace's racial hubris, but he suppressed his rage to maintain the trust and support of white Christians, who made possible his outreach to blacks." Meanwhile, Hogan seemed to give little heed to the controversy. In a private letter to Jimmie Lovell, a white friend and patron, Hogan expressed little surprise about Wallace's harangue, having previously been subjected to his vitriol. Lovell had asked Hogan if he had seen Wallace's essay. Hogan replied to the inquiry but only addressed the controversy in the final paragraph that began with a hint of exasperation: "Yes brother Lovell I saw the article in the Bible Banner written by brother Wallace." Indeed, Hogan's reply makes clear that the real source of Wallace's frustration was a recent situation in southern Texas when both men were holding revivals and "white people wouldn't stop attending my meeting to come and hear him." But Hogan also felt compelled to defend himself against some charges, asserting, "He is the first person . . . who has accused me of conducting myself in a way that shows that I am interested in 'mixing with the white people' or 'social equality.' Such has NEVER intered [sic] my mind and is no part of the truth." Hogan concluded, "I trust that God will forgive brother Wallace and the like of him, but I know that before God will forgive him he MUST repent. . . . [Y]ou may rest sssured [sic] that I'll press on. A number of the white people who saw that article have informed me that his paper shall enter their home no more."[11]

Hogan was writing to one of his primary white sponsors, an important source of income and support, so perhaps his reply was somewhat tempered. But his assessment of the controversy, while guarded in some respects, included no apology or particular deference toward Wallace, Lovell, or anyone else. Knowledge of Hogan's interaction with whites was clearly widespread, but he felt no reason to provide an explanation, except for Wallace's obvious jealousy. Hogan viewed such circumstances of "racial interchange" as coincidental. Evangelism was his primary concern, and the gospel was for everyone. He was not about to limit his audience to blacks. At the same time, Hogan made no special effort to promote "social equality," even as he carried and presented himself as an equal among whites.[12]

These comments are particularly interesting in light of Hogan's subsequent essays on segregated Christian colleges. While exhibiting no particular interest in "mixing with the white people," he clearly believed in racial equality and privately expressed enormous frustration with segregated Christian colleges. During this exchange in 1941, however, Hogan was resigned to focus his attention on evangelism, an endeavor upon which both blacks and whites presumably agreed. Wallace's tirade against this tepid race mixing apparently did little to sway his readers, as Hogan continued receiving numerous invitations to preach from black and white churches, including churches in Arkansas.[13]

In 1949, with his mentor Bowser in declining health, Hogan accepted the mantle of editing and publishing the *Christian Echo*. The publication was widely distributed among black churches, but numerous whites read the monthly and contributed articles too. Regardless of the author, articles typically consisted of biblical commentary, church news, or critiques of denominationalism that were intended to reinforce the sacrosanct idea that Churches of Christ were the true keepers of the faith. In this sense, blacks and whites echoed each other. They were consumed with confirming and reinforcing their collective identity as members of the one church. In 1954, in the same month that the US Supreme Court handed down its famous decision in *Brown v. Board of Education of Topeka, Kansas*, Hogan published an editorial in the *Christian Echo* that railed against denominationalism. "People everywhere should know that the Lord has but ONE CHURCH," he wrote. "People should know that in order to be saved, they MUST be members of that one church." Hogan further asserted, "Amid the many churches in our land today, the church of Christ stands unique. She has marks of identity which distinguish her from any other church in the land."[14]

In this strictly sectarian context, commentary about current events like the civil rights movement had no place. "Though the events of those years were surely the most revolutionary to transpire in America since the Civil War," wrote church historian Richard Hughes, "one scarcely would have known of them at all if one's only source of information during the period had been the *Firm Foundation*, the *Gospel Advocate*, or almost any other media outlet related to mainstream Churches of Christ." The same was true of the *Christian Echo*. Direct references to the civil rights movement or significant Supreme Court cases were largely absent, even though critiques of racial segregation in Churches of Christ appeared frequently. The most overtly political statement from this era appeared in 1960 and was not concerned with race but with religious orthodoxy. A regular contributor to the *Christian Echo* urged his readers to vote against John F. Kennedy for president because "it is impossible for any man to uphold the constitution of the U.S.A. and the constitution of the Catholic Church at the same time." When asked about other nominal Christians who were running for office, the writer noted, first, that they were not "New Testament Christians," before emphasizing that other churches were "not trying to unite the Church and State." Ironically, he voiced many of the same concerns expressed by white southerners who wondered about electing a Catholic president.[15]

No matter how aloof Churches of Christ seemed before the momentous events of the 1950s and 1960s, those with ears to hear and eyes to see knew that changes were afoot, especially with regard to racial segregation. The University of Arkansas law and medical schools admitted their first black students in 1948. Legal battles that began in Oklahoma and Texas culminated in Supreme Court rulings in 1948 and 1950 that clearly determined segregated public universities were unconstitutional. The five cases that were combined in the Supreme Court's 1954 *Brown* decision were initially filed in 1950 and 1951.[16] Amid these judicial milestones, black educators such as Bowser (who died in 1950) and Hogan continued to experience difficulties with building and maintaining institutions to serve black members of Churches of Christ. The latest example had been the Bowser Christian Institute that opened in Fort Smith, Arkansas, in 1938 but closed in 1946. This effort was not the last to operate a school for blacks in Churches of Christ, but as southern colleges gradually admitted black students, Hogan could no longer fathom whites' refusal to open doors to blacks, particularly brothers and sisters in the faith.[17]

Several contributors to the *Christian Echo* broached the subject of race relations in their articles, usually with a didactic approach and numerous biblical references. But the most prolonged attacks on racial discrimination came from Hogan. The biblical literalism and primitivism that characterized Churches of Christ also informed his writing about race and the civil rights movement. He began one editorial by observing, "Most of our Brethren who are in high places in the church of our Lord, are going to lose their souls because they are respecters of persons. That being a respecter is a sin is without question, for the Bible plainly says that it is a sin." Hogan quoted this phrase—"respecter of persons"—from a sermon by the apostle Peter, with which his readers would have been familiar. While Hogan's attacks were broadly aimed, he was especially appalled that racial discrimination persisted at what he termed "so-called christian [sic] schools." Administrators had previously hidden behind the law, Hogan noted, "but our government has informed the entire country that the practice of segregation because of race or color is unconstitutional. But christians [sic] shouldn't have to be told that." Even these comments appeared in 1959, five years after the initial *Brown* decision and even further removed from the Supreme Court's decisions regarding the desegregation of higher educational institutions. As he discussed colleges affiliated with Churches of Christ, Hogan would insert quotation marks around the term "Christian," suggesting that he questioned the credentials of a nominally Christian college that practiced racial exclusion. "The fact that Negroes are not allowed in these churches and schools is proof that God is not there; for where God is, no man is barred because of the color of his skin. Brethren, you may fallout with me because of this article, but you know that I am telling the truth and those guilty will do well to repent."[18]

Later in 1959, Hogan published an essay titled "Enemies of Righteousness," an unsubtle reference to a sorcerer whom the apostle Paul encountered in the Acts of the Apostles. The essay reported on a meeting of Christian college presidents, Hogan's "enemies of righteousness," who agreed to continue operating church colleges in the South on a segregated basis. Colleges outside of the South accepted blacks, Hogan noted, "but the Presidents of these western and northern schools . . . failed to point out the sin of the decision of the Presidents of the other schools." Hogan had grown weary of excuses and platitudes from whites who sought to maintain segregation. "Surely these people will not contend that they love the Negro when they refuse him admittance into their schools that are supposed to be christian." To those whites who counseled gradual change, Hogan opined that the "Negro has taken his time for a hundren [sic] years and I think it is a terrible thing to tell people to take their time in obeying God. Take their time in repenting of their sins. Just as well to tell a man who has been in the Baptist, Methodist or other denominational churches all of his life to take his time in coming out of that human institution." Again, Hogan conceived of Churches of Christ as the only true church, as a unique entity among a plethora of denominations. His critique was bound to the religious identity that he shared with so many whites, an identity that made him even more perturbed about their intransigence with regard to segregated schools.[19]

Charles Cannon, a white subscriber to the *Christian Echo* from southwestern Arkansas, responded to Hogan's complaints.[20] His remarks illustrate how the Bible was a battleground of sorts for those people who disagreed over providential intentions with regard to racial segregation. Cannon quoted Acts 17:26, "[God] hath made of one blood all nations of men for to dwell on all the face of the earth, and hath determined the times before appointed, and the bounds of their habitation." Ironically, both segregationists and integrationists utilized the verse in a battle over biblical justification and authority for their respective positions. The latter noted that humans were "of one blood," while segregationists emphasized that God had apparently prescribed boundaries for various peoples of the earth. Hogan responded in kind to what he called Cannon's "ridiculous arguments." He acknowledged that whites had helped blacks in a variety of ways, but this help was "nothing to brag about" because God commanded Christians to help each other. He also questioned how Cannon could speak of "their churches," a misnomer among the exclusivist Churches of Christ. Hogan concluded his rebuttal with an appeal: "I sincerely pray that my brethren, both White and Colored, will soon rid their hearts of hate, prejudice and pride and be satisfied with being simple New Testament christians, for regardless of the color of the skin, we are in the same kingdom, subject to the same King. Let's stop referring to other races as your brethren and to our own race as my brethren. Regardless of the race, if we are in Christ, we are all brethren."[21]

This integrationist and primitivist bent persisted throughout Hogan's writing about race, especially as he praised some whites who appeared enlightened about such things. In April 1960, Hogan reprinted comments from a white preacher who decried racially segregated churches in 1878. Two months later, Hogan penned another editorial praising the few white ministers among Churches of Christ who took similar positions. "There is no such thing in the Bible as a white church of Christ and a Colored church of Christ. I hope the time will soon come when my brethren will not allow the sign, 'church of Christ (Colored)' to be erected on their buildings, for God has no church of Christ, Colored. Neither does he have a church of Christ, white. . . . Prejudice, hate and segregation have no place in the true church of Christ." The fact that blacks could attend Christian colleges that were not affiliated with Churches of Christ did not affect Hogan's commitment to the "true church." But the sectarian faith that gave blacks and whites in Churches of Christ so much in common became the means by which blacks questioned segregation's persistence. "Where is the 'Thus saith the Lord' to practice the principles of racial discrimination in the Church of Christ?" one contributor to the *Christian Echo* rhetorically asked. Whites like Cannon also relied on the Bible to buttress their prejudices, but as other Christian denominations began building theological consensus around integration and the federal government began showing signs of change, Hogan's frustrations simmered.[22]

This sort of didactic appeal exemplified Hogan's writing about race relations in the 1950s and 1960s. While his criticisms of racial discrimination continued, he never encouraged any form of activism or protest and never made a specific reference to prominent civil rights activists. Hogan's laments evolved, however, as he grew disillusioned with the possibility that whites might make any meaningful changes. He occasionally made room in the *Christian Echo* to vent these frustrations, once instructing his black readers "to love all white people, for you will go to hell if you hate them, like some of them are going to hell for hating you." Hogan also decried the invisibility of Churches of Christ when racial strife overwhelmed cities such as Birmingham, Alabama, and Jackson, Mississippi. "Where are the Churches of Christ . . . during all of those disgraceful racial struggles in these places?"[23]

The most notable exception to this general omission of the civil rights movement from the pages of the *Christian Echo* appeared in June 1965. Hogan published a report of the Selma-to-Montgomery march from a black minister named Norman Adamson, an Arkansas native who was then working for a Church of Christ in Chicago. Adamson was well acquainted with racial discrimination in the church, having been initially accepted to the segregated Church of Christ Harding College before administrators discovered that he was black and rescinded his admission. Adamson later recalled how he made a passing remark expressing solidarity with the Selma campaign, when several ladies in his congregation challenged him to travel south and participate. His report outlined his motives at the time: "Realizing our Christian responsibility towards [segregationists], we . . . identified ourselves with the Non-violent Civil Rights' Movement, with our number one objective: the salvation of white men who have bigoted hearts, and our second objective—making this world a better place in which to live for all mankind, black and white." Neither voting rights nor any civil rights were mentioned in his report. Indeed, the report amounted to another homily on the evils of bigotry and segregation, with which *Christian Echo* readers were certainly familiar. Hogan undoubtedly approved of the report's content, in part because one could easily mistake Adamson's sojourn to Alabama as an evangelistic endeavor rather than a demand for voting rights. Participation in the march was about the extent of Adamson's activism, although he remained committed to racial justice throughout his life.[24]

Hogan's career as a preacher and writer reminds us of the complexities of race and religion in the twentieth century. At the very least, his life serves as a reminder that the experiences of blacks in predominantly white denominations should qualify our generalizations about a singular, monolithic black church. But Hogan's perspectives on race and religion additionally compel us to evaluate how racial and religious identities have competed within the psyches of individuals. Scholars commonly refer to W.E.B. DuBois's phrase "double consciousness" and the warring ideas entailed with being black and American. Yet such ideas have never been limited to race or nationality. In Hogan's case, religious identity prevailed upon him such that he regularly worked with whites to advance evangelism and education, but he also fiercely denounced racial discrimination without giving public support for traditional civil rights activism. The depth of this religious identity is the only explanation as to why Hogan would place himself in a predominantly white denomination.

Hogan also illustrates the need to further examine the black freedom struggle through the eyes of people who were not civil rights activists, even if they sympathized with many of the movement's premises or objectives. Churches of Christ did not associate with other denominations, so when the civil rights movement was assigned religious significance by some leading activists, Churches of Christ maintained a preexisting aversion to collective actions among churches. In the minds of many congregants and preachers, securing eternal salvation deserved greater attention than correcting contemporary social injustices. From this perspective, preachers who gave so much time and energy to the civil rights movement were neglecting their primary responsibility of saving souls. Hogan provides a compelling example of someone who was outspoken in opposition to white supremacy but had no desire to participate in a civil rights march. Re-imagining the freedom struggle in these ways will yield new insights into the lives of people who witnessed and sympathized with the freedom struggle, even if they did not participate in its most famous battles.

PART IV

From *Braceros* and Refugees to Citizens—New Perspectives on the Latina/o and Asian Experience in Arkansas

CHAPTER 10

The Bracero Program
Mexican Workers in the Arkansas Delta, 1948–1964

JULIE M. WEISE

"WIKE'S DRIVE INN (Restaurant)" read the photograph's caption. "It is at the outskirts of Marked Tree, Arkansas, heading towards Harrisburg, Arkansas. A well constructed and nice-looking establishment." It was November 1949 when Mexican consul Rubén Gaxiola traveled to Marked Tree, Arkansas, to investigate alleged discrimination against Mexicans. He recorded his findings with a camera: "No Mexicans" signs prominently displayed in front of eleven establishments. Additionally, one of the town's two movie theaters seated Mexican patrons only in the area reserved for blacks. Attaching the photos as evidence in his report to Mexico City, Gaxiola immediately recommended that Marked Tree's employers have their Mexican labor contracts cancelled. Gaxiola hoped that swift action would set an example for the rest of Arkansas, "as an energetic protest against these discriminatory acts against Mexicans."[1]

The signs would not remain for long. During the decade following their 1947 arrival in the Arkansas Delta, Mexican cotton workers successfully resisted Jim Crow–style exclusion through strategies this chapter will examine. The victory was ambiguous and gave way to a new, more fluid separation in which Mexicans had access to white public space but often felt more comfortable socializing with blacks. The first-class citizenship that Mexicans demanded with an end to their formal segregation never extended into the economic realm, where they fought for, but failed to win, broad guarantees of economic security.

Discrimination against Mexicans and consular interventions to prevent them were commonplace throughout the United States during the Bracero Program, which brought more than 4 million Mexican men to work in the United States between 1942 and 1964 on bilateral labor contracts. Like their counterparts in the Southwest, Arkansas's cotton farmers were hungry for labor during that time. Poor whites and blacks had migrated out of the area en masse, beginning during the decade of 1910 and in even greater numbers during World War II. When Arkansas extension agents and farmers' associations first introduced the possibility of contracting *braceros* in 1947 and 1948, the farmers' response was overwhelming. Wrote one county extension agent near the end of the 1948 picking season, "The farmers, as a whole, are very well pleased, and it looks as if there will be a demand for 5,000 such workers next year." Between 1948 and the program's demise in 1964, at least 300,000 braceros would arrive in Arkansas's fields to pick cotton, at times comprising a quarter of the cotton labor force there.[2]

The history of the Bracero Program in Arkansas has been overlooked by scholars yet is both analytically provocative and empirically significant. Braceros' tenure in Arkansas coincided with the decade of Jim Crow's fall. Five years after Consul Gaxiola captured the "No Mexicans" sign, the US Supreme Court negated the doctrine of "separate but equal" through its ruling in *Brown v. Board of Education*.[3] Three years after that, the federal government facilitated the integration of Central High School in nearby Little Rock. As the structures of eugenically based de jure segregation crumbled in the face of increasing black political power and the interventions of the federal government, battles over race and rights moved increasingly into cultural and economic territory.

The twin demands of racial equality and improved economic security for rural workers dogged white southern conservatives facing down New Deal liberals at mid-century, and braceros challenged them on both fronts. They rejected both poor labor conditions and social discrimination in Arkansas, calling upon the support of the local Memphis consulate of the Mexican Foreign Service. White conservatives responded by steadfastly protecting their economic and political advantages over labor, even if this meant compromise in the area of racial segregation. As such, braceros' activism laid bare the primacy of delta elites' economic investment in white supremacy even as they contributed to the system's demise.

Mexican workers signing up for the Bracero Program, whether for money, for adventure, or to make good on the program's promise of modernization, may have known something of the Mexican migrant experience in the United States from friends and relatives who had already journeyed to work there. Most likely, however, they had not heard about Arkansas. The two-day journey from bracero-contracting sites along the US-Mexico border in southeastern Texas to the cotton fields of the Arkansas Delta gave workers their first taste of the poor conditions to come. Particularly during the early years of the program, workers were given nowhere to sleep overnight, no restroom facilities, and nowhere to sit during the long ride. Bracero contracts enumerated very specific rules for transport vehicles, sleeping arrangements, and food along the way. But crew leaders, usually Mexican Americans from Texas known as *Tejanos*, often remained ignorant of these rules, were instructed by Arkansas farmers to ignore them, or flouted them of their own accord. For example, Tejano crew leader Pedro Villarreal Jr. was instructed to feed braceros only bread, but he pitied the workers and bought them canned sardines in addition.

On arrival in Arkansas, braceros were typically housed in abandoned sharecropper cabins, many of which had not been used for years since their inhabitants had left the cotton fields. Most had no bathroom or toilet. Workers routinely cited problems, including "grass filled mattresses, insufficient tables and benches, and insufficient cooking utensils." One worker told of being made to sleep in the farm's garage alongside its tractors. In another case, workers on C. E. Scott's plantation in England, Arkansas, lost all of their possessions and barely escaped with their lives when their cabin caught fire from a heating stove that had been installed "to avoid the furnishing of blankets and mattresses to the workers." With long distances from field to town and no public transport, braceros' mobility was limited and varied. Braceros employed by Claude Overton were gouged by their employer, who charged fifty cents a ride to go the twenty to twenty-five miles into nearby Pine Bluff. The workers of M. C. Baumann, on the other hand, once found their own transportation from Memphis back to Baumann's farm in Marion, rather than return along with their employer when they were upset with him.

Certainly, many braceros showed a willingness to tolerate poor living and working conditions in light of the earning potential that Arkansas represented. Gabino Solís Aguilera, who remembers being one of the first braceros to arrive at a particular Arkansas farm in 1948, described the area as "peaceful. It was a town where they didn't sell alcohol. I ended up there and I was happy with it." But that same year, a bracero in Pine Bluff found the conditions so depressing that he attempted suicide.

Charting a course in between these two responses, thousands of braceros employed varied resistance strategies to improve their lives in Arkansas. Indeed, just two years after the first braceros were contracted to Arkansas, the president of the Agricultural Council of Arkansas complained, "In 1948 . . . we thought our labor problem was solved, but we soon found that instead of having a seasonal labor supply we had a year-round headache." Though this comment referred specifically to the interventions of the Mexican and US federal governments, braceros themselves caused farmers plenty of "headaches" as well. Unlike Solís Aguilera, a vocal minority of braceros sought greater economic and social rights. Their challenges to farmers and authorities were often entwined with their expectations of citizenship in a modern nation, Mexico, which they believed should translate into modern living and social conditions. These braceros appealed directly to farmers for improved wages and conditions, organized their own strikes, fled farms altogether, and went to great lengths to appeal to the Mexican consulate for help.

Braceros dissatisfied with their wages and working conditions often began by raising their objections directly with the farmers that employed them or through middlemen. Tejano crew leader Joe García recalled braceros demanding a raise from their contracted rate of $2.50 per hundred pounds of cotton. García brought the concern to farmer E. D. McKnight, who approved a 25-cent raise.[4] Others communicated directly to employers. A group of braceros who had worked for Royce Stubblefield in Monette wrote a letter to Stubblefield once they were back in Mexico, stating that the truck driver who transported them to the border was supposed to disburse money for transit from the border to their hometowns in Mexico, but he did not do so. Pablo Soto Amaya and Cristóbal Vázquez Martínez asked farmer C. E. Hardin to bring medical attention to some sick compatriots; when Hardin didn't comply at first, the braceros continued to ask "an infinite number of times." These braceros perceived the farmers' dependence on their labor and believed they had enough bargaining power to demand their compliance with the bracero contract.

Even repeated an "infinite" number of times, however, simple requests from small groups of braceros usually were insufficient to win change. In escalating their efforts, braceros drew upon a nationalist Mexican consciousness that promised, and in some ways delivered, modernity and improvement. Most young male braceros in the late 1940s and early 1950s were born after the Mexican Revolution's consolidation of rule in the 1920s, reared during the land redistributions and oil nationalization of the 1930s, and educated, if only for a few years, in schools that had become deliberate parts of the nationalist project.[5] They came of age in the 1940s, a decade marked by uneven economic expansion and the growth of the state apparatus, and signed on to the Bracero Program, which promised to be an engine of both.[6]

Braceros' collective actions drew upon these nationalistic expectations in ways both subtle and overt. On an Arkansas farm during the picking season of 1948, braceros were disgusted by poor housing "once inhabited by blacks" and the pay of $2.00 per hundred pounds of cotton picked, when the contract guaranteed $3.00. They elected two of their own, Jose Luís Landa and Manuel Gallegos, to lead them in a work stoppage. On September 16, Mexican Independence Day, Landa, Gallegos and their group of sixty-five workers went on strike. They returned to the fields for a brief time after a Tejano interpreter insisted that $2.00 was the most the boss would pay. But soon, they "[knew] that there had been strikes in other fields," declared Landa and Gallegos, "and there was a visit from the Consul of Mexico in New Orleans, and it was then that they started to pay us $3." The braceros' choice of Mexican Independence Day for their strike reflected their use of Mexican nationalism as an internal rallying cry for resistance to abuse even when official Mexican government representatives were nowhere in sight. These braceros had come to think of themselves as full citizens of the Mexican modernizing nation, linked through this identity to diverse compatriots.

Braceros struck for higher wages, but control over labor, issues of dignity, and even traditionally feminine concerns, such as food and cooking, prompted work stoppages as well. On one Phillips County farm, three hundred workers wanted to replace their Tejano crew leader with a leader from their own ranks. To make their point, they "mutinied and were engaged in throwing their bunks and bed clothes through the windows and doors of the barracks in which they were lodged." Braceros on another farm, who lost all of their possessions in a fire, struck to force their employer to cover their losses. Those employed by the Miller Lumber Company in Marianna were upset that they were forced to buy food at the company restaurant, wanting instead to be provided with cooking utensils to make their own food at lower cost. They went on strike and refused to eat in the restaurant. Afraid of losing the workforce altogether, the company caved and provided cooking utensils and facilities. In other cases, the work stoppage was less dramatic. During a dispute over wages between Ignacio Paz Gordillo and the Young brothers, one of the Youngs hit Gordillo in the face. The Youngs immediately realized this action jeopardized their bracero contracts, so they reported the incident to their growers' association and sought ways to make amends. But the damage was done. The farm's braceros "remained very much disturbed and refused to continue to work for this employer." Rather than risk trouble for all of the area's farmers, the local growers' association kicked out the Young brothers and transferred their workers to another farm.

Other braceros—by some estimates at least one in ten—resisted their conditions in Arkansas by leaving the farms altogether. Though farmers sought Mexicans to replace a black labor force that had largely moved north, they found themselves confronting the same problem with Mexicans. One farmer complained, "1) Many aliens who enter are not agricultural workers and have no intention of working. They usually disappear or skip while en route to the farm or soon after their arrival. 2) Many after their arrival at the farm hear of high wages in some industrial cities or towns and leave for these jobs before the departure date. 3) Some of them become homesick and leave." Another noted in 1949 that of 641 braceros contracted, 88, or one in seven, had skipped their contracts. Still smarting over the exodus of their black workers, farmers reacted strongly to indications that braceros planned to leave their farms. In 1953, Mississippi Delta farmer E. J. Ganier asked the local sheriff to arrest bracero José Dionisio Sosa because Sosa had threatened "to influence other workers so that they would leave the place." Unlike braceros in California and Texas, who tended to desert the program for the Southwest's urban centers, Arkansas's braceros left the farms for a destination to which farmers had already lost countless racialized laborers: Chicago.

The symbolic meaning of Chicago to both braceros and white farmers was apparent in the case of Juán Braya Carlos, Angel Ramírez López, and Eduardo Gracios Mora. The men arrived to pick cotton on the farm of A. H. Barnhill in Bay, Arkansas, in 1953. They immediately rejected the dilapidated housing they were provided. Aware that the braceros planned to leave, Barnhill asked the local sheriff to arrest them. When the dispatched highway patrolman found the workers, he asked them if they wanted to go back to Mexico, to which they responded,

"No." Asked if they wanted to go to Chicago, the workers shrugged their shoulders and said, "Maybe." Yet, an inspection of the braceros' living quarters suggested that their intentions had been firmer. A map of Illinois lay in the rundown house "with the City of Chicago face up." The workers claimed the map was not theirs but was already there when they arrived, allegedly left behind by earlier groups of braceros or the African Americans that had previously inhabited the house.

While braceros resisted their conditions in Arkansas by making demands of crew leaders and farmers, staging ad hoc strikes, and fleeing to Chicago, they recognized that the Mexican government represented their greatest source of political power. Indeed, black and white workers had utilized all of the former strategies, even organizing the Southern Tenant Farmer's Union, but they faced brutal repression.[7] In contrast to their bracero counterparts, Tejano migrant workers who were US citizens had no local recourse at all and thus fared worse than braceros. Jacinto Sauceda, for example, died on the job in Arkansas, but his next of kin stood to benefit from an investigation into the circumstances of his death, until consular officials figured out that he was a Tejano and not a Mexican national and thus closed his case.

Mexican bureaucrats pursued literally thousands of bracero complaints in matters of economic consequence, such as unpaid wages or problems with health insurance, as well as those about social discrimination. The consulate's most significant tool for battle was the threat of blacklisting particular farmers or areas from the Bracero Program. This could imperil farmers' labor source, often after the crops had been planted. Historians have noted that the Mexican government's bargaining power in the Bracero Program slipped away after 1948, in part because the US government tacitly undermined it by allowing undocumented workers to enter the country.[8] In 1949, the Mexican government lost the right to blacklist entire areas and could blacklist only individual employers. By 1954, the Mexican government had relinquished the right to unilaterally blacklist altogether.[9] Yet while Texas farmers had easier recourse to Tejano or undocumented labor, the threat of blacklisting carried more weight in Arkansas even as the Mexican government's control over the process slipped away.[10] The Mexican consulate in Memphis did succeed in blacklisting employers during this period, and it went to extreme means to do so even when US officials did not cooperate. The consul refused to renew contracts for employers who had matters such as unpaid wages pending with the consulate, and evidence suggests that several Arkansas employers remained blacklisted for up to five years at a time. The consulate's threat of blacklisting in Arkansas was real, if incomplete.

While farmers had sought braceros because they believed that they would be a cheap and pliant workforce, in practice, braceros insisted on claiming the wages and working conditions due them in their contracts. Between 1948 and 1953, braceros filed at least four hundred complaints to their consulate. While some grievances were individual, many represented dozens of braceros. About a third focused on unpaid wages, with transportation, lodging, discrimination (usually wage discrimination), and medical care each representing a significant share as well. These claims echoed those that the poor whites and blacks in the Southern Tenant Farmers' Union had made more than a decade before. Mexican workers, in effect, were petitioning for economic security. Miguel Santiago complained that he had been forced to pay for his own medicine when it should have been the farmer's responsibility. Others decried poor housing conditions. Workers demanded that Byron Landres pay them for additional days of work they lost when the labor contractor's truck broke down on its way to Arkansas. Others demanded pay, as stipulated in the contract, when poor weather made it impossible to pick.

In all, these braceros advocated for shifting the burden of risk from workers to employers. Labor Department official P. M. Kenefick acknowledged as much in a private conversation with Arkansas congressman E. C. Gathings in 1953. Decrying Mexican consul Angel Cano's "megalomaniac" actions on behalf of Mexican workers, Kenefick noted that neither drought nor economic conditions would sway the consul into accepting less for Mexican workers. "Cano takes the position that these things have no bearing," Kenefick complained. "He says we gamble on the weather." An official from the nearby Mississippi Delta, testifying before Congress in 1950, expressed mid-South farmers' fundamental concern that organized labor would say, "All right, you have entered into an agreement with the Mexican Government to furnish certain facilities, bedding, housing, insurance, a guaranty of minimum work hours. . . . We feel that we want that for our domestic workers as well." The question of who would "gamble" on unforeseen circumstances and make a "guaranty" struck at the heart of the New Deal reforms that had benefited urban workers but excluded those in agriculture.

The role Mexican workers and consulates played in undermining the farmers' fight against New Deal worker protections in agriculture became apparent by 1952–53, when Mexicans became the first workers in Arkansas's fields to earn a minimum wage. Bracero agreements stated that braceros should be paid the local prevailing wage or an amount "necessary to cover their living needs," whichever was higher. During the early 1950s, consulates set a floor of 50 cents per hour or $2.50 per hundred pounds of cotton. During the 1953–54 picking season, farm jobs in other bracero-receiving areas had prevailing wages as low as 45 to 60 cents per hour in Texas and as high as $1.00 to $1.25 per hour in Oregon. In Arkansas, however, prevailing hourly wages were 30 to 40 cents. Only in Arkansas was the prevailing hourly wage substantially below the Bracero Program's 50-cent floor. Thus, only in Arkansas did the Mexican government effectively set a minimum wage for its workers.

Arkansas farmers were uniquely and primarily troubled by the prospect that a minimum wage in agriculture, something they had fought to stave off for more than a decade, would become a reality thanks to the Mexican government. Farmer Earl Beck Jr. worried, "If we would all start paying 50 cents an hour to the Mexicans our common day labor would expect the same, no matter if they are worth it or not." Another accused Consul Cano of "trying to jack up the total wage for the area." E. D. McKnight, head of the Parkin Farmers' Association, declared, "I do not believe that our farmers or our government should be put in the position so that Mexico can dictate the wage for our farm workers." Farmers had recruited braceros specifically to keep labor costs down, yet they now faced the prospect that consular intervention would have the opposite effect.

Farmers fought off US federal intervention into the labor conditions on their farms for decades, only to face this intervention from a different federal government during the Bracero Program. When J. S. Cecil found himself on the ineligible list, he threw up his hands and declared that he did not want any more Mexican workers anyway. But consular interventions and contractual obligations notwithstanding, most farmers desperately wanted to continue employing Mexicans, and they fought hard to do so. They fought back by making their case to Arkansas congressman E. C. Gathings, the Mexican Embassy in Washington, the consul himself, or US Employment Services (USES) representatives. Leo Powell tried to circumvent his blacklist status by contracting braceros under his father's name. Convinced that the only real problem with the bracero arrangement was Consul Cano's "personality problem," farmers conspired with Representative Gathings and Senator J. W. Fulbright to have Cano removed from his post. They portrayed Cano as an outside agitator, suggesting that braceros themselves had no problem with their living and working conditions in Arkansas. A. H. Barnhill, for example, complained, "It was not until after they talked to the consul that they complained of the blankets being wet." His comment, of course, ignored the fact that bracero complaints brought Cano to his farm in the first place.

While the vast majority of issues raised by braceros and consuls related to wages and to working, living, and transport conditions, concerns that echoed generations of white and black agricultural workers' pleas, others took on matters of race. Contrary to farmers' assertions, braceros themselves, not consular interlopers, initiated battles over discrimination. Both braceros and their consular officials were acutely aware of blacks' inferior position in the delta, and they were committed to ensuring that Mexicans, as citizens of somewhere, did not suffer the same fate. Just as Mexicans sought to influence their wages and working conditions on the farms, so too did they work to control discrimination in the Jim Crow landscape of the delta's towns.

The consulate's first major intervention in a racially charged matter occurred in November 1949. In the middle of that year's cotton-picking season, Tejano Nick C. Amador and two Mexican nationals approached the Mexican consulate in Memphis. The workers were picking cotton near Marked Tree, Arkansas, and reported that anti-Mexican discrimination was rife there. Consul Ruben Gaxiola initiated a joint investigation together with the US Labor Department and recommended the cancellation of the area's contracts. A week later, Gaxiola traveled to the town to gather information. He found that eleven establishments bore "No Mexicans" signs. In his report to Mexico City officials, Gaxiola linked southern race relations to Mexican nationalist concerns about class and modernity. With each photograph of a business displaying "No Mexicans" signs, Gaxiola noted details of the establishment's construction and appearance, explaining whether it was a "nice" establishment or more lower class. He also noted that the town's movie theater, run by the son of its largest employer, E. Ritter, consigned Mexicans to the seats reserved for blacks.

Though they had openly and mightily resisted bracero minimum wages, work guarantees, and the monitoring of their housing and transportation conditions, social discrimination was an area in which local officials and farmers were willing to compromise in an effort to preserve their source of labor. In Marked Tree, local officials immediately agreed to bring discrimination against Mexicans to an end. Failure to do so, members of the US Farm Placement Service explained to farmer E. Ritter, could lead to the cancellation of Marked Tree's contracts by mutual agreement of the US and Mexican governments. Marked Tree's mayor personally approached the offending businesses, as did Ritter. "As of five thirty," reported Ritter on November 22, 1949, the signs had all been removed. "To our knowledge there are no other signs being displayed now in Marked Tree." By Christmas of 1949, all of the signs were down.

The following year braceros in nearby Osceola lodged similar complaints about discrimination. A. Zacarias and Mateo Flores approached the consulate in November 1950, concerned about discrimination taking place in Osceola. A consular visit confirmed the allegations that March. As in Marked Tree, local officials in Osceola offered no resistance to the consulate on matters of social discrimination. "I am sure that within the next few days these signs will be removed," assured the mayor. The US Labor Department official who traveled to investigate assured Consul Cano that what discrimination did exist in Osceola and neighboring Luxora did "not reflect the feeling or the attitude of the major portion of this community." Yet, much of the evidence he gathered suggested the contrary. At the Rock Garden restaurant, for example, proprietor Mr. Allen said, "We have a very high class trade that would leave if my place was filled up with Mexicans. I would close up before I would serve them." For the following picking season, the towns of Osceola and nearby Luxora were blacklisted from receiving braceros.

Yet these battles were not so easily won. A few months later, complaints once again surfaced in Marked Tree, showing that the consulate's 1949 "victory" in that area had been illusory. The very same "No Mexicans" sign was back up on Wike's Drive Inn. Many other businesses had taken down signs to appease the consulate, but they still refused to serve Mexicans. And in locations refusing to serve Mexican nationals, "no distinction was made between Mexican Nationals and citizens of the United States of Mexican extraction." Despite farmers' desire to have continued access to Mexican labor, many white Arkansans were not prepared to begin admitting Mexicans and Mexican Americans into their establishments.

Over the next year, the consul repeatedly pushed to have the Marked Tree area contracts cancelled. Local officials, desperate to keep their labor, signed affidavits promising to afford Mexicans the same rights "as the local citizens," which all parties understood to mean whites. Business owners wrote declarations affirming their intention to treat Mexicans equally. Local officials showed movies "favorable to Mexico" in town. Still, the discrimination continued. Agustín Gallego and Jesús Ortiz Lutieros filed complaints with the consulate after having been refused service at the Holland Cafe. In response, consular and USES officials met up in Marked Tree to conduct an "experiment," sending a bracero "who was dressed in clean work clothes" to order a cup of coffee in several establishments. Bryant's Cafe refused him service. At Knott Hole Cafe, the bartender as well as several customers pointed the bracero to the back of the establishment, where a separate bar was available for Mexicans. As consular officials and US Department of Labor representatives plainly saw, anti-Mexican practices in Marked Tree were both store policy and popular sentiment. In neighboring Trumann, too, the chief of police admitted that discrimination against Mexicans persisted. There, four Tejanos, reaping more benefit from their Mexican ethnicity than their US citizenship, told USES and Mexican consular officials of widespread discrimination in local restaurants.

In Marked Tree, the consulate received a USES agreement late in the picking season of 1951 to blacklist E. Ritter, the area's main employer, though they did not succeed in withdrawing labor from the area's other farmers and associations, nor in cancelling Ritter's contract mid-season. Yet, even this limited victory was sufficient to prompt change in Marked Tree. Making a last-ditch attempt to secure workers for the 1952 picking season, local officials employed new and inventive means to stymie discrimination. The Marked Tree City Council published an ordinance in the *Marked Tree Tribune* stating that any person or business discriminating against Mexicans would be fined between $10 and $50, "and each act of discrimination shall constitute a separate offense." The Police Department changed its compensation structure so as to remove officers' incentives to make superfluous arrests of Mexican workers. The farmers' association even purchased outright two restaurants that refused to comply with the mandate not to discriminate.

Though the consulate was not able to enforce every threat of blacklisting and contract cancellation, by 1953 it had flexed enough power to have most white establishments in the Arkansas Delta admit Mexicans. Consulate documentary records show that discrimination complaints after 1953 were few, far between, and far less severe than they had been previously. More importantly, oral history interviews suggest that while the long-term results of these political battles over anti-Mexican discrimination were uneven, overall, Mexicans in Arkansas did gain admission to white establishments in Arkansas by the mid-1950s. Claude Kennedy, whose father owned a small farm near Marianna, recalled the resentment that many African Americans like himself felt about Mexicans' superior access to public space. "They could go to the movies with whites, where black people still had to go upstairs," Kennedy said. "That was something that black people could not understand." He remembered his mother, a schoolteacher, explaining to him why Mexicans were not subject to the painful discrimination of Jim Crow. "Their government would not allow them to be treated that way," he recalled. "That was the agreement. It was common knowledge that you can use them, but you've got to give them the respect of being equal to the white man. They could go anywhere they wanted to go." Bernard Lipsey, the son of Jewish storeowners, remembered a Mexican boy attending the white school with him around 1957, before Lepanto's schools had desegregated. The boy's assignment to the white school had seemed natural to Lipsey at the time, suggesting that within the binary world of the 1950s Arkansas Delta, locals eventually accepted that Mexicans would fall into the white category.[11]

Accepting Mexicans as white for Jim Crow purposes, however, did not mean whites accepted them socially. And Mexicans' access to white public space did not connote a feeling of affinity with whites. Both whites and African Americans also recalled that, like poor white cotton workers, Mexicans certainly were not made to feel welcome in every town establishment. Unlike poor whites, Mexicans often favored black sides of town in their leisure time. Harrison Locke, an African American man reared near Brinkley, recalled local authorities forbidding Mexicans from entering black establishments, even though they felt "more comfortable" in them.[12] The son of a white farmer, John Collier, remembered that when he rounded up braceros in Parkin to return to the farm on Saturday nights, those who did not report for the ride were most likely to be found in black "honky-tonks" or beer joints or seeking the services of black prostitutes.[13] And though he resented Mexicans' ability to sit with whites in the movie theater, Claude Kennedy also recalled braceros seeking social contact in black establishments. On one occasion, a Mexican man who spoke no English came into a black barbershop where Kennedy was getting a haircut. Kennedy understood that the man had been a barber in Mexico who missed practicing his trade. Kennedy and the barber let the man cut Kennedy's hair, even though the result left his locks a bit longer than they would have liked. As the stories show, Mexicans in 1950s Arkansas fought for access to white establishments because they rejected discrimination, not because they disdained African Americans or considered themselves white in the Jim Crow sense of the word.

The major decade of bracero contracting to Arkansas was the one in which de jure segregation fell. Braceros had arrived in Arkansas in the wake of a war fought in segregated battalions, and they left just before the passage of the Civil Rights Act of 1964. In the intervening years, the US Supreme Court struck down the doctrine of separate but equal and Arkansas segregationists lost the battle over school integration with the federal government. Having spent decades fighting against both racial integration and a shift in economic risk from agricultural employee to employer, farmers sought temporary Mexican workers, who seemed the ideal solution to meet labor needs without further threatening a crumbling social order. Unfortunately for farmers, the racialized workers who arrived had in many ways, like their Memphis- and Chicago-bound black counterparts, come to see themselves as modern citizens with rights. In Mexicans' case, they also belonged to a nation that championed the cause of working people. Unlike their rural black counterparts, Mexicans had access to a transnational source of power strong enough to effect rapid change through the emigration-minded Mexican government and its local consulate.

Race and class overlapped imperfectly in mid-century battles over social and economic rights, and only in Arkansas, with its large black population, did the Mexican consulate abet both strands of the liberal agenda: economic security and an end to de jure racial discrimination. Mexican workers, appealing to their consulate for support, succeeded in forcing farmers to reject overt anti-Mexican discrimination and to admit dark-skinned foreigners into white establishments as early as 1948. By all accounts, this gain stood, if imperfectly, throughout braceros' tenure in the Arkansas Delta. In the economic arena, where farmers resisted the consulate more vehemently, Mexicans' gains were more inconsistent. Notably, however, at key moments in the early 1950s, they did force white farmers and their Democratic allies to pay a minimum wage in agriculture—the first in the state's history—not only to braceros but, inadvertently, also to blacks and whites.

Though braceros themselves raised these demands, the success of their challenge to Jim Crow and their sometime ability to claim higher and fairer pay depended directly on the intervention of a robust Mexican government retaining real control over farmers' access to labor. After all, as Mexicans' actual choice to continue frequenting black bars and businesses showed, the race and class politics of the Arkansas Delta did not "naturally" afford Mexicans rights or acceptance of any sort. The Mexican government's control over bracero contracting and its ability to blacklist employers declined substantially in the early 1960s, leaving in its wake a region where locals were generally willing to view Mexicans favorably and tolerate their presence in white establishments but where Mexicans' wages were stagnant and working conditions were deplorable. Bracero Juan Loza, who worked near Helena in 1962, recalled once, but not always, being asked to leave a lunch counter there. He also remembered one Sunday that year when he and other braceros went to Helena's Catholic Church. They sat together in a pew, and a white couple joined them at the other end of the bench. "When the mass was over, it was only us there," he said. "I don't even know when they moved." Rejected, but not ejected, by the church's whites, Loza's predicament encapsulated that of braceros in Arkansas in the early 1960s. These men eluded the rigid structures of Jim Crow but did not escape the economic, social, and cultural caste system it had created.

CHAPTER 11

A Tenuous Welcome for Latinas/os and Asians
States' Rights Discourse in Late Twentieth-Century Arkansas

PERLA M. GUERRERO

THE LATINA/O POPULATION in Arkansas doubled from 2000 to 2010 to more than 186,000, constituting 6.4 percent of Arkansans.[1] Latinas/os greatly drove Arkansas's diversification, accounting for 41 percent of the overall growth and 83 percent of youth of color.[2] There are areas and districts with a substantial Latina/o community, such as Senate District 7 in Washington County, where Latinas/os make up almost one-third of the population.[3] In the same decade, the Asian population grew by nearly 80 percent to constitute 1.2 percent of Arkansans. The numbers tell part of the story about these newest southerners, but there is still a lot more to learn about Latinas/os and Asians in Arkansas.[4] The groups entered the state in various ways and with different legal categories, but in each instance the debates that ensued over their presence brought into sharp contrast long-standing tensions in the state and region.

On April 28, 1975, the Pentagon announced it had chosen Fort Chaffee as one of three bases to serve as processing and relocation centers for Vietnamese people fleeing the country at the end of the war. In response to a distraught constituent who objected to the use of the base, Arkansas governor David Pryor wrote that Arkansans needed to "accept the inevitable responsibilities which result from the Federal Government deciding to utilize the facilities at Fort Chaffee."[5] Five years later, Fort Chaffee was again chosen as a processing center, this time for Cubans leaving from the port of Mariel during Fidel Castro's "Back Door Policy."[6] The processing of this cohort of Cubans was slow going.

After several incidents on the base, a group of around two hundred Cubans broke the camp perimeter and headed to the nearby town of Barling. County sheriffs and city police officers halted their progress. The event outraged Arkansans. In the aftermath, Gov. Bill Clinton asked Arkansas attorney general Steve Clark about pursuing an inquiry into the possibility that federal action or inaction at Fort Chaffee "resulted in objectionable or harmful encroachments upon the normal field of state functions and powers."[7] Clark investigated the military's inaction based upon Arkansas Statute Annotated § 5-401, which allowed the attorney general to "determine whether federal legislation imposes objectionable burdens on our State."[8]

A decade later Latinas/os, mainly ethnic Mexicans, began migrating and immigrating to the state in substantive numbers and settling in areas that had been overwhelmingly white for most of the twentieth century. At the turn of the twenty-first century, as the Latina/o community continued to establish roots and grow, some Arkansans began mobilizing anti-immigrant organizations and legislation. In 2005 Jim Holt, a state senator and Republican from Springdale, a city that experienced dynamic Latina/o growth, announced the formation of Protect Arkansas Now.[9] Joe McCutchen of Fort Smith, chairman of the organization, said that President George W. Bush was not protecting the United States from "Mexican invaders."[10] Holt proposed the Arkansas Taxpayer and Citizen Protection Act and argued that Arkansas was a "safe haven" for "illegal immigrants."[11]

At the end of the twentieth century and turn of the twenty-first century, states' rights rhetoric undergirded the debate between local, state, and federal officials when Latina/o and Asian refugees and immigrants arrived in Arkansas. States' rights ideology has moved men and women to violence and secession in its defense and drastically shaped US history. Although this principle is not unique to the region itself, it has deep historical meaning, given the other times it has been deployed, mainly to prevent African American struggles for equality. Twenty years after the desegregation of Little Rock's Central High School, the rhetoric was deployed again in matters of racial difference, but this time in reference to Asians and, later, Latinas/os. This understudied and overdue history of Asians and Latinas/os in Arkansas and their role as refugees and immigrants provides a new window to learn about the long life of states' rights discourse and ideology and how it is used when dealing with racial difference. More importantly, and in line with what historian Vicky Ruiz proposed, Asian and Latina/o history is indelibly Arkansas and southern history.[12]

On April 25, 1975, the *Arkansas Gazette* reported that Fort Chaffee was going to be used as a refugee center, yet at the time the news was treated as a preposterous rumor. The story was not given much weight for three likely reasons: firstly, the news came through "unnamed" sources; secondly, state officials and congressmen claimed that they did not know of any such plan; and thirdly, army officers at the fort had heard nothing. That day, Arkansas senator John L. McClellan, a Democrat, said Chaffee was not being considered because he was "assured by the State Department that no such decision has been made concerning Fort Chaffee and that it will not be made without further consultation."[13] The next day Pentagon officials declared Fort Chaffee was being considered as a site.[14] On April 28, the Pentagon announced that it had chosen Fort Chaffee, in Arkansas, Eaglin Air Force Base, in Florida, and Camp Pendleton, in California, as processing centers.

L. Dean Brown, director of the Interagency Task Force for Indochinese Refugees (ITFIR), which was established by President Gerald Ford, announced that the camps would house up to twenty thousand refugees for ninety days or more with the hope of relocating them within two weeks.[15] When the *Arkansas Gazette* printed the story, another noteworthy headline shared the page: "State Lawmakers Accept Proposal with Qualms." Senator McClellan and Rep. John Paul Hammerschmidt, a Republican who represented Arkansas's Third Congressional District, where Fort Chaffee was located, balked at the federal decision. The newspaper did not quote Hammerschmidt directly but reported that the representative's questions "reflected concern for the economic and social ramifications of placing a refugee center in the Fort Smith area."[16]

McClellan and Hammerschmidt were upset about the choice of Arkansas as site for the refugees. As McClellan bluntly put it, "We're all unhappy about this situation developing." Hammerschmidt more pragmatically reflected, "I wish the situation didn't exist and wish it was not in Arkansas . . . but it is and we have to face it."[17] Both were so displeased that McClellan thought about trying to reduce the $327 million appropriation the Ford administration sought for humanitarian aid to South Vietnam, while Hammerschmidt voted against it "out of protest of where the refugee centers were located."[18] Neither was convinced by administration officials or meetings with President Ford and Secretary of State Henry Kissinger, who both insisted that the refugee center would not cause regional economic and social damage to the area.[19]

Dr. Lam Van Thatch, the informal leader of the group, wore a brown, tailored suit as he led seventy exhausted Vietnamese from the airplane into the chilly Friday afternoon on May 2, 1975.[20] About four hundred people from surrounding communities, including church leaders and members, Girl Scouts, and one white supremacist, welcomed them to northwest Arkansas. The Vietnamese arrivals stood in the rain and fifty-five-degree weather, some without coats, at the municipal airport as Mayor Jack Freeze and Gov. David Pryor welcomed them to Fort Smith, to Arkansas, and to the United States.[21] There were welcome signs in English and Vietnamese. Unwelcoming signs were largely absent except for one that read, "RESCUE USA from REDS FIRST!!! WHiTE MAN UNiTE!!! AND FigHT!! [sic]," with a Star of David and a swastika in the background.[22] As the governor gave his speech, the man with the racist sign constantly yelled that the refugee presence was a Zionist conspiracy. In turn, others in attendance tried to drown him out by shouting, "Welcome, Welcome!" At one point a woman tried to tear down the Nazi sign, but a minister stopped her and a scuffle ensued as members of the welcoming group asked and tried to prevent national news photographers from taking the man's picture and capturing his response to the Vietnamese.[23]

Despite attempting to paint the situation in a positive light, Governor Pryor could not ignore voices of dissent, which objected, sometimes in strident terms, to the arrival of Vietnamese refugees to US shores and, particularly, to their placement in Arkansas. The ceremony itself was marred by the constant yelling of the "professional protester from Hot Springs," but there were also incidents prior to the refugees arriving that demonstrated how unhappy some people were about Fort Chaffee being used as a refugee-processing center and camp.[24] A group of five young people held signs on Highway 59, a road that leads to Fort Chaffee and the one on which refugees traveled, that said, "Go Back to Vietnam" and "Would They Do The Same For Us?"[25] A homeowner who lived close to Chaffee made a sign that read, "Gooksville, three miles."[26] But dissent did not stop at making signs. On April 30, residents of Barling and Greenwood, two towns close to Fort Chaffee, were organizing a protest so that, according to Johnnie Calhoun, "those slant-eyes can see they're not wanted." She was so incensed about Vietnamese refugees in Fort Chaffee that she told a reporter: "They say it's a lot colder here than it is in Vietnam. With a little luck, maybe they'll all take pneumonia and die."[27] Calhoun was not alone in her outrage. The mayor of one of the towns assured a local reporter that "the people here are 100 percent against it. They don't want them moving into this community."[28]

Governor Pryor reacted publicly on April 30, after he and Arkansas senator Dale Bumpers, a Democrat, returned from a trip to Washington, D.C. They told their constituents that Fort Chaffee would only provide transitory housing of up to two weeks for a period of six months and that the undertaking should not cause much burden to local governments. Bumpers emphasized that the Vietnamese refugees' arrival, processing, and placement were a "national problem, and it will be borne out on a national scale," thereby allaying those fears that Arkansas was going to unfairly carry the burden.[29] Although Pryor made supportive statements in public and in correspondence to constituents, he also appeared less than happy with the situation. When Larry J. Cornish wrote him a letter voicing his concerns, the governor replied, "Arkansas has a role to play in the evacuation of Vietnamese refugees. You must accept the inevitable responsibilities that result from the Federal Government deciding to utilize the facilities at Fort Chaffee. I believe that we must do all we can to cooperate with both the federal officials and the voluntary agencies to see that the unfortunate circumstances surrounding the presence of the Vietnamese are quickly relieved."[30]

In May, the Department of Defense increased the number of Vietnamese at Fort Chaffee by four thousand, and again in mid-June it raised the number by another one thousand, much to Hammerschmidt's dismay and over his "strong opposition."[31] This made Southeast Asian refugees the largest nonwhite group in northwest Arkansas since the area's African American population consisted of less than seven thousand. It represented a significant demographic shift and one that created anxieties. This was resolved, at least in part, when the Vietnamese were sponsored out of the camp and dispersed across various places in the United States. At the end of the year Arkansans sponsored a total of 2,061 Vietnamese into various communities.[32] Since then the Asian American community, especially Southeast Asian, has grown slowly but steadily in the region.

Five years after the arrival of Vietnamese, the US government decided to use Fort Chaffee as a processing center again, this time for Cubans leaving from the Port of Mariel. From April to October 1980, around 125,000 Cubans left the island after Castro initiated his "Back Door Policy," which allowed many people who wished to leave the island to do so. The majority arrived in the United States, where they were temporarily detained in Florida before being sent to be processed elsewhere. Initially, the US press reacted positively to the news because they saw the Cubans as only the latest cohort fleeing the communist regime and anti-communism was still a potent point of mobilization. The media coverage changed quickly as Castro cast them as criminals, mentally ill, homosexuals, and parasites in an effort to discredit the group.[33] In the end, the US government determined that less than 2 percent of these Cubans were serious criminals and denied them asylum.[34]

Obtaining an accurate number about how many gay men and women left Cuba during the Mariel boatlift is difficult, but estimates ranged from 400 to 20,000, while reports from the Cuban-Haitian Task Force estimated that between 1,000 to 2,500 gay men arrived.[35] By the end of May there were more than 19,000 Cubans, more than 70 percent of them men.[36] Additionally, Fort Chaffee's nonwhite population was nearly double the Mariel cohort average, at almost 40 percent, with almost 30 percent black and 7 percent mulatto.[37] This meant that Arkansas's "11th largest city" was also almost half nonwhite, a significant demographic change in northwest Arkansas's overwhelmingly white landscape.[38]

Fort Chaffee was chosen to serve as a holding center, at least in part because of its experience with Vietnamese refugees, but processing appeared to be very slow while their confinement did not make sense to Cubans because they knew prior cohorts of their compatriots that had arrived on US shores were greeted as "welcomed exiles" and were quickly provided a path to legalization.[39]

All of the parties involved, including Cubans from the Mariel boatlift, volunteer agencies inside the camp, and Cuban Americans and Arkansans outside the camp, were getting anxious about the slow processing rate, but none more so than the refugees themselves. On the night of Monday, May 26, about 350 Cubans who had been protesting their detention broke through the southwest gate and into the neighboring community of Jenny Lind. According to one report, the military and park police did not attempt to stop them because of "questions about the military police's authority over civilians."[40] On the afternoon of Friday,

May 30, about 30 Cubans assembled on Fourth Avenue roughly a thousand yards from the gates. They were threatening a hunger strike to protest their slow processing. However, camp officials were able to calm the situation.

On Sunday, June 1, 1980, at mid-morning about 100 Cubans began to gather on Fourth Avenue inside of Fort Chaffee and approached one of the gates. A Cuban refugee talked to the group and they dispersed. At noon they "returned with rocks and empty bottles," which they threw at Military Police and state troopers stationed at the gate. Three were injured.[41] At 1:30 p.m. about 200 Cubans broke through the entrance on Highway 22. "They encountered no resistance, other than verbal commands from Army guards to retreat. Upon reaching the highway, the refugees appeared puzzled and confused until one, shouting '*Libertad!*' struck out toward Barling." The crowd followed him toward a bridge a few hundred yards west of the gate while continuing the chant of "Liberty!" Two Arkansas State Police cars stopped in front of them, and then "two troopers, wielding nightsticks, attempted to confront Cubans until an unidentified Army major, jumping between the troopers and refugees, shouted, 'Don't hit them!'" More state police vehicles blocked the road, but Cubans ran around the barricade; then state troopers and local policemen formed a "human barricade and managed to turn back about half of the crowd. Officers chased retreating refugees to the front gates, kicking and clubbing the Cubans on the heads, backs and arms. The 75 or more refugees who slipped through this barricade were finally halted about 50 yards from the Barling city limit by a line of local police and deputies." By the following week, Fort Chaffee was fortified with "barbed concertina wire and guarded by more than 2,000 federal troops."[42]

Governor Clinton arrived at Fort Chaffee in the early hours of June 2 and "was furious" over the "long disputed" question of whether the military could use force to control Cubans.[43] The next day, at a meeting with outraged Barling residents, he defended himself by placing the failure squarely on the shoulders of President Jimmy Carter and, by extension, the federal government: "In spite of what I was told on election day by the highest authority at the White House, there was still no security on that Fort, and the only thing between you and it were the State Police, who risked themselves to protect you."[44]

The governor's aide Robert Lyford told Clinton he needed to ask President Carter for a document that defined the Cubans' status because the governor's staff had been previously told that "they were applicants for asylum, not detainees refugees [*sic*], or aliens. Whatever their status it needs to be committed to writing. Also the authority or lack thereof for a local law enforcement officer to return a Cuban to the base needs to be clarified."[45] Clinton asked Christian R. Holmes, director of the Cuban-Haitian Task Force (CHTF), who responded: "State and local authorities may arrest and/or detain only for violation of the laws of the State of Arkansas."[46] Attorney General Clark made the point explicit when he said: "Six thousand Cubans walking on Highway 22 adjacent to Fort Chaffee aren't guilty of anything."[47] As a lawyer and former attorney general for Arkansas, Clinton understood the ramifications of Holmes's reply but sought Clark's opinion nonetheless. The governor asked him, "What authority, if any, do State and local law enforcement officials have to arrest or detain Cuban entrants who leave Fort Chaffee without permission?"[48]

If the federal government failed to act, then it was time for state action based on the US Constitution's Tenth Amendment, "which provides that states have the authority to exercise police power except in those areas specifically pre-empted by the federal government."[49] Clark proposed that Clinton might need to file a suit in US District Court, Western District, "seeking declaratory judgment as to the construction of federal immigration laws and actions arising there under. This suit should address the issue of legal authority of the federal government to act in the area of law enforcement in contrast to the authority of state and local officials."[50]

Clark also suggested that Clinton might consider seeking "injunctive relief" to prevent the transfer of more Cubans to Chaffee until the questions were resolved. After a flurry of correspondence between the governor's office and the president's office about the Cubans' legal categorization and who had the ability to detain them, the issue was settled. Camp authorities would notify state officers if they learned that any Cubans escaped, but the officers could only pick them up if they violated local or state laws. Otherwise the local and state officials had to notify the Border Patrol because it was "the only agency authorized by law to arrest illegal aliens."[51]

In contrast to the Southeast Asian community, which grew post-sponsorship, Cubans left the area, probably due to the intense animosity toward them. By 2001, only about fifteen Cubans from

Mariel lived in the area.⁵² In the end the legal title assigned to Cubans in Arkansas mirrored that of undocumented immigrants as they were "illegal aliens" who had not been admitted to the country. It is perhaps telling that Cubans, a Latina/o group, preceded Mexican immigrants as "illegal aliens" in Arkansas. The rhetoric about criminality is also something the two groups would come to share since Latina/o immigrants are often presumed to be undocumented and, therefore, lawbreakers and criminals who threaten communities in Arkansas.

Latinas/os began moving to Arkansas in large numbers in the 1990s. For some migrants Arkansas was a second or third site of settlement. They moved to Arkansas after years or decades of living in more traditional states of immigrant settlement, such as California and Texas. They were working-class people who thought that they had found their US homes, only to realize that their livelihoods were threatened or eliminated in the recession of the 1990s.⁵³ Other factors, such as the 1986 Immigration Reform and Control Act, which legalized hundreds of thousands of people, facilitated the migration and settlement of these new southerners. But as Steve Striffler puts it, "The role of chicken cannot be underestimated."⁵⁴ The poultry industry was searching for more low-wage workers and especially workers that it could exploit more easily and that offered year-round employment. The lax enforcement of immigration documents and the state's low cost of living served to provide Latinas/os with opportunities of upward mobility and homeownership unavailable in traditional states of immigrant reception and settlement.

Although there were some varied responses to Latina/o immigrants, they were overwhelmingly constructed as illegal aliens. The discourse of illegal aliens racialized all Latinas/os as undocumented, criminal, and Mexican. As the years went by, Latinas/os bought homes, created communities, and established roots in Arkansas. But not everyone was happy about those developments. Alderman John Womack beat John Sampier, a seventeen-year incumbent, in the 1998 Rogers mayoral election when he ran the campaign on a platform of "zero tolerance" for undocumented immigrants. He depicted Sampier as supporting "illegal immigration."⁵⁵ In contrast to Womack, Sampier had been at the forefront of attempts to incorporate Latinas/os into the local community, and he had been co-chairman of the Governor's Hispanic Relations Task Force.

In another election in 2001, Gunner DeLay, a Republican from Fort Smith, said at a forum sponsored by the Washington County Republican

Women that "illegal immigration" was the "defining issue in the race" for Arkansas's Third Congressional District. The issue needed an immediate remedy, and he said he would consider using the military to secure the US-Mexico border.[56] The other candidates considered undocumented immigration to be important but asked voters to remember that Latina/o growth in the area was also due to legal immigration and to Spanish-speaking US citizens.[57] Ultimately, DeLay lost the race and John Boozman of Rogers won. Boozman then joined the Congressional Immigration Reform Caucus, which proposed denying citizenship to US-born children of undocumented immigrants.[58]

In 2005, Jim Holt, a state senator and Republican from Springdale, announced the formation of Protect Arkansas Now, modeled after the Arizona group that successfully lobbied to pass Proposition 200. Joe McCutchen of Fort Smith and chairman of the organization said that President Bush was not protecting the nation from "Mexican invaders" and that "no society can withstand this type of invasion, particularly Third Worlders, who are uneducated and very poor."[59] Holt proposed the Arkansas Taxpayer and Citizen Protection Act, which would halt state spending on undocumented immigrants. The wording copied the Arizona legislation and argued that Arkansas was a "safe haven" for "illegal immigrants." Among other provisions, the law would require state employees to report suspected immigration violations or face misdemeanor charges.[60]

These attempts by Arkansas elected officials and community organizations to exert control over the supposed large numbers of undocumented immigrants reflect the fears of some Arkansans and the ongoing tensions between state and federal government policy in the state. Yet the relationship between the state and the federal government was not always acrimonious. By February 2005, two Republican brothers, both state representatives, Jeremy Hutchinson and Timothy Hutchinson, proposed House Bill 1012, which sought the participation of Arkansas State Police officers in US Immigration and Customs Enforcement's 287(g) training program, which provided for the "performance of immigration officer functions by state officers and employees."[61] The bill passed and made Arkansas the third state, after Florida and Alabama, to participate in the program. By September 2007, four northwest Arkansas law enforcement agencies had signed the Memorandum of Agreement: the Benton County Sheriff's Office, the Rogers Police Department, the

Washington County Sheriff's Office, and the City of Springdale Police Department.[62] Tellingly, these law enforcement agencies are located in cities and counties that experienced the most dynamic Latina/o growth.

When Fort Chaffee was selected as a processing and relocation center for Vietnamese, there was considerable resentment about the lack of agency the state had in deciding whether it wanted one of its federal bases to be used for such an endeavor. Arkansas government officials often asserted that it was a federal mandate that the state and Arkansans had to bear. Five years later, when Fort Chaffee was once again chosen to process Cubans, the state and its people resented the federal government more deeply than they had in the case of the Vietnamese. Many Arkansans and their state officials believed that the federal government was shirking its responsibilities and failing to protect its citizenry by allowing Cuban "criminals" into the United States. In response to Latina/o immigrants in the 1990s, Arkansans blamed the federal government for ineffectively guarding the Mexico-US border while the state paid and its people suffered the consequences.

States' rights discourse and actions in 1975 and 1980 Arkansas foreshadowed events in 1990s California and 2000s Arizona when those states' governors argued that the federal government was failing to protect US citizens from an invasion of foreigners, particularly undocumented Mexican immigrants. Gov. Pete Wilson and Jan Brewer respectively argued that they did what the federal government had failed to do and were acting in their states' best interests as they attempted to establish programs that would halt immigration and consequently diminish public expenditures. Arizona's actions in successfully passing Proposition 200, in turn, influenced Arkansans' efforts as some organizations and politicians sought to organize in the same way to pass a carbon copy of that legislation. These instances are about dealing with racial difference and with people who are deemed outside of the norm. The result is that people are seen as threatening to the community, state, and nation, and that consequently creates a need to "protect" those deemed as insiders. In Arkansas, these fears drew on states' rights discourse, indicating the extent to which this particular legacy has to be reckoned with and the extent to which it can be adapted to new groups as they seek to make Arkansas home.

CHAPTER 12

Soy el Jefe
How Hispanic Entrepreneurs Are Changing the Economic Landscape of Northeast Arkansas

MELANY BOWMAN

LIKE MANY HISPANICS moving to Jonesboro, Arkansas, Luis Flores came to the area from El Salvador in pursuit of a better life than his home country could provide for him and his family. In addition to his fulltime job as a pharmacy technician at St. Bernard's Hospital, Flores also serves as a pastor for the First Baptist Church Hispanic Ministries Outreach. As pastor, Flores incorporates many of the traditions, customs, and music popular in the Hispanic world into the worship service. While his congregation consists of a small but devoted group of worshipers, Flores notes that many Hispanics in the area forego attending church in search of job opportunities. "Logically, Hispanics are not here [in the United States] to look for a church. He is not here seeking the answer to spiritual questions. He is here out of economic necessity," noted Flores.[1]

But for some, economic necessity has turned into economic opportunity. As the Hispanic population grows in Jonesboro and northeast Arkansas, so does the number of Hispanic-owned and -operated businesses. In addition to providing Hispanic entrepreneurs an opportunity to work for themselves instead of others, Hispanic businesses are very important to the quality of life and social space of Hispanic newcomers to this area. This essay explores how Hispanic-owned and -operated businesses are not only contributing to the local economy but also meeting the social and cultural needs of the growing Hispanic community in nrtheast Arkansas.

For this study, a total of forty-six field interviews with Hispanic and non-Hispanic community leaders in Jonesboro were conducted between 2009 and 2012. Feature stories about local Hispanic businessmen and women appearing in the city's newspaper, the *Jonesboro Sun*, supplement information gleaned from field interviews. Together, the interviews and feature stories will paint a portrait of an intrepid group of individuals who contribute to the general economy of Jonesboro and also serve a vital role in the Hispanic community.

Jonesboro serves as the economic hub of northeast Arkansas. The latest census figures listed Jonesboro's population as 67,263, a growth of 11,748 people since the 2000 census. Jonesboro mayor Harold Perrin noted that the boost in population "increases our stature and responsibility as a regional hub and shows we are a destination city."[2] In recent years, Jonesboro has been the destination of major industries like Unilever, a company that produces beauty and personal care products, Nordex, a wind turbine manufacturer, and Nice-Pak, a producer of wet wipes. These major corporations have joined agriculture and food-processing industries such as Riceland Foods, Swanson, Nestlé, Frito-Lay, and Post in bringing hundreds of new jobs to this area.

The industrial sector of Jonesboro's economic engine is part of a diverse economy of the region that includes agriculture and education. Communities surrounding Jonesboro produce acres of rice, cotton, and other agricultural products. As the educational hub of northeast Arkansas, Jonesboro is home to a thriving university and progressive public schools. Recently, Arkansas State University reached a record enrollment of more than thirteen thousand students.[3] Local public schools are making investments in facilities and technology to accommodate the growing number of students in the classroom.[4] The Jonesboro School District will spend $18.5 million on campus improvement projects.[5] Also within the city of Jonesboro, the Nettleton School District and the Valley View School District have proposed votes on property tax increases to build new facilities and improve technology.[6] Arkansas State University (ASU) and the public schools, kindergarten through twelfth grade, are also placing a greater emphasis on welcoming international students and teaching the community about world cultures. The spring 2011 international student population at ASU increased 42.4 percent (648 students) over spring 2010 figures (445 students).[7] Jonesboro Public School's International Magnet School reached out to prospective students and families by hosting a multicultural showcase featuring an exhibition of South American countries presented by second-grade students.[8]

The quality education and diverse economy in Jonesboro that has contributed to the overall growth of the town has also been an attractive lure for Hispanics. According to the Pew Hispanic Center, Arkansas ranks fifth nationally among states with the highest percentage of growth in the Hispanic population (114 percent).[9] Jonesboro and Craighead County have seen the number of Spanish-speaking people living in the area skyrocket. The American Community Survey estimates that the Hispanic population in Craighead County grew from 1,739 in 2000 to 4,277 in 2010, an increase of 146 percent.[10] According to the 2010 US Census, the Hispanic population in Jonesboro is 3,503, more than doubling the number of Hispanics since 2000.[11]

The diversity of job opportunities and the stability of the local economy have opened many new job opportunities and contributed greatly to the tremendous rise in the Hispanic population in Jonesboro and Craighead County. For some Hispanics their stay in northeast Arkansas is short-lived. They come to earn money and return to their home countries once they have earned the desired amount of money. "They look for work on Sundays because the more they work, the more they earn and save and can hasten their return to their home country," said Luis Flores. "There are some who are here because they are in need of a great sum of money and they return to their countries later."[12]

The migratory pattern of seeking temporary work and returning to their native country is nothing new to this region of the state. From World War II through the mid-1960s, Mexican workers called *braceros* worked in farm fields during cotton-picking season before returning home with their earnings.[13] In recent years, Hispanics have moved to Arkansas in record numbers, more than doubling the state's Hispanic population from 86,866 in 2000 to 186,050 in 2010.[14] The major reason why Hispanics came to Arkansas during the past decade was simple: jobs. In a 2006 interview with League of United Latin American Citizens (LULAC) member Alejandro Aviles, she noted that employment in construction and agricultural is a major attraction for Hispanics coming to Arkansas.[15]

Despite the prospect for employment, many Hispanics in Arkansas struggle financially. According to the Pew Hispanic Center, 43 percent of Hispanics seventeen years old or younger live in poverty. The annual personal earnings for Hispanics in Arkansas total $19,000. More than a third of Hispanics in the state (37 percent) have no health insurance.[16]

Despite the low wages, Arkansas still remains a destination for many immigrants seeking employment opportunities in the United States.

Self-employment is one way some Hispanics work and boost their earning potential. Entrepreneur Luis Madera's journey has taken him from his home in Jalisco Guadalajara, Mexico, to Chicago before settling in Jonesboro. For Madera, Jonesboro not only offered an opportunity to start his own business, but provided a great place to raise a family. "We looked in Arkansas and settled on Jonesboro because it was one of the places that we liked the most," said Madera. "The educational system is very good for our children." In addition to providing his family with a great quality of life and educational opportunities for his children, Madera saw Jonesboro as a place to fulfill his dream of being self-employed. After years of working for a company in Chicago, Madera made the decision to move to Jonesboro and open his own restaurant specializing in Mexican food popular in his hometown of Jalisco. Like any new business, Madera struggled in the beginning. But hard work and perseverance has paid off for him and his family. "At first it was hard but now it is successful and with that comes opportunity."[17]

Madera's success with his restaurant business in Jonesboro also means opportunities for other Hispanics looking for work in this area. Madera supports the Hispanic community in Jonesboro by employing many Spanish-speaking workers in his restaurant. "There are a lot of people who come here looking for work," observed Madera. "I think the reason there is growth in the number of Hispanic business is that Jonesboro is a town that gives opportunities. As the Hispanic [population] grows, it requires more businesses to support that population."[18]

The support provided by entrepreneurs to the Hispanic community extends beyond job opportunities. As a professor in Boston University's School of Social Work, Melvin Delgado, observed, "Latino businesses can take on the role of nontraditional social service centers" where information important to the migrant community can be exchanged with family and friends.[19] These network centers often serve as bridges between those Hispanics already established in the community and newcomers who need help adjusting to new surroundings and assistance in locating housing or finding employment.[20] Los Arcos, a Hispanic-owned restaurant, grocery, and dry goods store in Jonesboro, features foods and products popular throughout the Latino world. Patrons can grocery shop, dine at one of the tables in the restaurant section, or watch soccer matches on televisions mounted through the store. This type of setting allows Hispanics to gather in an informal setting while providing a venue that "facilitate(s) conversation, and the exchange of concerns and advice, minimizing the stigma for those seeking assistance."[21] Hispanic businesses are more than just a place for commerce but become important sites for social networking.[22]

While Hispanic-owned and -operated businesses serve the commercial and social needs of the growing Hispanic community, non-Hispanic businesses are becoming aware of the consumer potential of the growing Hispanic market. Walmart and Walgreens locations in Jonesboro are devoting small sections of shelf space to food items and other goods popular in Spanish-speaking countries. Likewise, locally owned Jonesboro businesses are reaching out to the growing Hispanic consumer market by stocking goods associated with Latino culture, providing bilingual services, and reaching out to Hispanic customers with bilingual advertising. Fred Pearson, owner of Payless Rent-to-Own Furniture and Appliances and Payless Rent-to-Own Cars, never considered tapping into the local Hispanic market until a Hispanic lady came into his business looking for a job in sales. "She said there are a lot of Hispanics moving into this area. In fact, there are a lot already here," said Pearson. "What she said began to click with me because I had seen the Hispanic population in a lot of places. And I said she was probably right." Pearson quickly realized that his business would have a distinct advantage with Hispanic customers over other rent-to-own businesses by employing someone with Spanish-speaking skills. Upon hiring his new Spanish-speaking salesperson, Pearson saw immediate results after promoting that his business had someone on staff with bilingual skills. "So I thought if I put out a sign that said, 'We speak Spanish,' that is a good way to attract Spanish speaking people. And we did."[23]

Like Pearson, Larry McElvoy, owner of the costume and party supply store Golden Grotto, saw an increase in the number of Hispanic customers coming through his store. McElvoy devoted shelf space to *quinceañera* supplies and hired someone with Spanish-speaking skills to interact with his Hispanic customers. "Then you started to see a few Spanish people," said McElvoy. "Now you see a lot of Spanish people." The rise in the Hispanic population in northeast Arkansas has also had a positive impact on McElvoy's business. "I would say maybe 10 percent (are Hispanic customers). That's obviously growing."[24]

Throughout Jonesboro, there is increasing evidence that non-Hispanic business owners are reaching out to attract Hispanic consumers. Local publications feature advertisements that promote "Se Habla Español." Signage written in both English and Spanish is becoming increasing visible, all in an effort to cater to Hispanic consumers. These are just a few examples of how local non-Hispanic businesses in Jonesboro are changing their view of the Hispanic consumer, according to Henry Torres, instructor in the ASU College of Business and a successful businessman. "I think people in the business community have changed," said Torres. "They realize that the money in the pockets of those people, it's green, just like the rest of the money."[25]

Jonesboro mayor Harold Perrin understands the importance of reaching out to the Hispanic community and developing a loyal customer base. Prior to becoming mayor, Perrin was a bank consultant with several clients in northwest Arkansas. As the Hispanic population grew in that region of the state, Perrin advised his clients to institute policies and procedures that appeal to Spanish-speaking customers. "Every new account was bilingual," noted Perrin. He brings that same philosophy of outreach to the Hispanic community in his role as Jonesboro mayor. He supports Hispanic Community Services, Incorporated, a nonprofit organization that assists area Hispanics with a variety of social, legal, educational, health, and cultural services.[26] Perrin regularly attends events sponsored by the organization, such as the Hispanic Celebration in May, a showcase for Hispanic culture and traditions, as well as the annual fall multicultural dinner. As a businessman and chief executive of the city of Jonesboro, Perrin understands the importance of the Hispanic community on the economy of Jonesboro. "They have been very successful in getting employment," said Perrin. "And when they do that, then obviously, they spend money like you and I, so the sales tax base goes up."[27]

But not all the money earned in Jonesboro remains in Jonesboro. According to a Congressional Research Service report on the economic relationship between the United States and Mexico, "remittances are the second highest source of foreign currency" in Mexico, coming mostly from workers in the United States who send money to family members in their native country.[28] Recognizing the business potential for transferring money from one country to another, some Hispanic entrepreneurs provide services to Mexicans to maintain contact with relatives back home and to transfer money to Mexico. In addition to serving her customers with the genuine taste of breads and cakes popular in many Latin American countries, Linda López, owner of Panadería El Buen Gusto (The Good Taste Bakery), expanded her business by selling phone cards and offering money transfer services so that her Hispanic customers can send remittances to their home country.[29]

While the amount of transfers to Latin American countries declined in 2010 due to worldwide economic problems and increasing unemployment in the United States, poor economic conditions such as high poverty and unemployment in Mexico continue to drive thousands of people to the United States in hope of a better economic life. For those who chose Jonesboro and northeast Arkansas as their destination to find job opportunities, the search for jobs takes place seven days a week. "The majority of Hispanics work on Sunday," said Pastor Luis Flores. "They look for work on Sunday because the more they work, the more they earn and save and can hasten their return to their home country."[30]

The increased presence of Hispanic immigrants has created a need for food and other products, thus providing opportunities for entrepreneurs like Linda López, Luis Madera, and others who have found a simple model to establish their own business: find an audience, provide a service, and work hard to be a success. While such a formula is typical for many successful ethnic entrepreneurs across the nation, a growing number of Hispanics find Jonesboro and northeast Arkansas an ideal location to start a business. Luis Madera believes Arkansas truly lives up to its motto as the Land of Opportunity. "I think that the reason there is growth in the number of Hispanic businesses [is] that Jonesboro is a town that gives opportunities," said Madera. "As the Hispanic growth shows, it requires more businesses to support that population. So the growth goes hand in hand. It has grown tremendously in the last ten years."[31]

As mentioned earlier, many Hispanic businesses offer products and services that appeal to the Hispanic market. But while serving a niche market is the key to success for many entrepreneurs, some Hispanic businesses must also reach out to non-Hispanic customers for their enterprise to grow and prosper. For years Andrés Acosta dreamed of owning and operating his own business instead of working for others. Recently Acosta's dream came true when he opened a bilingual childcare and daycare service. To increase his chance of success, Acosta reaches out to non-Hispanic customers in Jonesboro and surrounding areas. "My clients are 90 percent American, Anglos, if you will; 10 percent of my customers are Hispanic." To meet the language demands of both his American and Hispanic clients, he employs both English- and Spanish-speaking employees. For Acosta, the chance of coming to the United States and starting his own business is the realization of a dream. "This country offers opportunities for one to be their own boss, to own their own business."[32]

For some Hispanics, the dream of owning and operating a business is tempered by the reality of legal and bureaucratic hurdles associated with being an entrepreneur in the United States. Understanding all the rules and regulations related to starting a business can be bewildering to most people, especially to an immigrant unfamiliar with US business practices. Learning to navigate through administrative paperwork can be challenging for Hispanics opening a new business, according to Acosta: "The system is new to us. We come from other countries where things are done differently, right? And so, it was a bit difficult to establish a business with the permits, rules, regulations, and so forth. All that is more complicated here than in our countries."

In addition to the bureaucratic obstacles of owning and operating a business in this country, cultural differences in doing business also provide challenges for Hispanic business owners. Henry Torres has experience improving efficiency for major corporations like Neiman Marcus and Walmart. Now as an instructor in the College of Business at ASU in Jonesboro, Torres has advised local businessmen on how to start and sustain successful companies and helped transform Jonesboro's Hispanic Community Service, Incorporated, into a 501C3 organization.[33] As someone who works closely with the Hispanic community in Jonesboro and northeast Arkansas, Torres has observed how cultural differences in conducting business have been the downfall of several Hispanic entrepreneurs. Bargaining with customers reluctant to pay prices associated with goods and services is a common practice in many Latin countries. Hispanic entrepreneurs bring this practice with them to their new business operations in the United States, often reducing the price of their products and services by half in order to do business with a customer. These types of price reductions can have serious effects on the bottom line. "So they kind of shoot themselves in the foot," observed Torres. "All these guys that have created these little businesses shoot themselves because of the haggling mentality they bring with them from their culture"[34]

Cultural differences and the unfamiliarity of US business practices are just a few of the challenges facing Hispanic entrepreneurs. The national discourse surrounding illegal immigration has created a difficult environment for many Hispanics to conduct business. Alejandro Lorenzana is an entrepreneur who owns several businesses, including a cleaning company, a construction company, a graphic design company, and teaches dance lessons. Lorenzana's latest venture is the publication of *Mid-South Latino Magazine*. The magazine is unique because it is a bilingual publication featuring inspirational stories appealing to both Spanish- and non-Spanish-speaking audiences. "For example, we did our main article on the first Miss Arkansas Latina in 2005," said Lorenzana. "She is a model and she end up with ovarian cancer. So she has this great story. It is a story that everybody can read, not just Spanish people but Americans." Yet despite the crossover appeal in his magazine's content, Lorenzana noted reluctance by some non-Hispanic businesses to advertise and invest in the publication because of the inflammatory rhetoric surrounding Hispanic immigration to this country. "A lot of people concentrate on that," said Lorenzana. "So by the time I try to sell them advertising and talk to them about the magazine, they don't want to hear it." Lorenzana observed, "Some of them don't even want to invest in this because they care a lot of what their friends are going to think or they think that if they advertise they are promoting illegal immigration."[35]

Despite these obstacles, Lorenzana is determined to use his skills as a publisher to promote a positive image of Hispanics and their culture within his magazine. In doing so, Lorenzana believes he can bridge any gaps that exist between Hispanics and non-Hispanics. "We are doing articles that everybody will be interested in reading, not just Hispanic people," said Lorenzana. "But we are doing it also with in mind that we want to promote our culture . . . the Hispanic culture. We want everybody to understand our culture. And that's why we do it in English and Spanish." Lorenzana hopes to combat the negative stories appearing daily in the US press about the problems associated with the economy and living conditions in Mexico by publishing stories that humanize the growing Hispanic population in this country. "And we kind of want to focus the magazine on positive things with our culture and show, at the same time, we are not so different than everybody else."[36]

While stories in *Mid-South Latino Magazine* promote universal human qualities shared by all people, Luis Madera wants the general public to know that Hispanics bring a unique richness to the community through their language and culture. "One thing I would like people to know is that I am proud to be Hispanic. We speak two languages and our culture is very rich." This rich culture is reflected in several public events, including the Hispanic Celebration in May and the Multicultural Dinner and Dance, both sponsored in part by the Hispanic Community Services. These public events allow Hispanics to celebrate their own culture while introducing the non-Hispanic community to the food, music, dance, and other cultural features from throughout the Latin world. The Hispanic Celebration in May and the Multicultural Dinner and Dance also allow both Hispanic and non-Hispanic business and civic leaders an opportunity to interact in a fun and informal setting. This type of interaction brings the communities together in a spirit of cooperation and demonstrates the important contributions Hispanics can make to Jonesboro and northeast Arkansas. "I wish that all the Americans would realize how important we are for this community," said Luis Madera. "We came here to participate in this community."[37]

Participation in local civic activities and organizations is a standard method of doing business for many business owners. It is no different for Hispanic entrepreneurs. Attending public events, joining community groups, and volunteering for charitable causes allow business people to network with others in the community, exchange information, and promote their businesses. The additional benefit of participating in civic activities for Hispanic entrepreneurs is that it helps create a positive awareness of Hispanics in Jonesboro. Hispanic Community Services executive director Gina Gómez is a highly visible member of the Hispanic community. Gómez participates in a variety of social functions and is an active member of the Greater Jonesboro Chamber of Commerce. Part of her chamber of commerce experience includes membership on the Non-Profit Committee and participation in the annual Chamber of Commerce Business Expo.[38] The Business Expo provides Gómez with an opportunity to network with area businesses and introduce them to the Jonesboro Hispanic community by distributing information about the organization and the Hispanic population. Because the chamber of commerce has limited resources to help Hispanics, Gómez and the staff of the Hispanic Community Services work with chamber of commerce officials on translation services.

Alejandro Lorenzana is also active in the Greater Jonesboro Chamber of Commerce. In addition to participating in its functions, Lorenzana is active in several charitable organizations in Jonesboro, including the Cardiology Associates, a Jonesboro-based group of doctors who promote heart care and healthy lifestyles through a variety of educational outreach programs, and the Women's Discovery Center, a nonprofit organization offering support, services, and enrichment opportunities to women in the community. According to Lorenzana, participation in community activities is not only good for his business and for increasing awareness about Hispanics in the area, but also helps build trusting relationships with members of the greater Jonesboro community. "A lot of the times it's that Hispanics are afraid to talk to people from another culture," said Lorenzana. "So that is a big issue when it comes to our culture, they kind of isolate themselves from being part of the community, in a way. I think that is because they are scared. They don't know what to expect."[39]

Overcoming this fear and isolation will be a challenge for both the non-Hispanic civic leaders unfamiliar with Hispanic culture and the Hispanic newcomers to the United States. Building trust between the two groups will require effort toward a better understanding of how to reach out to each community. In his article "Latino Outreach Strategies for Civic Engagement," Greg Keiden describes several strategies communities could use to reach out to Hispanic, including the following: (1) practice relationship-building with Latino leaders; (2) recruit trusted organizations to serve as intermediaries with the Latino community; (3) demonstrate how participation in civic activities is beneficial to the individual; (4) encourage organizational networks within the Hispanic community to issue invitations to community events; (5) enlist religious leaders and church organizations to recommend participation in community activities; (6) publicize activities through Latino media; (7) offer inducements and acknowledge participation; (8) hold events in locations "comfortable and familiar to Latinos"; (9) personalize invitations through phone calls and direct contact; and (10) coordinate transportation with the assistance of Latino community members.[40] The inclusion of Latinos and a commitment to outreach will ease fears and create a sense of participation among groups who often feel marginalized in their new homeland.

Like other ethnic business owners, Hispanic entrepreneurs experience many challenges owning and operating a business. Navigating through confusing regulations and bureaucracies, overcoming language and cultural differences, and facing prejudices marginalize the existence of some Hispanic entrepreneurs and create obstacles for success in communities where the non-Hispanic population dominates. Despite these challenges, Hispanic entrepreneurs persevere in their attempts to achieve financial independence and pursue lifelong dreams of owning their own businesses. In doing so, the Hispanic entrepreneurs not only contribute to their own personal economic well-being, but also serve as an important support system by providing a location for newcomers to network with other Hispanics, exchange information, and ease the transition from their native land to a new country. Additionally, Hispanic-owned and -operated businesses add cultural richness to the general population.

NOTES

1. Black and White on Slavery's Frontier: The Slave Experience in Arkansas

1. Ira Berlin, *Many Thousands Gone: The First Two Centuries of Slavery in North America* (Cambridge, MA: Belknap Press, 1998) and *Generations of Captivity: A History of African-American Slaves* (Cambridge, MA: Belknap Press, 2003); Edward E. Baptist, *Creating an Old South: Middle Florida's Plantation Frontier before the Civil War* (Chapel Hill: University of North Carolina Press, 2002); Anthony Gene Carey, *Sold Down the River: Slavery in the Lower Chattahoochee Valley of Alabama and Georgia* (Tuscaloosa: University of Alabama Press, 2011); Orville Taylor, *Negro Slavery in Arkansas* (1958; repr., Fayetteville, University of Arkansas Press, 2000).

2. S. Charles Bolton, *Remote and Restless: Arkansas, 1800–1860* (Fayetteville: University of Arkansas Press, 1998); Jeannie M. Whayne, et al., *Arkansas: A Narrative History* (Fayetteville: University of Arkansas Press, 2002); S. Charles Bolton, *Fugitives from Injustice: Freedom-Seeking Slaves in Arkansas, 1800–1860* (Omaha, NE: National Park Service, 2006); Carl H. Moneyhon, "The Slave Family in Arkansas," *Arkansas Historical Quarterly* 58 (Spring 1999): 24–44.

3. See "Migration Generations" in Berlin, *Generations of Captivity*, 161–244; Steven Deyle, *Carry Me Back: The Domestic Slave Trade in American Life* (New York: Oxford University Press, 2005), 43.

4. Joseph C. G. Kennedy, *Population of the United States in 1860, Compiled from the Original Returns of the Eighth Census* (Washington, DC: Government Printing Office, 1864), 12–13, 503–4.

5. For some examples, see George Lankford, *Bearing Witness: Memories of Arkansas Slavery* (Fayetteville: University of Arkansas Press, 2003), 36, 66, 104, 126, 134, 45, 53, 104, and Edward E. Baptist, "'Stol' and Fetched Here': Enslaved Migration, Ex-slave Narratives, and Vernacular History," in *New Studies in the History of American Slavery*, ed. Edward E. Baptist and Stephanie M. H. Camp (Athens: University of Georgia Press, 2006), 243–44, 252–54.

6. Steven Deyle, *Carry Me Back*, 44; Lankford, *Bearing Witness*, 24. See also Michael Tadman, *Speculators and Slaves: Masters, Traders, and Slaves in the Old South* (Madison: University of Wisconsin Press, 1989); and Walter Johnson, *Soul by Soul: Life inside the Antebellum Slave Market* (Cambridge, MA: Harvard University Press, 1999).

7. Sarah Brooke Malloy, "The Health of Our Family: The Correspondence of Amanda Beardsley Trulock, 1837–1868" (MA thesis, University of Arkansas, 2005), 1–2, 22.

8. Wagram Plantation Journal, series 5, box 30, folder 457, Rice C. Ballard Papers, Southern Historical Collection, University of North Carolina, Chapel Hill (hereafter cited as Ballard Papers); James M[illegible] to Col. R. C. Ballard, series 1.3, box 7, folder 108, Ballard Papers.

9. Lankford, *Bearing Witness*, 15.

10. *Anderson v. Dunn* (1858), 19 Ark. 651–66. (The court cases are from *Reports of Cases at Law and in Equity Argued and Determined in the Supreme Court of Arkansas*.)

11. *Pond v. Obaugh* (1855), 16 Ark. 95.

12. *Humphries v. McCraw* (1848), 9 Ark. 92–98.

13. Jn. B. Pelham to Col. Ballard, October 23, [1857], subseries 1.3, box 17, folder 261, Ballard Papers.

14. Lankford, *Bearing Witness*, 195–96, 94, 96; *Case v. Maffitt* (1858), 19 Ark. 645–46; Manuscript census returns, US Bureau of the Census, *Eighth Census of the United States*, 1860, Schedule 1 (Free Inhabitants) and Schedule 2 (Slave Inhabitants), Independence County, AR (microfilm, University of Arkansas Libraries, Fayetteville).

15. Bolton, *Fugitives from Injustice*, 84, 65–66; Roman J. Zorn, "An Arkansas Fugitive Slave Incident and Its International Repercussions," *Arkansas Historical Quarterly* 16 (Summer 1957): 139–49.

16. Kelly Houston Jones, "'A Rough, Saucy Set of Hands to Manage': Slave Resistance in Arkansas," *Arkansas Historical Quarterly* 71 (Spring 2012): 6–9.

17. *Costar v. Davies* (1847), 8 Ark. 213.

18. Jones, "'A Rough, Saucy Set of Hands to Manage,'" 8–9; *Lindsay v. Wayland* (1856), 17 Ark. 385.

19. Peete & Raglan to Mr. Ballard [April 1858], series 1.3, box 18, folder 277, Ballard Papers; W. Cox & Co. to Col. R. C. Ballard, May 6, 1858, series 1.3, box 18, folder 278, Ballard Papers; C. M. Rutherford to Coln. Ballard, May 16, July 5, 6, 1858, series 1.3, box 18, folder 283, Ballard Papers.

20. Anthony Kaye, *Joining Places: Slave Neighborhoods in the Old South* (Chapel Hill: University of North Carolina Press, 2007), 8, 32.

21. Lankford, *Bearing Witness*, 290.

22. Ibid., 24, 294, 320, 295.

23. Ibid., 13, 102.

24. Ibid., 13, 15, 23, 102, 104, 136, 379, 122, 164, 197, 370–71.

25. Ibid., 371, 4, 102, 305, 244, 124, 216.

26. Margaret Jones Bolsterli, ed., *A Remembrance of Eden: Harriet Bailey Bullock Daniel's Memories of a Frontier Plantation in Arkansas, 1849–1872* (Fayetteville: University of Arkansas Press, 1993), 49; *Rose v. Rose* (1849), 9 Ark. 507.

27. Lankford, *Bearing Witness*, 366, 30, 215, 165.

28. Ibid., 185, 376, 24, 317–18, 164, 165.

29. Ibid., 48, 140, 102; Jno. Pelham to Col. Ballard, November 15, 21, 1857, folder 263, box 17, subseries 1.3, Ballard Papers.

30. John W. Brown Diary, August 18, 1852, January 25, 1853, February 4, 1853, February 15, 1853, April 9, 1853, microfilm, University of Arkansas Libraries, Fayetteville.

31. Ibid., October 13, 1852, January 14, 1853, January 25, 1853.

32. Maggie E. Walker Diary, Stebbins Supplement, Small Manuscripts Collection, folder 6, Arkansas History Commission, Little Rock.

33. Jones, "A Rough, Saucy Set of Hand to Manage,'" 10–11, 16.

34. See the letters from John Pelham and H. L. Berry to Col. Ballard, subseries 1.3, Ballard Papers.

35. Anthony Kaye and Anthony Gene Carey find much more market activity among slaves in the frontier Natchez and Chattahoochee regions than the documents

show for most of Arkansas. Both locales had higher population concentrations as well as larger slave populations than Arkansas overall in 1860. Kaye, *Joining Places*, 103–9, 114, 186, 221; Carey, *Sold Down the River*, 99–103, 43.

36. Josiah Gould, *A Digest of the Statutes of Arkansas: Embracing all laws of a general and permanent character in force at the close of the session of the General Assembly of 1856, together with notes of the decisions of the Supreme Court upon the statutes, and an appendix containing forms for justices of the peace* (Little Rock: Johnson & Yerkes, 1858), 1032, 1035, 1051–52, 382, 1031.

37. Paul D. Lack, "An Urban Slave Community: Little Rock, 1831–1862," *Arkansas Historical Quarterly* 41 (October 1982): 263–66, 258.

38. Pulaski County Indictment Records, 1848–1863, Books B–C, Arkansas History Commission, Little Rock.

39. *Powell v. The State* (1860), 21 Ark. 509–11.

40. *Omey v. The State* (1861), 23 Ark. 281; Manuscript census returns, US Bureau of the Census, *Eighth Census of the United States*, 1860, Schedule 1 (Free Inhabitants), Crawford County, AR (microfilm, University of Arkansas Libraries, Fayetteville).

41. *Ridge v. Featherston* (1854), 15 Ark. 160; Manuscript census returns, US Bureau of the Census, *Seventh Census of the United States*, 1850, Schedule 1 (Free Inhabitants) and Schedule 2 (Slave Inhabitants), Benton County, AR (microfilm, University of Arkansas Libraries, Fayetteville). One man, Wagoola, was accused of using his gun to shoot a neighbor's mare that had been trampling the fence. Ridge was a near neighbor of Cephas Washburn, the well-known missionary to the Cherokees.

42. Lankford, *Bearing Witness*, 128–29.

43. *Rose v. Rose* (1849), 9 Ark. 508.

44. Jones, "'A Rough, Saucy Set of Hands to Manage,'" 15–16, 18–19.

45. *Moss v. Sandefur* (1854), 15 Ark. 381–88.

46. *Daniel v. Guy* (1857), 19 Ark. 121–38 and (1861) 23 Ark. 50. Abby Guy's case is explored in more detail in Robert S. Shafer, "White Persons Held to Racial Slavery in Antebellum Aransas," *Arkansas Historical Quarterly* 44 (Summer 1985): 134–43.

47. *Sadler v. Sadler* (1856), 16 Ark. 634; Jones, "'A Rough, Saucy Set of Hands to Manage,'" 4–5. All of Rice C. Ballard's overseers at Wagram Plantation in Chicot County reported visits from neighboring planters. See R. C. Ballard letters, series 1.3, Ballard Papers.

48. *Cornelius v. The State* (1852), 12 Ark. 782.

2. Race and the Struggle for Freedom: African American Arkansans after Emancipation

1. George P. Rawick, ed., *The American Slave: A Composite Autobiography: Arkansas Narratives* (Westport, CT: Greenwood Publishing Company, 1972), vol. 8, pt. 1, 47.

2. Edwin M. Stanton to Lorenzo Thomas, March 25, 1863, and Circular, October 27, 1863, in *The War of the Rebellion: A Compilation of the Official Records of the Union and Confederate Armies*, US War Department, 128 vols. (Washington, DC: GPO, 1880–1901), series 3, vol. 3, 100, 939.

3. Nate Coulter, "The Impact of the Civil War upon Pulaski County, Arkansas," *Arkansas Historical Quarterly* 41 (Spring 1982): 71.

4. Rawick, *The American Slave*, 8:110.

5. Quarterly Report of Refugees and Freedmen for Eastern District of Arkansas, June 30, 1865, Letters Received, Department of Arkansas, 7th Army Corps and 4th Military District, Record Group 393, National Archives (hereafter cited as RG, NA); Carl H. Moneyhon, "From Slavery to Free Labor: The Federal Plantation Experiment in Arkansas," *Arkansas Historical Quarterly* 53 (Summer 1994): 137–60.

6. John Eaton, *Report of the General Superintendent of Freedmen, Department of the Tennessee and the State of Arkansas for 1864* (Memphis, 1864), 36 and 67; Joseph Warren, comp., *Extracts from Reports of Superintendents of Freedmen* (Vicksburg, MS: Freedmen Press Print, 1864), 16.

7. J. L. Thorp to John Tyler, January 6, 1867, Records of the Assistant Commissioner for Arkansas, Letters Received, Bureau of Refugees, Freedmen and Abandoned Land (hereafter cited as BRFAL), RG105, NA.

8. E. A. Young to C. H. Fowler, February 4, 1864, American Missionary Association Manuscripts, NA; Joel Grant, Report, May 31, 1865, Field Office Records, Arkansas, BRFAL, RG105, NA.

9. William Stuart to John Tyler, October 31, 1865, Records of the Assistant Commissioner for Arkansas (hereafter cited as RACA), Letters Received, BRFAL, RG90, NA.

10. Testimony of Gen. John B. Sanborn, US Congress, *Report of the Joint Committee on Reconstruction*, 39th Cong., 1st sess., pt. 3, 77.

11. *Little Rock Evening Republican,* June 4, 1867; *Arkansas Gazette* (Little Rock), June 4, November 19, 1867; Buckner H. "Ariel" Payne, *The Negro: What Is His Ethnological Status?* (Charleston, SC: Joseph Walker, 1867), 48.

12. *Proceedings of the Convention of Colored Citizens of the State of Arkansas, Held in Little Rock, Thursday, Friday, and Saturday, November 30, December 1, and 2* (Helena, AR, 1866), 10; *House Reports*, 39th Cong., 1st sess., no. 30.

13. *Arkansas Gazette*, May 30, 1857; June 15, 1858. See also December 27, 1856; April 6, 1855.

14. *Arkansas Gazette*, January 10, 1857.

15. *Arkansas Gazette*, September 13, 1866; *Western Clarion* (Helena, Arkansas), December 16, 1865.

16. *Arkansas Gazette*, September 19, 1866.

17. John W. Sprague to John Thorp, December 19, 1865, RACA, Letters Sent, BRFAL, RG90, NA.

18. Randy Finley, *From Slavery to Uncertain Freedom: The Freedmen's Bureau in Arkansas, 1865–1869* (Fayetteville: University of Arkansas Press, 1996), 72.

19. W. A. Britton to E. M. Gantt, December 18, 1865, in (Arkadelphia) Field Office Records, BRFAL, RG105, NA.

20. *Arkansas Gazette*, September 3, October 24, 1867.

21. *Arkansas Gazette*, March 26, 1867.

22. *Arkansas Gazette*, December 17, 1867.

23. William Stuart to John Tyler, October 31, 1865, RACA, Letters Received, BRFAL, RG90, NA.

24. V. V. Smith, July 9, 1867, RACA, Reports, BRFAL, RG1, NA.

25. Anthony Taylor, *Arkansas Narratives, The American Slave*, 2nd ser. (Westport, CN: Greenwood Press, 1972), vol. 11, pt. 7, 157.

26. V. V. Smith to John Bennett, July 17, 1867, Field Office Records, Arkansas, BRFAL, RG105, NA; General Orders No. 19, Headquarters 4th Military District,

August 13, 1867, in *Arkansas Gazette*, August 27, 1867; William Bryan Report, April 30, 1868, RACA, Reports, BRFAL, RG90, NA; "Letter from E. O. C. Ord in Relation to the Treatment of Freedmen in Arkansas, November 24, 1866," *House Miscellaneous Documents*, 39th Cong., 2d sess., no. 14, 1–2.

27. Rawick, *The American Slave*, vol. 8, pt. 2, 147.

28. Finley, *From Slavery to Uncertain Freedom*, 130–31.

29. "Letter from E. O. C. Ord in Relation to the Treatment of Freedmen in Arkansas, November 24, 1866"; *Arkansas Gazette*, December 17, 1867; S. Geisreiter to John Tyler, March 26, 1867, RACA, Letters Received, BRFAL, RG90, NA.

30. *Arkansas Gazette*, December 20, 1867; December 10, 1867; June 4, 1867; February 4, 1867.

31. *Arkansas Gazette*, August 20 1867; December 17, 1867.

32. *Arkansas Gazette*, November 19, 1867; Payne, *The Negro: What Is His Ethnological Status?*, 48.

33. Tom Baskett Jr., ed., *Persistence of the Spirit: The Black Experience in Arkansas* (Little Rock: Arkansas Endowment for the Humanities, 1986), 22.

34. Carl H. Moneyhon, *Arkansas in the New South, 1874–1929* (Fayetteville: University of Arkansas Press, 1997), 75.

35. *Arkansas Gazette*, August 28 and 29, 1883.

3. "Send Forth More Laborers into the Vineyard": Understanding the African American Exodus to Arkansas

1. *Philadelphia (PA) Christian Recorder*, December 13, 1888; Blake Wintory, "African-American Legislators in the Arkansas General Assembly, 1868–1893," *Arkansas Historical Quarterly* 65 (Winter 2006): 385–434.

2. Reprinted as "Conditions in Arkansas" in the *New York Age*, December 29, 1888, and "New Eldorado" in the *Indianapolis (IN) Freeman*, January 5, 1889.

3. Story Matkin-Rawn "'The Great Negro State of the Country': Arkansas's Reconstruction and the Other Great Migration," *Arkansas Historical Quarterly* 72 (Spring 2013): 2.

4. According to intercensal estimates, roughly 56,000 African Americans migrated to Arkansas in the 1880s, with Pennsylvania at a distant second, attracting roughly 24,000 African American migrants. Using mortality-corrected state-of-birth figures, demographer William Edward Vickery recalculated these numbers at 59,539 for Arkansas and 26,236 for Pennsylvania. See William Edward Vickery, *The Economics of the Negro Migration, 1900–1960* (New York: Arno Press, 1977), 20, 169.

5. Vickery, *The Economics of the Negro Migration*, 169.

6. *New York Age*, March 30, 1889.

7. Carl H. Moneyhon, *The Impact of the Civil War and Reconstruction on Arkansas* (Fayetteville: University of Arkansas Press, 2002), 177–79; *New York Times*, January 23, 1867.

8. Joel Williamson, *After Slavery: The Negro in South Carolina during Reconstruction, 1861–1877* (Chapel Hill: University of North Carolina Press, 1965), 108; *Macon (GA) Telegraph*, quoted in "Nomadic Negroes of the South," *Little's Living Age* 1195 (April 27, 1867): 430. Howard estimated that 66,000 freedpeople left Georgia between the end of the war and early 1867, roughly 15 percent of the state's black population. See "The Colored People of the South," *Friend's Review*, March 2, 1867.

9. Steven Hahn, *A Nation under Our Feet: Black Political Struggles in the Rural South from Slavery to the Great Migration* (Cambridge, MA: Belknap Press, 2003), 54–55, 65–66, 131–32; Francis A. Tolliver, "The Lost Black History of White County," *White County Heritage* 40 (2002): 28–42. For other firsthand accounts of a typical journey, see the interview with William Dunwoody in *The American Slave: A Composite Autobiography*, ed. George P. Rawick, 9 vols. (Westport, CT.: Greenwood Publishing Company, 1972), vol. 8, *Arkansas Narratives*, pt. 2. See also Harriet Hill, vol. 9, pt. 3; Walter Jones, vol. 9, pt. 4; Warren McKinney, vol. 10, pt. 5; Emma Morris, vol. 10, pt. 5; Henry Pettus, vol. 10, pt. 5, all in Rawick, *The American Slave*.

10. James Danky, "Reading, Writing, and Resisting: African American Print Culture History, 1880–1940," in *The History of the Book in America*, ed. Carl Kaestle and Janice Radway (Chapel Hill: University of North Carolina Press, 2008), 4:341–42.

11. *Macon (GA) Weekly Telegraph*, February 15, 1867. According to the *Fort Valley (GA) Mirror*, January 14, 1875, wages after an exodus jumped to $100 to $135 dollars a year, whereas in a "normal" year, they offered $60 to $85 and board.

12. Randy Finley, "The Freedmen's Bureau in Arkansas" (PhD diss., University of Arkansas, Fayetteville, 1993), 293; *Morning Republican* (Little Rock, AR), July 23, 1870; *Arkansas Gazette* (Little Rock), October 17, 1872; *Memphis (TN) Appeal*, January 24, 1873.

13. See *Weekly Telegraph*, January 2, 1873; *New National Era*, reprinted in the *Weekly Louisianan* (New Orleans), December 7, 1872; *New York Times*, January 3, 1873; *Arkansas Gazette*, January 19, 1873; *Southern Watchman* (Athens, GA), July 23, 1873.

14. *Charleston (NC) Daily News*, January 2, 1873; *Augusta (GA) Chronicle*, January 18, 1873; *Albany (GA) News*, December 3 and 10, 1874; *Augusta Chronicle*, October 8, 1875; Joseph P. Reidy, *From Slavery to Agrarian Capitalism in the Cotton Plantation South: Central Georgia, 1800–1880* (Chapel Hill: University of North Carolina Press, 1995), 297 n60.

15. *Columbus (GA) Daily Sun*, January 18, 1873; "The Georgia Conference," *Christian Recorder*, May 8, 1873.

16. Michael B. Dougan, *Arkansas Odyssey: The Saga of Arkansas from Prehistoric Times to Present: A History* (Little Rock, AR: Rose Publishing Co., 1995), 131–32, 141–42; Brooks Blevins, *Arkansas/Arkansaw: How Bear Hunters, Hillbillies, and Good Ol' Boys Defined a State* (Fayetteville: University of Arkansas Press, 2009), 12–16, 34–35, 45–46; Melinda Meek, "The Life of Archibald Yell," *Arkansas Historical Quarterly* 26 (Winter 1967), quotation from page 356.

17. *Christian Recorder*, July 15, 1878, February 23, 1882. For another lament over Arkansans' heathenish ways, see L. W. Elkins, "Hot Springs District," *Southwestern Christian Advocate* (New Orleans, LA), August 16, 1883.

18. *Christian Recorder*, January 27, 1881; Loren Schweninger, *Black Property Owners in the South, 1790–1915* (Champaign: University of Illinois Press, 1997), 170.

19. Schweninger, *Black Property Owners*, 164, 170; *Morning Republican*, July 21, 1869; *Arkansas Gazette*, August 28, 1883.

20. Arkansas had improved 1,983,313 acres as of 1860. The state covered roughly 34,464,000 acres. US Census Office, *Agriculture in the United States in 1860* (Washington DC: GPO, 1864), vii; Claude F. Oubre, *Forty Acres and a Mule: The Freedmen's Bureau and Black Land Ownership* (Baton Rouge: Louisiana State University Press, 1978), 86–94, 103–9; Stephen E. Wood, "The Development of Arkansas Railroads, Part 1," *Arkansas Historical Quarterly* 7 (July 1948): 120, 125–40.

21. For movement out of Tennessee and Alabama, see *Memphis Appeal,* April 26, 1873; *Weekly Enquirer* (Columbus, GA), January 21, 1874; *Hinds County (AL) Gazette,* January 21, 1874; *Arkansas Gazette,* January 23, 1874, and February 6, 1875; *Morning Republican,* March 19, 1874; *Chicago Daily Tribune,* May 10, 1875; *Enquirer Sun* (Columbus, GA), reprinted in *Macon Weekly Telegraph,* March 21, 1876.

22. John William Graves, *Town and Country: Race Relations in an Urban-Rural Context, Arkansas, 1865–1905* (Fayetteville: University of Arkansas Press, 1990), 38–58; Kenneth C. Barnes, *Journey of Hope: The Back-to-Africa Movement in Arkansas in the Late 1800s* (Chapel Hill: University of North Carolina Press, 2004), 14–16; Fon Louise Gordon, *Caste and Class: The Black Experience in Arkansas, 1880–1920* (Athens: University of Georgia Press, 1995), 10 ("to assure"); *Chicago Daily Tribune,* May 10, 1875 ("labor supply"). See also "The South," *Chicago Tribune,* May 8, 1875.

23. *Arkansas Gazette,* May 10 and 20, 1879; Nell Irvin Painter, *Exodusters: Black Migration to Kansas* (New York: Alfred A. Knopf, 1976), chapters 14, 15, and 17. The American Colonization Society facilitated the resettlement of 972 persons during the 1870s. See P. J. Staudenraus, *The African Colonization Movement, 1816–1865* (New York: Columbia University Press, 1961), 251. Add to this 206 African Americans who sailed in an independent venture on the ship *Azor* in 1878. See Barnes, *Journey of Hope,* 11. A detailed estimate of black migration to Kansas can be found in William Cohen, *At Freedom's Edge: Black Mobility and the Southern White Quest for Racial Control, 1861–1915* (Baton Rouge: Louisiana State University Press, 1991), Appendix B, 301–11.

24. Vickery, *The Economics of the Negro Migration,* 172. The number of black Arkansan emigrants to Liberia can be found in Barnes, *Journey of Hope,* 25, 31. His is also the best description of the decline in emigration movements after the 1880 election and the improving situation for Arkansas's black voters in the early 1880s (Barnes, *Journey of Hope,* 33–36). According to William Cohen's figures, 893 black residents of Kansas listed Arkansas as their state of birth in the 1870 census. That number had fallen to 768 in 1880, making Arkansans the only group of southern transplants in Kansas to decline over the 1870s. See Cohen, *At Freedom's Edge,* 170.

25. Cohen, *At Freedom's Edge,* chapters 6 and 7; Hahn, *A Nation under Our Feet,* 330–337 (quotation, 333); Painter, *Exodusters,* 158–59, 170–71, 177–80, 184–96.

26. Edmund Drago, *Black Politicians and Reconstruction in Georgia: A Splendid Failure* (Athens: University of Georgia Press, 1992), chapters 4 and 6; Reidy, *From Slavery to Agrarian Capitalism,* 203–7, 211–32; Richard Bailey, *Neither Carpetbaggers nor Scalawags: Black Officeholders during the Reconstruction of Alabama, 1867–1878* (Montgomery, AL: New South Books, 2009), 179, 215–60. The Ida Blackshear Hutchinson interview is in Rawick, *The American Slave,* vol. 9, *Arkansas,* pt. 3, 378.

27. Aiken, Barnwell, Edgefield, and Laurens Counties were particularly active in the Liberian exodus movement and all saw the departure of large numbers of freedpeople for Arkansas in the 1880s. "Bound for Arkansas," *News and Courier* (Charleston, SC), December 29, 1881; Cohen, *At Freedom's Edge,* 154–57; *News and Courier,* January 1, 2, and 3, 1881; *Anderson (SC) Intelligencer,* December 14, 1884; *Galveston (TX) Daily News,* December 22, 1886.

28. *Christian Recorder,* July 14, 1881.

29. Hahn, *A Nation under Our Feet,* 333; *New York Times,* May 12, 1874; *Scribners Monthly* 8 (October 1874): 641.

30. *Christian Recorder,* December 14, 1872, May 6, 1875; Richard R. Wright,

Centennial Encyclopedia of the African Methodist Episcopal Church (Philadelphia, PA: Book Concern of the A.M.E. Church, 1916), 10.

31. The census of 1880 recorded Arkansas's population as 73.7 percent white in 1880. US Bureau of the Census, *Compendium of the Tenth Census* (Washington, DC: GPO, 1883), 2–3.

32. Travelers' impressions of nineteenth-century Arkansas are drawn from Dallas T. Herndon, "A Little of What Arkansas Was Like a Hundred Years Ago," *Arkansas Historical Quarterly* 3 (Summer 1944): 97–124; Robert L. Morris, "Three Arkansas Travelers," *Arkansas Historical Quarterly* 4 (Autumn 1945): 215–30; Don C. Bragg, "Natural Presettlement Features of Ashley County, Arkansas Area," *American Midland Naturalist* 149 (January 2003): 1–20; Don C. Bragg, "General Land Office Surveys as a Source for Arkansas History: The Example of Ashley County," *Arkansas Historical Quarterly* 63 (Summer 2004): 166–84. Useful primary sources include "Letter from Arkansas," *Macon Weekly Telegraph,* June 3, 1873 ("covered over"); "Lonoke, a Queen of the Prairies," *Arkansas Gazette,* August 5, 1883; and travel accounts by Geo. F. Codd, W. A. Webber, and N. P. Prentiss, all in T. B. Mills, ed., *A History of the Northwestern Editorial Excursion* (Little Rock: T. B. Mills and Co., 1876), 63–78, 236–43, and 244–61 ("cotton height," 250), respectively.

33. Bragg, "Natural Presettlement Features," 14; Gordon D. Morgan, *Black Hillbillies of the Arkansas Ozarks* (Fayetteville: Dept. of Sociology, University of Arkansas, 1973), 106; Conevery Bolton Valencius, *The Health of the Country: How American Settlers Understood Themselves and Their Land* (New York: Basic Books, 2002), 114–32.

34. Written accounts praising the land are so numerous as to be beyond documenting. A sample includes *Morning Republican,* July 16, 1869, February 8, 1873; *Christian Recorder,* July 10, 1876, January 27, 1881, October 16, 1890; *Arkansas Mansion* (Little Rock), July 14, 1883; *Southwestern Christian Advocate,* December 3, 1885; *Christian Index* (Memphis, TN), January 14, 1888.

35. *Christian Index,* June 1885; V. H. Bulkley, *The Truth about Arkansas* (Sumpter, SC: Watchman and Southron Print, 1883), 4; *Christian Recorder,* September 21, 1882.

36. *Christian Recorder,* May 6, 1875; Bulkley, *The Truth about Arkansas,* 8; Letter from Charles Zigler to the Editor, *The Bee* (Washington, DC), March 17, 1887; Story Matkin-Rawn, "We Fight for the Rights of Our Race: Black Arkansans in the Era of Jim Crow," (PhD diss., University of Wisconsin, Madison, 2009), 47–49, 273 n66.

37. Kenneth C. Barnes, *Who Killed John Clayton? Political Violence and the Emergence of the New South, 1861–1893* (Durham, NC: Duke University Press, 1998), and Graves, *Town and Country,* provide a useful overview of the state's third-party movements and interracial political organizing in the 1880s. *Southwestern Christian Advocate,* December 30, 1886. For references to Joshua 9:23, see "Shall We Have Farms or Not?," *Christian Recorder,* December 30, 1875; "Reply to Bro. Chambers," *Christian Recorder,* October 25, 1877; "A Trip in the West," *Christian Recorder,* September 21, 1882.

38. R. T. Louis, "Editorial Perambulations," *Southwestern Christian Advocate,* December 3, 1885; Marshall Taylor, "The Negro Solving His Own Problem," *Southwestern Christian Advocate,* June 2, 1887.

39. Letter from the Ocmulgee Farmers Club No. 7 to the Editor, *Telegraph and Messenger* (Macon, GA), February 4, 1873; "New Exodus," *Christian Recorder,* January 12, 1882.

40. *Southwestern Christian Advocate*, June 25, 1885; *Christian Recorder*, October 16, 1890; John M. Collins, "Arkansas to Georgia," *Christian Recorder*, September 3, 1885.

41. *Arkansas Mansion*, July 14, September 22, 1883; Mifflin Wistar Gibbs, *Shadow and Light: An Autobiography with Reminiscences of the Last and Present Century* (Washington, DC: M. W. Gibbs, 1902), 85–86; US Bureau of the Census, *Report on Farms and Homes: Proprietorship and Indebtedness in the United States at the Eleventh Census: 1890* (Washington, DC: GPO, 1896), 566–68; Loren Schweninger, "A Vanishing Breed: Black Farm Owners in the South, 1651–1982," *Agricultural History* 63 (Summer 1989): Appendix B.

42. See "Shall We Have Farms or Not?," *Christian Recorder*, December 30, 1875; "Emigration," *Christian Recorder*, July 14, 1881; "Two Arkansas Conferences," *Christian Recorder*, May 12, 1881; "A Trip in the West," *Christian Recorder*, September 21, 1882; "It Is a Mistake to Go North," *Southwestern Christian Advocate*, June 25, 1885; Bulkley, *The Truth about Arkansas*, 6, 8.

43. Frankye Geraldine Tollette Charles, "The History of Tollette," n.d., author's private papers; Alice Crawford Branch, "Desha County's Unique Town Liberia City," *Desha County Historical Society 1983 Program* 10 (Spring 1984): 62–64; "Immigrants Who Throve," *Indianapolis Freedman*, July 8, 1893; Gracie Jemerson Morgan, "Immanuel High School, Almyra, Arkansas County," *Grand Prairie Historical Bulletin* 50 (April 2007): 36–43; Women's Civil League of Menifee, *Menifee—Past and Present* (Menifee, AR: 1976).

44. *New York Herald*, September 20, 1889; Vickery, *The Economics of the Negro Migration*, 165, 176. Documentation on the North Carolina Emigration Association is stronger than for almost any other movement. See *News and Observer* (Raleigh, NC), March 17, 1889; *Anderson Intelligencer*, September 28, 1889; and a long interview with NCEA representatives in the *Arkansas Gazette*, August 25, 1889.

45. Graves, *Town and Country*, chapters 7, 8, and 9; Barnes, *Who Killed John Clayton*, chapters 3 and 4.

46. Vickery, *The Economics of the Negro Migration*, 172; Emmett J. Scott, *Negro Migration during the War* (New York: Oxford University Press, 1920), 63–65.

47. Arkansas's rate of out migration was 18 in 1,000 black residents during the 1870s and 1880s, compared to 53 and 55, respectively, for the South as a whole in those decades. By the 1890s, the rate of emigration for the South had risen to 83 in 1,000 blacks, and Arkansas's jumped to 57. Vickery, *The Economics of the Negro Migration*, 26, 165, 184.

48. "Now or Never," *Christian Recorder*, October 16, 1890; "North Carolina Notes," *Christian Recorder*, March 21, 1889. For other examples of this sort of direct advice to prospective migrations to Arkansas and the Southwest on where and how to settle, see "Bishop Harris on the Race Problem—Judicious Immigration," *Southwestern Christian Advocate*, December 11, 1890; "A Wild Goose Chase," *Southwestern Christian Advocate*, May 7, 1891; E. W. Johnson, Letter to the Editor, *Southwestern Christian Advocate*, October 27, 1892; and the "Shall We Go or Stay" series in the *Southwestern Christian Advocate*, November 2, 1893, and February 1, 1894.

49. "South and West," *Christian Recorder*, July 25, 1878.

4. Sundown Towns: Racial Cleansing in the Arkansas Delta

1. James. W. Loewen, *Sundown Towns: A Hidden Dimension of American Racism* (New York: New Press, 2005), 71, 74; Jacqueline Froelich and David Zimmerman, "Total Eclipse: The Destruction of the African American Community of Harrison, Arkansas, in 1905 and 1909," *Arkansas Historical Quarterly* 58 (Summer 1999): 133–59; Guy Lancaster, "'They Are Not Wanted': The Extirpation of African Americans from Baxter County, Arkansas," *Arkansas Historical Quarterly* 69 (Spring 2010): 28–44.

2. Steven Hahn, *A Nation under Our Feet: Black Political Struggles in the Rural South from Slavery to the Great Migration* (Cambridge, MA: Harvard University Press, 2003), 427.

3. O. L. Dalton, "More about St. Francis . . . ," *Piggott Banner* (Piggott, AR), August 30, 1963, 2.

4. Letter from C. E. (Nub) Jewell, published in column titled "Some More about Greenway," *Piggott Banner*, September 27, 1963, 13; Sherry Laymon, *Pfeiffer Country: The Tenant Farms and Business Activities of Paul Pfeiffer in Clay County, Arkansas, 1902–1954* (Little Rock: Butler Center Books, 2009), 73–75. For more information on the Ku Klux Klan in the county, see Robert T. Webb, *History and Traditions of Clay County* (Mountain Home, AR: Shiras Brothers Print Shop, 1933), 25–27, 58; "Two More," *Arkansas Gazette* (Little Rock), January 1, 1885; "Captain of the Ku Klux," *Arkansas Gazette*, January 2, 1885; "Ten Short Days," *Arkansas Gazette*, January 20, 1885; "End of a Ku Kluxer," *Arkansas Gazette*, January 31, 1885. A late 1887 outbreak of "black diphtheria" in Clay County apparently also resulted in many African Americans leaving the place (see "A Deadly Malady and Its Results in Clay County," *Arkansas Gazette*, December 4, 1887).

5. "A Bad State of Affairs in a Portion of Lawrence County," *Arkansas Gazette*, October 14, 1887.

6. "Whitecaps," *Arkansas Gazette*, January 17, 1894, 2; "Negroes Ordered out of the County," *New York Times*, January 17, 1894, 8. The fact that African Americans were driven out of neighboring towns may have played a role in Black Rock whitecappers seeking to drive out black laborers, especially if the all-white makeup of these other towns was widely seen as something to be desired. Froelich and Zimmerman suggest that such a contagion, as it were, may have been in effect following the Harrison race riots, given that the neighboring counties of Madison and Carroll also reported steep drops in their respective black populations between the 1900 and 1910 censuses. See Froelich and Zimmerman, "Total Eclipse," 156.

7. "Armed Quiet in Black Rock," *New York Times*, January 19, 1894, 6. See also "Indignant Citizens," *Arkansas Gazette*, January 20, 1894; "The Facts in the Case," *Arkansas Gazette*, January 21, 1894. Whitecappers did continue to operate in the county, though their actions are mentioned only in concert with a multiple murder that happened in Black Rock in 1898. At approximately 2:00 a.m. on Sunday, November 20, the local marshal discovered Henry White, an African American, apparently stealing a hog (he was "carrying a pig in a sack") and, according to the *Arkansas Gazette*, deputized a number of citizens to assist in White's apprehension; the *New York Times*, in contrast, identifies this band of people as "White Caps," without reference to any official capacity in which they might have been operating. As they approached the jail, White pulled a pistol and began firing, killing two and badly wounding one in the process of making his escape. The published reports add that

"whitecappers had operated in the county for a few weeks past and several negroes had been whipped." "Negro's Bloody Deed," *Arkansas Gazette*, November 23, 1898; "White Caps Shot in Arkansas," *New York Times*, November 24, 1898.

8. "Disgraceful if True," *Arkansas Gazette*, April 21, 1888; "The Paragould Outrage," *Arkansas Gazette*, April 27, 1888.

9. "Ordered to Leave the County," *Arkansas Gazette*, November 1, 1892.

10. "Negroes Are Leaving Paragould by Hundreds," *Arkansas Gazette*, August 8, 1899; "Paragould Whitecappers," *Arkansas Gazette*, August 9, 1889.

11. "Paragould Has Lost Cotton Compress," *Arkansas Gazette*, October 21, 1903.

12. "Negroes Ordered out of Paragould," *Arkansas Gazette*, April 9, 1908. For more information on racial cleansing in Paragould, see Guy Lancaster, "'Negroes Are Leaving Paragould by Hundreds': Racial Cleansing in a Northeast Arkansas Railroad Town," *Arkansas Review: A Journal of Delta Studies* 41 (April 2010): 3–15.

13. Clarence B. Moore, "Antiquities of the St. Francis, White, and Black Rivers, Arkansas," *Journal of the Academy of Natural Sciences of Philadelphia* 14 (1910): 256. Online at http://www.archive.org/details/antiquitiesofstfoomooruoft (accessed February 17, 2012).

14. "Buffalo Island Drainage District No. 16 of Mississippi County, Arkansas . . . Then and Now!" (n.p.: Drainage District No. 16, 1987). The author went on to add, "There were no plantations on Buffalo Island, but there was plenty of cheap labor, predominantly the white persons who were available for hire by the lumber industries, the farmers and the merchants."

15. L. A. "Buddy" Diebold Jr., "My Home Town—Hickory Ridge, Arkansas," May 22, 1961, Folklore Class Reports, Mary Celestia Parler Research Materials, Special Collections, University of Arkansas Libraries, Fayetteville.

16. "Race Troubles Are Feared in Trumann," *Arkansas Gazette*, August 17, 1908; "Fear Race War in Arkansas," *Chicago Daily Tribune*, August 17, 1908.

17. "Danger of Riot at Trumann Ends," *Arkansas Gazette*, August 18, 1908.

18. Wanda Moss, *Memories of Yesteryear: A Photographic Account of Trumann since 1894* (Trumann, AR: self-published, 1990), 12.

19. Richard Allen Burns, "The Shotgun Houses of Trumann, Arkansas," *Arkansas Review: A Journal of Delta Studies* 33 (April 2002): 46. Employment of African Americans in Trumann by the Singer Company did not protect them from local hostilities, even before they were expelled en masse. In September 1918, one W. G. Criss (or Crist), proprietor of a poolroom in Trumann, shot and killed a black employee of the Singer Company for reportedly refusing to "leave to town" and then laughing when the proprietor repeated his demand. The black employee, unnamed in the newspaper account, was apparently waiting around to receive his pay from the company (see "Negro Shot at Trumann, Tuesday," *Marked Tree Tribune*, September 6, 1918).

20. Burns, "The Shotgun Houses of Trumann," 44. Burns cites "political pressure" on the Singer Company, and there is a decent chance that this pressure came from the familiar quarters of the Ku Klux Klan. H. L. Mitchell, one of the organizers of the Southern Tenant Farmers' Union, records that the KKK had started organizing in Trumann in the early 1920s and soon "represented a majority of voters in the Trumann district." See H. L. Mitchell, *Mean Things Happening in This Land: The Life and Times of H. L. Mitchell, Co-founder of the Southern Tenant Farmers Union* (Norman: University of Oklahoma Press, 2008), 40. Some of the impetus behind Klan organization may be that the town, "since 1912, had been a hotbed of socialism" (39), according

to Mitchell. He names a number of prominent local socialists and adds that the American Federation of Labor led a strike against the Singer plant soon after World War I.

21. Burns, "The Shotgun Houses of Trumann," 49.

22. "Citizens Join to Protect Negroes," *Jonesboro Evening Sun*, April 18, 1912; "Citizens Join to Protect Negroes," *Arkansas Gazette*, April 19, 1912. Of course, these self-appointed "protectors" of the black residents still used language perhaps better suited to the whitecappers when they wrote, "When you go after the nigger, be sure you are not caught."

23. "Walnut Ridge Negroes Ordered to Leave by Whites, Militia Called," *Jonesboro Evening Sun*, April 22, 1912.

24. "Whites Dynamite Home of Negro," *Arkansas Gazette*, April 21, 1912.

25. "Militia in Camp at Walnut Ridge," *Arkansas Gazette*, April 22, 1912.

26. "Governor Offers Rewards," *Atlanta Constitution*, February 11, 1898.

27. "Shoot into the Negroes' Cabins," *Arkansas Gazette*, April 10, 1908.

28. Jeannie Whayne, *Delta Empire: Lee Wilson and the Transformation of Agriculture in the New South* (Baton Rouge: Louisiana State University Press, 2011), 121.

29. "Negroes Warned to Leave Pine Bluff," *Arkansas Gazette*, March 15, 1915; "Night Walkers Scare Negroes," *Pine Bluff Daily Graphic*, March 3, 1915. The neighborhood in question was comprised of Twelfth and Texas, Missouri, Indiana, East Thirteenth, Fourteenth, and Fifteenth Streets, and many of the recipients of the warnings were shopkeepers (see "Notices Warning Them to Leave Town Greatly Excites Negroes," *Pine Bluff Commercial*, March 2, 1915). The *Daily Graphic* reported that authorities were considering three possibilities for the origin of these messages, "one that a negro is responsible, he being perhaps mentally unsound; another, that white men are playing a joke, just to scare the negroes; and the third, that an effort is being made to 'bluff' the negroes into moving away, that their property might be purchased below its real value." Contrary to that first possibility, the *Commercial* quoted a witness who saw three white men acting suspiciously in the neighborhood prior to the posting of the notices. The *Commercial* even issued an editorial against the posting of notices (see "Nightriders," *Pine Bluff Commercial*, March 2, 1915).

30. "One Negro Killed and 500 Shots Fired as Result of Panic among Negroes Early Sunday Morning," *Pine Bluff Commercial*, March 15, 1915; "Negroes Warned to Leave Pine Bluff," *Arkansas Gazette*, March 15, 1915; "Colored People Shouldn't Worry," *Pine Bluff Daily Graphic*, March 16, 1915.

31. More black-owned houses were destroyed by fire on March 21. See "Fire at Pine Bluff," *Arkansas Gazette*, March 22, 1915. However, this latter article does not link the fires with the previous week's nightriding activities.

32. "Negro Held for Stealing Shotgun," *Pine Bluff Commercial*, March 16, 1915.

33. "Night Riders in Mississippi County," *Osceola Times*, March 19, 1915. The *Osceola Times* reflected Judge Driver's determination to stamp out nightriding in an editorial that compared one of the notices posted near Rosa, just southwest of O'Donnell Bend, with a letter received from Revered E. D. Hathom, a black resident of Osceola, for purposes of emphasizing the illiteracy of the nightrider's notice: "The stone of his screed shows him to be far lower, both mentally and morally, than the average negro plantation hand whom he so despises" (see "Two Letters—A Contrast," *Osceola Times*, March 26, 1915). The newspaper had previously editorialized against

nightriding in nearby Pemiscot County, Missouri (see "Night Riders in Southern Missouri," *Osceola Times*, March 12, 1915).

34. "Faces Term in Pen in Nightrider Case," *Arkansas Gazette*, March 24, 1915; "Jury Says Guilty of Night Riding," *Osceola Times*, March 26, 1915; "Captain of 'Riders' Gets 8-Year Term," *Arkansas Gazette*, March 26, 1915; "Rogers Given Seven Years and a Half," *Osceola Times*, April 2, 1915; Mississippi County Circuit Court Criminal Record, Osceola District, Book 2, 258–59. Rogers's name is rendered "Rodgers" in some reports, while Swafford is sometimes rendered "Swofford." According to reporting in the *Gazette*, local authorities had "evidence incriminating more than 100 persons as a result of the confessions obtained from the men under indictment (see "100 Implicated in Nightrider Cases," *Arkansas Gazette*, March 16, 1915).

35. This is not to assert that lynching and racial cleansing may be understood as much the same phenomenon on account of their extreme nature. Indeed, there are numerous conceptual problems in applying the scholarship of lynching to a study of racial cleansing, though on occasion a lynching formed part of an instance of racial cleansing. See Guy Lancaster, "Review of *White Man's Heaven: The Lynching and Expulsion of Blacks in the Southern Ozarks, 1894–1909*," *Arkansas Review: A Journal of Delta Studies* 42 (April 2011): 62–64.

36. Vilhelm Moberg, *A History of the Swedish People*, vol. 1: *From Prehistory to Renaissance*, trans. Paul Britten Austin (Minneapolis: University of Minnesota Press, 2005), 6.

37. Story L. Matkin-Rawn, "'We Fight for the Rights of Our Race': Black Arkansans in the Era of Jim Crow" (PhD diss., University of Wisconsin–Madison, 2009), 97–98.

5. Race, History, and Memory in Harrison, Arkansas: An Ozarks Town Reckons with Its Past

1. Jacqueline Froelich and David Zimmermann, "Total Eclipse: The Destruction of the African American Community of Harrison, Arkansas, in 1905 and 1909," *Arkansas Historical Quarterly* 58 (Summer 1999): 131–59.

2. Loren Watkins, "Some History of Boone County, Arkansas," *Boone County Historian* 7, no. 1 (1984): 282.

3. *Arkansas Gazette* (Little Rock), October 6, 1905.

4. Manuscript Census Returns, *Twelfth Census of the United States*, Carroll County, Arkansas, 1900, Eureka Springs Historical Museum.

5. Froelich and Zimmermann, "Total Eclipse," 133.

6. Ralph Rea, *Boone County and Its People* (Van Buren, AR: Argus, 1955): 119, 121.

7. Froelich and Zimmermann, "Total Eclipse," 136.

8. *Arkansas Gazette*, October 7, 1905.

9. Certain Harrison property records at the Boone County Courthouse circa 1905 show red pencil marked-out names of African Americans replaced by white property owners.

10. *Carroll Progress* (Berryville, AR), October 21, 1905.

11. US Attorneys and Marshals Records of the Western District of Arkansas, Grand Jury Minutes, Harrison Division, October 1905, 78, RG 1, 18.

12. Interview, March 4, 1998, with Dr. Katherine Lederer, author of *Many*

Thousands Gone: Springfield's Lost Black History (Springfield: Southwest Missouri State University, 1986).

13. Jacqueline Froelich, "Tulsa Race Riot," National Public Radio KUAF, news feature, broadcast June 4, 1998.

14. Ibid.; Jacqueline Froelich, "Eureka Springs in Black and White: The Lost History of an African-American Neighborhood," *Arkansas Historical Quarterly* 56 (Summer 1997): 174.

15. Froelich, "Eureka Springs in Black and White," 166.

16. L. J. Kalklosch, *The Healing Fountain* (Eureka Springs, AR, 1881), 82.

17. Froelich, "Eureka Springs in Black and White," 167.

18. Ibid., 170.

19. Ibid., 171.

20. Ibid., 174.

21. Ibid.

22. Froelich and Zimmermann, "Total Eclipse," 133.

23. *Arkansas Democrat* (Little Rock), March 25, 1909.

24. Froelich and Zimmermann, "Total Eclipse," 154.

25. "Muskogee Negro Is Hanged in Arkansas," *Muskogee Times-Democrat*, March 14, 1909.

26. "Hang a Negro Man Cram Him in Box," *San Antonio Light*, March 26, 1909.

27. Froelich and Zimmermann, "Total Eclipse," 152.

28. Ibid.

29. Jacqueline Froelich's interviews with Gerald L. K. Smith historian Glen Jeansonne, May 5, 1998, Fayetteville, Arkansas; Thom Robb, January 20, 2001, Harrison, Arkansas; and Mike Hallimore, February 4, 2003, Harrison, Arkansas.

30. This sentiment has been shared with the author at numerous public-speaking settings.

31. Versions of "Total Eclipse" were also published as an *Arkansas Democrat-Gazette* feature article, August 1, 1999, and broadcast as a KUAF National Public Radio documentary, April 12, 2003.

32. George Holcomb, "Racist Image Haunts Town," *Harrison Daily Times*, January 27, 2003.

33. Jacqueline Froelich, interview for broadcast on KUAF Public Radio with Wayne Kelly, Harrison, Arkansas, April 16, 2003.

34. Ibid.

35. Ibid.

36. Jacqueline Froelich, interview with Mayor Bob Reynolds, Harrison, Arkansas, April 16, 2003.

37. Jacqueline Froelich, interview with Mike Hallimore, Harrison, Arkansas, June 21, 2003.

38. Ibid.

39. Ibid.

40. Mike Hallimore, Kingdom Identity flyer.

41. Jacqueline Froelich, interview with D. Jeff Christiansen, Harrison, Arkansas, June 21, 2003.

42. Proclamation, City of Harrison, May 1, 2003.

43. Advertisement, *Harrison Daily Times,* January 22, 2006, 8&9A.

44. Jacqueline Froelich, interview with Harrison Race Task Force members, Harrison, Arkansas, May 7, 2011.

45. George Holcomb, "Researchers Donate Summer," *Harrison Daily Times*, September 23, 2005.

46. Jacqueline Froelich, interview with Harrison Race Task Force members, Harrison, Arkansas, May 7, 2011.

47. Ibid.

48. Ibid.

49. Ibid.

50. Jacqueline Froelich, interview with Layne Ragsdale, Harrison Chamber of Commerce, Harrison, Arkansas, May 7, 2011.

51. Jacqueline Froelich, public radio broadcast, November 14, 2012, http://www.kuaf.org/content/organized-hate-groups-crumbling-arkansas.

52. Marco Williams, prod., *Banished: American Ethnic Cleansings* (Two Tone Productions, 2007).

53. Jacqueline Froelich, interviews with anonymous residents, Harrison, Arkansas, April 2, 2012.

54. Wikipedia entry: http://en.wikipedia.org/wiki/Harrison,_Arkansas (accessed March 18, 2012).

55. Jeannie Nuss, "Arkansas Town Known for Ties to KKK Tries to Rebrand," *Arkansas Democrat-Gazette*, March 27, 2012.

56. Thom Robb's Ku Klux Klan "empire" is comprised of several novelty stores and churches.

57. Bryan Hix, "Debunking a Non-racist Present; 'Do Not Speak for Me,'" *Harrison Daily Times,* April 11, 2012.

58. US Census Bureau, generated by Jacqueline Froelich, using CensusViewer, *Harrison, Arkansas Population, Census 2010*, http://censusviewer.com/city/AR/Harrison (accessed February 12, 2013).

59. Froelich and Zimmermann, "Total Eclipse," 155.

60. Smith, quoted in Rea, *Boone County and Its People*, 141.

61. Jacqueline Froelich, interview with Joyce Coker for KUAF Public Radio broadcast, August 1, 2011.

62. Jacqueline Froelich, interview with Joyce Coker for KUAF Public Radio broadcast, April 6, 2011.

63. While a flag of the Confederacy is on display, a Confederate battle flag, widely considered a symbol of hate and racism, was removed by Harrison Race Reconciliation Task Force request in 2008.

64. Jacqueline Froelich, telephone interview with Harrison Race Task Force member Carolyn Cline, Harrison, Arkansas, July 20, 2014.

6. The Twenty-One Deaths Caused by the 1959 Fire at the Arkansas Negro Boys Industrial School: An Isolated Case of "Neglect" or an Instance of Racial Violence?

1. These letters and telegrams are found in the Orval Faubus Papers, box 301, folder 12, Special Collections, University of Arkansas Libraries, Fayetteville.

2. *Arkansas Democrat* (Little Rock), March 5, 1959. Though publisher K. August Engel only rarely wrote editorials himself, his position as a board member for the agency overseeing state social welfare programs would have provided him the information and opinions contained in the editorial.

3. For a broad overview of the fire, see Grif Stockley, *Ruled by Race: Black/White Relations in Arkansas from Slavery to the Present* (Fayetteville: University of Arkansas Press, 2009), 287–96.

4. *Arkansas Gazette* (Little Rock), March 6, 1959.

5. David Y. Thomas, ed., *Arkansas and Its People: A History, 1541–1930*, vol. 2 (New York: American Historical Society, 1930); Erle Chambers, "Correctional Institutions," 1930, 503–4.

6. In 1937 the school at Wrightsville became a full-fledged prison farm for the older adolescent boys. Over thirty farm structures and houses for employees were improved or erected, including a cotton gin and barns for animals and farm.

7. Quoted in Stockley, *Ruled by Race*, 290. Eleventh Biennial Report, Arkansas Boys' Industrial School," June 30, 1940, Phillip Back Papers, Butler Center for Arkansas Studies, Little Rock, Arkansas.

8. "Hill Ousted as Superintendent of Boys School," August 22, 1945, clipping, Governor Ben Laney Scrapbook, University of Central Arkansas Archives.

9. *Arkansas State Press* (Little Rock), September 12, 1947.

10. Ed McCuistion, quoted in the Francis Cherry Papers, box 37, folder 59, "Report of Five Person Committee for Study of State Training Schools," March 26, 1952, Arkansas History Commission, Little Rock.

11. Bernice Ratliff, letter to Neva Talley, August 25, 1952, Francis Cherry Papers, box 37, folder 59, Arkansas History Commission, Little Rock.

12. Ibid.

13. Charles Bussey, letter to Gov. Francis Cherry, February 11,1953, Francis Cherry Papers, box 37, folder 59, Arkansas History Commission, Little Rock.

14. Arkansas Act 511 of 1953.

15. Gordon Morgan, "The Arkansas Negro Boys' Industrial School: A Case Study in Institutional Organization" (MA thesis, University of Arkansas, 1956), 42. A comprehensive summary of the conditions noted by Dr. Morgan, as well as similar reports of state officials and an independent inspection team, details the conditions at the school. See Stockley, *Ruled by Race*, 287–96.

16. Frank Lawrence, recorded interview with Howard Lee Nash, June 19, 2009: "Somebody would get a whipping every night. I got about five or six whippings . . . big ole strap wide as your hand . . . give you ten or fifteen licks . . . [and] if you wouldn't take it had boys hold you. . . . [S]trap tore your butt up . . . [and they] didn't give you nothing for it." The author wishes to express his appreciation to Lawrence, brother of one of the victims, for generously sharing his research about the fire.

17. Faubus, quoted in the *Arkansas Democrat*, March 5, 1959, and *Arkansas Gazette*, March 6, 1959.

18. "Final Report of the Public Institutions Committee of the Pulaski County Grand Jury," March 4, 1960, Pulaski County Circuit Clerk.

19. *Arkansas Democrat,* March 5–6, 1959; *Arkansas Gazette*, March 6–7, 1959.

20. See Grif Stockley, *Daisy Bates, Civil Rights Crusader from Arkansas* (Jackson: University Press of Mississippi, 2005), 108–9. Though Daisy Bates considered Harry

Ashmore the "most liberal" white in Little Rock in 1957, Ashmore argued passionately for preserving the "separate but equal" doctrine in his 1958 book, *Epitaph for Dixie.*

21. As far back as 1902, the widely known Helena, Arkansas, Baptist minister and black leader E. C. Morris recognized that it is racial prejudice that "gives employment to every Negro preacher, every Negro teacher, doctor, lawyer, that built all the Negro churches, and schools, started every Negro store, hotel and restaurant, every bank, every insurance company, and in act every enterprise owned and operated by the race." At the end of the century, the president of the Scipio A. Jones alumna association in North Little Rock told a reporter she "would welcome a return to separate but equal. . . . [T]hat is, if the schools for black children were truly equal." Quoted in Stockley, *Ruled by Race*, 136, 450.

22. John William Graves, in his seminal work, *Town and County Race Relations in an Urban-Rural Context, Arkansas, 1865–1905* (Fayetteville: University of Arkansas Press, 1990), follows C. Van Woodward in documenting many exceptions, especially in urban eras of the state, but in a general sense, even successful black Arkansans still faced overwhelming social barriers.

23. *Arkansas Gazette*, March 19, 1949.

24. *Encyclopedia of Religion in the South* (Macon, GA: Mercer University Press, 1984), 681.

25. Stockley, *Ruled by Race*, 1.

26. Bureau of Labor Statistics on-line calculator, http://data.bls.gov/cgi-bin/cpic (accessed July 24, 2013); Ed McCuistion, quoted in the *Arkansas Gazette*, April 5, 1949.

27. *Arkansas Gazette*, April 13, 1949.

7. Empowering Families and Communities: African American Home Demonstration Agents in Arkansas, 1913–1965

1. Mary S. Hoffschwelle, "'Better Homes on Better Farms': Domestic Reform in Rural Tennessee," *Frontiers: A Journal of Women Studies* 22 (2001): 52.

2. Stephen F. Strausberg, *A Century of Research: A Centennial History of the Arkansas Agricultural Experiment Station* (Fayetteville: Arkansas Agricultural Experiment Station, University of Arkansas, 1989), 30; Alfred Charles True, *A History of Agricultural Education in the United States, 1785–1925* (New York: Arno Press, 1969), 280–81, 365.

3. Jeannie M. Whayne, Thomas A. DeBlack, George Sabo II, and Morris S. Arnold, eds., *Arkansas: A Narrative History* (Fayetteville: University of Arkansas Press, 2002), 308.

4. Florence E. Ward, "Home Demonstration Work under the Smith-Lever Act, 1914–1924," Circular No. 43, June, 1929, US Department of Agriculture, Washington, DC; Hoffschwelle, "'Better Homes on Better Farms,'" 53.

5. Gary Zellar, "H. C. Ray and Racial Politics in the African American Extension Service Program in Arkansas, 1915–1929," *Agricultural History* 72 (Spring 1999): 431, 433; Mena Hogan, "A History of the Agricultural Extension Service in Arkansas" (MA thesis, University of Arkansas, 1940), 139; T. R. Betton, "A Brief History of Agricultural Extension Work among Negroes in Arkansas" (n.p., 1962), box 8, folder 3, 2, University of Arkansas Cooperative Extension Service Records, 1914–1988, Special Collections, University of Arkansas Libraries, Fayetteville.

6. Carmen Harris, "Grace under Pressure: The Black Home Extension Service in South Carolina 1919–1966," in *Rethinking Home Economics: Women and the History of a Profession*, ed. Sarah Stage (Ithaca, NY: Cornell University Press, 1997), 207.

7. Hogan, "A History of the Agricultural Extension Service," 155.

8. Ibid., 139.

9. Whayne et al., *Arkansas: A Narrative History*, 309.

10. Zellar, "H. C. Ray and Racial Politics," 433; Whayne et al., *Arkansas: A Narrative History*, 309; Hogan, "A History of the Agricultural Extension Service," 147.

11. "Government Extension Agents Aid Farmers," *Chicago Defender* (national edition), September 20, 1924, http://search.proquest.com/docview/492010135?accountid=8363 (accessed March 27, 2012); Strausberg, *A Century of Research*, 30.

12. Betton, "A Brief History of Agricultural Extension Work."

13. Donald Holley, *Uncle Sam's Farmers: The New Deal Communities in the Lower Mississippi Valley* (Urbana: University of Illinois Press, 1975), 134.

14. Hogan, "A History of the Agricultural Extension Service," 141.

15. Ibid., 147, 148.

16. Betton, "A Brief History of Agricultural Extension Work," 3; Whayne et al., *Arkansas: A Narrative History*, 309; Nan Woodruff, *American Congo: The African American Freedom Struggle in the Delta* (Chapel Hill: University of North Carolina Press, 2003), 146.

17. "Many Win Prizes at Arkansas State Fair," *Chicago Defender* (national edition), November 22, 1924, http://search.proquest.com/docview/492043547?accountid=8363 (accessed March 26, 2012).

18. Pete Daniel, *Deep'n as It Come: The 1927 Mississippi River Flood* (Fayetteville: University of Arkansas Press, 1996), 36, 144.

19. "Coolidge Projects Inland Waterways for Flood Control," *New York Times*, October 4, 1927, http://search.proquest.com/docview/104061122?accountid=8363 (accessed March 26, 2012); Whayne et al., *Arkansas: A Narrative History*, 314; Zellar, "H. C. Ray and Racial Politics," 441–42; Daniel, *Deep'n as It Come*, 137, 144.

20. "Movable Schools Bring Modern Farm Methods to Rural Homes," *Chicago Defender* (national edition), September 20, 1924, http://search.proquest.com/docview/492034870?accountid=8363; "Movable Schools," *New York Amsterdam News*, December 9, 1925, http://search.proquest.com/docview/226244596?accountid=8363 (accessed March 30, 2012); Betton, "A Brief History of Agricultural Extension Work," 3–4; Karen J. Ferguson, "Caught in 'No Man's Land': The Negro Cooperative Demonstration Service and the Ideology of Booker T. Washington, 1900–1918," *Agricultural History* 72 (Winter 1998): 34–37.

21. "Tells How Famous Movable School Started," *Chicago Defender* (national edition), October 12, 1940, http://search.proquest.com/docview/492590771?accountid=8363 (accessed March 30, 2012); Lynne A. Rieff, "'Go Ahead and Do All You Can': Southern Progressives and Alabama Home Demonstration Clubs, 1914–1940," in *Southern Women: Hidden Histories of Women in the New South*, ed. Virginia Bernhard, Betty Brandon, Theda Purdue, and Elizabeth Turner (Columbia: University of Missouri Press, 1994), 139; Zellar, "H. C. Ray and Racial Politics," 444; Allen W. Jones, "The Role of Tuskegee Institute in the Education of Black Farmers," *Journal of Negro History* 60 (April 1975): 262–65.

22. Zellar, "H. C. Ray and Racial Politics," 444.

23. Ibid.; Hogan, "A History of the Agricultural Extension Service in Arkansas," 149.

24. Bernice V. Shepherd, Negro Home Demonstration Agent, Narrative Report of the (Woodruff) County Home Demonstration Agent, December 1, 1943, to October 31, 1944, reel 106, Arkansas Annual Reports, 1917–1970, Record Group 33, Federal Extension Service, National Archives and Records Administration (hereafter cited as NARA) archive, Fort Worth, Texas; Ben F. Johnson III, *Arkansas in Modern America, 1930–1999* (Fayetteville: University of Arkansas Press, 2000), 34.

25. Rieff, "'Go Ahead and Do All You Can,'" 136–37; Eunice Heywood, "Home Demonstration Clubs and Council," in *The Cooperative Extension Service*, ed. H. C. Sanders (Englewood Cliffs, NJ: Prentice-Hall, 1966), 253.

26. Mrs. J. Howard Crawford, President, Arkansas Council of Home Demonstration Clubs, Arkadelphia, "Home Demonstration Work in Arkansas," *Proceedings of the Arkansas Academy of Science* 4 (1951): 183, http://libinfo.uark.edu/aas/issues/1951v4/v4a26.pdf (accessed August 21, 2012).

27. Arkansas Extension Homemakers Council, *History of Home Demonstration Work in Arkansas 1914–1965: Extension Homemaker Work, 1966–1975* (n.p., 1978), 311; "Arkansas Farmers in 16th Annual Meet," *Chicago Defender* (national edition), September 5, 1936, http://search.proquest.com/docview/492484725?accountid=8363 (accessed June 28, 2012); Elizabeth Griffin Hill, *A Splendid Piece of Work: One Hundred Years of Arkansas's Home Demonstration Extension Homemakers Clubs, 1912–2012* (Lexington, KY: CreateSpace, 2012), 260.

28. "Arkansas Farmers in 16th Annual Meet"; "Two Agricultural Employes [sic] Receive Superior Awards," *Atlanta Daily World* (1932–2003), June 9, 1956, http://search.proquest.com/docview/491087723?accountid=8363; "National Home Demonstration Agents Hold First Annual Meeting in Ark," *Chicago Daily Defender* (daily edition), November 1, 1958, http://search.proquest.com/docview/493711724?accountid=8363; and "Photo Standalone 5—no Title," *Atlanta Daily World (1932–2003)*, June 12, 1956, http://search.proquest.com/docview/491085263?accountid=8363 (all accessed April 3, 2012). Her husband, Albert C. Boone, was principal of Burdette Negro High School in Mississippi. He died in Luxora, Arkansas, in 1951. See Sadie A. Thompson, "Little Rock Pebbles," *Chicago Defender* (national edition), December 15, 1951, http://search.proquest.com/docview/492834445?accountid=8363 (accessed April 3, 2012); and "Albert C. Boone, Burdette School Principal Dies," *Blytheville Courier News* (Blytheville, AR), November 24, 1951, www.newspaperarchives.com (both accessed April 3, 2012). In 1956, Fannie Mae Boone received a superior service award from the USDA. She was the only home demonstration agent from Arkansas to receive such an honor. See "Marianna," *Arkansas State Press* (Little Rock), July 6, 1956.

29. T. M. Campbell, "Home Demonstration Work among Negroes in South Has Aided Many," *Atlanta Daily World* (1932–2003), February 6, 1935, 2, http://search.proquest.com/docview/490446815?accountid=8363 (accessed March 27, 2012); Barbara R. Cotton, *The Lamplighters: Black Farm and Home Demonstration Agents in Florida, 1915–1965* (Tallahassee, FL: United States Department of Agriculture in Cooperation with Florida Agricultural and Mechanical University, 1982), 53; Melissa Walker, *All We Knew Was to Farm: Rural Women in the Upcountry South, 1919–1941* (Baltimore, MD: The Johns Hopkins University Press, 2000), 113.

30. "Farm Conference at Fargo College," *Chicago Defender* (national edition),

April 9, 1932, http://search.proquest.com/docview/492364880?accountid=8363 (accessed June 21, 2012).

31. "Farmers Plan Meet Exhibit in Arkansas: Home Improvement Is Urged at Osceola Monthly Confab," *Chicago Defender* (national edition), December 25, 1937, http://search.proquest.com/docview/492479849?accountid=8363 (accessed June 21, 2012).

32. The home demonstration club in Dermott, for example, was founded in 1955. See "Dermott," *Arkansas State Press*, January 28, 1955.

33. "Arkansas Women Stage 'Cotton Dress' Revue," *Atlanta Daily World*, June 10, 1940, http://search.proquest.com/docview/490622494?accountid=8363 (accessed March 27, 2012). A National Better Homes Movement was initiated in 1922 and started in Arkansas in 1924. African Americans did not have a Better Homes chairperson until 1930. See Hogan, "A History of the Agricultural Extension Service in Arkansas," 227, 232.

34. "Dixie Sleeps Well, Due to U. S. Mattress Projects," *Chicago Defender* (national edition), February 21, 1942, http://search.proquest.com/docview/492573824?accountid=8363 (accessed March 27, 2012); Mildred S. Davis, Negro Home Demonstration Agent, Report of the (Monroe) County Home Demonstration Agent, December 1, 1943, to November 30, 1944, reel 104, Arkansas Annual Reports, 1917–1970, RG 33, Federal Extension Service, NARA archive, Fort Worth, Texas.

35. "Arkansas Extension Homemakers Council, History of Home Demonstration Work in Arkansas 1914–1965: Extension Homemaker Work, 1966–1975," 328.

36. "Negro Farmer Confab Slated for Arkansas," *Chicago Defender* (national edition), July 4, 1942, http://search.proquest.com/docview/492623829?accountid=8363; "Negro Farmers Part in Victory Drive to Be Thrashed Out Soon," *Atlanta Daily World*, July 6, 1942, http://search.proquest.com/docview/490682870?accountid=8363; "800 Attend AAA Meets in Arkansas," *Atlanta Daily World*, July 22, 1942, http://search.proquest.com/docview/490683664?accountid=8363 (all accessed March 27, 2012). It was also known as the "Food for Victory Campaign."

37. Ibid.; T. R. Betton, "On the Agricultural Front with the U.S. Department of Agriculture," *Arkansas State Press*, April 13, 1945.

38. Edmund deS. Brunner, *Rural America and the Extension Service* (Menasha, WI: George Banta Publishing Company, 1949), 87.

39. Jeannie M. Whayne, "The Segregated Farm Program in Poinsett County, Arkansas," *Mississippi Quarterly* 45 (1992): 436; Woodruff, *American Congo*, 146; Lena H. Eddington, Negro Home Demonstration Agent, Report of the (Poinsett) County Home Demonstration Agent, December 1, 1943, to October 11, 1944, reel 104, Arkansas Annual Reports, 1917–1970, RG 33, Federal Extension Service, NARA archive, Fort Worth, Texas.

40. Pamela Webb, "By the Sweat of the Brow: The Back-to-the-Land Movement in Depression Arkansas," *Arkansas Historical Quarterly* 42 (Winter 1983): 338; Charles Morrow Wilson, Editorial Correspondence, "Arkansas Moves to Guard Future," *New York Times*, February 15, 1931, http://search.proquest.com/docview/99135507?accountid=8363 (accessed June 20, 2012); "Arkansas Farmers Win," *Atlanta Constitution*, November 1, 1931, http://search.proquest.com/docview/501192736?accountid=8363 (accessed June 20, 2012); Earle E. Griggs, "Backbone and Spareribs," *Atlanta Constitution*, November 1, 1931, http://search.proquest.com/docview/501195863?accountid=8363 (accessed June 20, 2012); photograph of Lena H.

Eddington, *Arkansas State Press*, June 4, 1954. In 1954, Eddington was the home demonstration agent for Pulaski County.

41. Harris, "Grace under Pressure," 217; June L. Rhue, "Arkansas H-D Agent Finds Meals Balanced (2)," *Chicago Defender* (national edition), October 6, 1951, http://search.proquest.com/docview/492767001?accountid=8363 (accessed March 27, 2012); Brunner, *Rural America and the Extension Service*, 87; Johnson, *Arkansas in Modern America*, 34.

42. James H. Purdy Jr., "Farmers Win Live-at-Home County Prizes," *Chicago Defender* (national edition), December 20, 1941, http://search.proquest.com/docview/492625201?accountid=8363; "Arkansas Family Wins Inter-State Farm Award," *Chicago Defender* (national edition), December 30, 1944, http://search.proquest.com/docview/492785970?accountid=8363 (both accessed March 27, 2012).

43. "Live-at-Home Competition in 3 States," *Chicago Defender* (national edition), March 11, 1939, http://search.proquest.com/docview/492514228?accountid=8363, (accessed June 20, 2012).

44. Hoffschwelle, "'Better Homes on Better Farms,'" 53.

45. Zellar, "H. C. Ray and Racial Politics," 429, 434.

46. "Woodruff Co.," *Arkansas State Press*, February 10, 1950.

47. The cypress "knees" are the part of the tree that is above water. See "Lake Village," *Arkansas State Press*, February 2, 1955.

48. "Dermott," *Arkansas State Press*, March 2, 1955.

49. "250 Arkansas Farm Families Lift Themselves by Their Own Bootstraps," *Arkansas State Press*, July 31, 1959.

50. Sixteenth Annual Meeting of the Arkansas Negro State Home Demonstration Council, September 11–12, 1952; Twenty-Third Annual Meeting of the Arkansas Negro State Home Demonstration Council, September 2–4, 1959; Twenty-Fifth Annual Meeting of the Arkansas Negro State Home Demonstration Council, August 30–September 1961, all in box 8, folder 3, University of Arkansas Cooperative Extension Service Records, 1914–1988, Special Collections, University of Arkansas Libraries, Fayetteville.

51. Mrs. Elveria Heard, Home Demonstration Council President, to Dr. John Tyler Caldwell, President, University of Arkansas, December 19, 1956, box 8, file 3, University of Arkansas Cooperative Extension Service Records, 1914–1988, Special Collections, University of Arkansas Libraries, Fayetteville.

52. "Arkansas Town Takes a New Lease on Life," *Chicago Defender* (national edition), February 6, 1960, http://search.proquest.com/docview/493008033?accountid=8363 (accessed April 3, 2012).

53. Ibid.

54. "Faulkner County Extension News," *Arkansas State Press*, March 10, 1950; "Upchurch," *Arkansas State Press*, February 2, 1954; "Lake Village," *Arkansas State Press*, June 10, 1955.

55. Maxine E. Reeves, *The History of the National Extension of Home Economists, 1933–1975* (n.p., 1976), 5.

56. "National Negro Home Demonstration Agents Association (NNHDAA), 1957–1965," http://www.neafcs.org/content.asp?pageID=2087 (accessed April 2, 2012). Mrs. Margaret William, 2nd Vice President (El Dorado); Miss Carreather Banks, Secretary (Forrest City); Mrs. Iola Rhone, Parliamentarian (Texarkana); and Mrs. Jennie B. Wright, Chaplain (Lake Village).

57. "Study Needs of Rural Families," *Chicago Defender* (national edition), November 15, 1958, http://search.proquest.com/docview/492980171?accountid=8363 (accessed April 3, 2012).

58. See http://www.neafcs.org/content.asp?pageID=2087 (accessed April 3, 2012).

59. "Extension Titles Are Changed," *Hope Star* (Hope, AR), December 10, 1966, www.newspaperarchive.com (accessed June 21, 2012); Charline J. Warren, ed., *An Official History of National Extension Homemakers Council, Inc.: 1930–1990* (Burlington, KY: National Extension Homemakers Council, 1991), 44. In 1968, it became the Arkansas Cooperative Extension Service.

8. It Should Be More Than Just a Simple Shout: The Life of Elias Camp ("E. C.") Morris

1. National Historic Landmark Nomination, Centennial Baptist Church, Helena, Arkansas, 4.

2. E. C. Morris, *Sermons, Addresses, and Reminiscences and Important Correspondence, With a Great Picture Gallery of Eminent Ministers and Scholars* (Nashville, TN: National Baptist Publishing Board, 1901), 181.

3. Vertie L. Carter, *Dr. E. C. Morris: May 7, 1855–September 5, 1922* (Little Rock, AR: VLC Research and Biographical Technical Enterprise, 1999), 36.

4. Ibid., 10.

5. Bobby L. Lovett, "Roger Williams University," *Tennessee Encyclopedia of History and Culture* online, http://www.tennesseeencyclopedia.net/entry.php?rec=1147 (accessed July 25, 2013).

6. Carter, *Dr. E. C. Morris*, 10–11.

7. 2004 Historical Census Browser online, from the University of Virginia, Geospatial and Statistical Data Center, http://mapserver.lib.virginia.edu/collections/stats/histcensus/index.html (accessed July 25, 2013). Also see Calvin White Jr., *The Rise to Respectability: Race, Religion, and the Church of God in Christ* (Fayetteville: University of Arkansas Press, 2013), 41.

8. Carter, *Dr. E. C. Morris*, 12.

9. White, *Rise to Respectability*, 14.

10. Leon F. Litwack, *Trouble in the Mind: Black Southerners in the Age of Jim Crow* (New York: Alfred A. Knopf Publishing, 1998), 380. See also White, *Rise to Respectability*, 14.

11. Carter, *Dr. E. C. Morris*, 15, 21.

12. Morris, *Sermons, Addresses, and Reminiscences*, 17.

13. Carter, *Dr. E. C. Morris*, 51. See also White, *Rise to Respectability*, 14–15.

14. For a more detailed account see David Daniels, "The Cultural Renewal of Slave Religion: Charles Price Jones and the Emergence of the Holiness Movement in Mississippi" (PhD diss., Union Theological Seminary, 1992), 7; Evelyn Brooks Higginbotham, *Righteous Discontent: The Women's Movement in the Black Baptist Church, 1882–1920* (Cambridge, MA: Harvard University Press, 1993), 7–12; Glenda Elizabeth Gilmore, *Gender and Jim Crow: Women and the Politics of White Supremacy in North Carolina, 1896–1920* (Chapel Hill: University of North Carolina Press, 1996); and Paul Harvey, *Redeeming the South, Religious Culture and Racial Identities among Southern Baptists, 1865–1925* (Chapel Hill: University of North Carolina Press, 1997), 111.

15. Morris, *Sermons, Addresses, and Reminiscences*, 32; Daniels, "The Cultural

Renewal of Slave Religion," 178–79; John Giggie, *After Redemption: Jim Crow and the Transformation of African American Religion in the Delta, 1875–1915* (New York: Oxford University Press, 2007), 176; White, *Rise to Respectability*, 19.

16. Morris, *Sermons, Addresses, and Reminiscences*, 17.

17. Ibid., 33.

18. For more information on Mason, Jones, and the fight between the progressives and the conservers, see Daniels, "The Cultural Renewal of Slave Religion"; White, *Rise to Respectability*; and Giggie, *After Redemption*.

19. Morris, *Sermons, Addresses, and Reminiscences*, 80–81.

20. Ibid., 56–61; Carter, *Dr. E. C. Morris*, 22.

21. Morris, *Sermons, Addresses, and Reminiscences*, 56–61

22. John Hope Franklin, *From Slavery to Freedom: A History of African Americans* (New York: McGraw Hill Publishers, 2000), 311–13. For more information on the National Negro Business League, see David H. Jackson, *Booker T. Washington and the Struggle against White Supremacy: The Southern Educational Tours, 908–1912* (New York: Palgrave Macmillan, 2008).

23. White, *Rise to Respectability*.

24. Carter, *Dr. E. C. Morris*, 17.

25. Ibid., 28.

26. Abner, quoted in Morris, *Sermons, Addresses, and Reminiscences*, 182.

27. Carter, *Dr. E. C. Morris*, 28.

28. Franklin, *From Slavery to Freedom*, 383–85.

29. "Six More Are Killed in Arkansas Riots," *New York Times*, October 3, 1919. For more on the Elaine race riots, see Grif Stockley Jr., *Blood in Their Eyes: The Elaine Race Massacre of 1919* (Fayetteville: University of Arkansas, 2001); and Robert Whitaker, *On the Laps of Gods: The Red Summer of 1919 and the Struggle for Justice that Remade a Nation* (New York: Crown, 2008).

30. "Six More Are Killed in Arkansas Riots."

31. Ibid.

32. Morris, *Sermons, Addresses, and Reminiscences*, 81.

33. Ibid.

34. Richard C. Cortner, *A Mob Intent on Death: The NAACP and the Arkansas Riot Cases* (Middletown, CT: Wesleyan University Press, 1988).

35. Carter, *Dr. E. C. Morris*, 42.

9. Civil Rights Inactivism: Richard Nathaniel Hogan and the "Enemies of Righteousness"

1. Jacquelyn Dowd Hall, "The Long Civil Rights Movement and the Political Uses of the Past," *Journal of American History* 91 (March 2005): 1233–63.

2. Peter C. Murray, *Methodists and the Crucible of Race, 1930–1975* (Columbia: University of Missouri Press, 2004), xiv; and Paul Harvey, *Redeeming the South: Religious Cultures and Racial Identities among Southern Baptists, 1865–1925* (Chapel Hill: University of North Carolina Press, 1997), 73.

3. David Edwin Harrell Jr., "The Sectional Origins of the Churches of Christ," *Journal of Southern History* 30 (August 1964): 277. Recent histories of the denomination include Richard T. Hughes, *Reviving the Ancient Faith: The Story of Churches of Christ in America* (Grand Rapids, MI: William B. Eerdmans Publishing Company,

1996); and David Edwin Harrell Jr., *The Churches of Christ in the 20th Century: Homer Hailey's Personal Journey of Faith* (Tuscaloosa: University of Alabama Press, 2000).

4. R. Vernon Boyd, *Undying Dedication: The Story of G.P. Bowser* (Nashville, TN: Gospel Advocate Company, 1985), 15–42.

5. Ibid., 64–67. The phrase "spiritual and financial paternalism" appears in David Edwin Harrell Jr., *White Sects and Black Men in the Recent South* (Nashville, TN: Vanderbilt University Press, 1971), 43–44.

6. G.P. Bowser, special insert, *Christian Echo* 38 (August 20, 1943): 6; Letter from Sister Rosa Turner, *Christian Echo* 36 (November 5, 1941): 4; Letter from G.P. Bowser, *Christian Echo* 42 (September 5, 1947): 6.

7. "A Working Group in Oklahoma City," *Christian Echo* 35 (August 5, 1940): 7; Letter from Sister Reuben H. Harrison, *Christian Echo* 35 (August 20, 1940): 5.

8. Marshall Keeble, "Report of Work," *Gospel Advocate* 71 (January 10, 1929): 48, quoted in Edward J. Robinson, ed., *A Godsend to His People: The Essential Writings and Speeches of Marshall Keeble* (Knoxville: University of Tennessee Press, 2008), 23; M. Keeble to B.C. Goodpasture, July 28, 1931, box 5, folder "Correspondence, Marshall Keeble, 1930–37," B.C. Goodpasture Papers, Disciples of Christ Historical Society, Nashville, Tennessee.

9. Hughes, *Reviving the Ancient Faith*, 184; Foy E. Wallace, "Negro Meetings for White People," *Bible Banner* 3 (March 1941): 7. Available online at http://www.bible.acu.edu/crs/ItemDetail.asp?Bookmark=1606 (accessed September 14, 2012).

10. Wallace, "Negro Meetings for White People," 7.

11. Edward J. Robinson, *Show Us How You Do It: Marshall Keeble and the Rise of Black Churches of Christ in the United States, 1914–1968* (Tuscaloosa: University of Alabama Press, 2008), 96; R. N. Hogan to James L. Lovell, April 18, 1941, box 15, folder "Historical (Church)," James Lovell Papers, Center for Restoration Studies, Abilene Christian University, Abilene, Texas. Available online at http://www.bible.acu.edu/crs/ItemDetail.asp? Bookmark=1597 (accessed September 14, 2012).

12. The phrase "racial interchange" is first employed in a similar sense in Paul Harvey, *Freedom's Coming: Religious Culture and the Shaping of the South from the Civil War through the Civil Rights Era* (Chapel Hill: University of North Carolina Press, 2005), 3.

13. Ira Y. Rice Jr., "Dear Brethren," *Singapore-Far East Newsletter* (June 28, 1960): 1–2; Mt. Sequoyah Encampment flier [July 11–19, 1953], series 6, box 5, folder 6, Center Street Church of Christ Records, 1897–1986, Special Collections, University of Arkansas Libraries, Fayetteville.

14. *Brown v. Board of Education of Topeka*, Kansas, 347 US 483, 74 S. Ct. 686, 98 L. Ed. 873 (1954); Boyd, *Undying Dedication*, 100; R. N. Hogan, "My Personal Observations," *Christian Echo* 50 (May 1954): 2.

15. Hughes, *Reviving the Ancient Faith*, 284; G.P. Holt, "Stand Up and Be Counted," *Christian Echo* 55 (October 1960): 1, 4.

16. On the legal origins of the civil rights movement see Richard Kluger, *Simple Justice: The History of* Brown v. Board of Education *and Black America's Struggle for Equality* (New York: Alfred A. Knopf, 1976); and Michael Klarman, *From Jim Crow to Civil Rights: The Supreme Court and the Struggle for Racial Equality* (New York: Oxford University Press, 2004).

17. Boyd, *Undying Dedication*, 91–102.

18. R. N. Hogan, "The Sin of Being a Respecter of Persons," *Christian Echo* 54 (June 1959): 2, 5.

19. R. N. Hogan, "Enemies of Righteousness," *Christian Echo* 54 (August 1959): 2. Acts 13:9–12 (KJV) states, "Then Saul, (who also is called Paul) filled with the Holy Ghost, set his eyes on him. And said, O full of all subtlety and all mischief, thou child of the devil, thou enemy of all righteousness, wilt thou not cease to pervert the right ways of the Lord? And now, behold, the hand of the Lord is upon thee, and thou shalt be blind, not seeing the sun for a season. And immediately there fell on him a mist and a darkness; and he went about seeking some to lead him by the hand. Then the deputy, when he saw what was done, believed, being astonished at the doctrine of the Lord."

20. Cannon's reply apparently appeared in the December 1959 issue of the *Christian Echo*, but there are no extant copies of this issue.

21. R. N. Hogan, "Brother C.A. Cannon of Saratoga, Ark., Replies to My Article on Segregation in the Lord's Church?," *Christian Echo* 55 (January 1960): 2–4.

22. "Race Prejudice," *Christian Echo* 55 (April 1960): 2; R. N. Hogan, "Brother David Lipscomb Stood with God on Race Prejudice in the Church of Christ," *Christian Echo* 55 (June 1960): 2–3; Roosevelt Word, "What Kind of Love Does a True and Faithful Soldier Have for Christ?," *Christian Echo* 55 (June 1960): 2–4.

23. R. N. Hogan, "My Personal Observations: Is It the Law or Down-Right Prejudice?," *Christian Echo* 58 (June 1963): 3.

24. Norman Adamson, interview by author, April 27, 2007, Nashville, Arkansas; Norman Adamson, "Reflections . . . On Selma and Montgomery," *Christian Echo* 60 (June 1965): 1–2. Harding College admitted its first black students in 1963.

10. The Bracero Program: Mexican Workers in the Arkansas Delta, 1948–1964

1. This chapter is based primarily on archival research at the Secretariat of Foreign Relations in Mexico City and at Arkansas State University in Jonesboro, Arkansas. Full and complete citations of all archival sources can be found in chapter 3 of Julie M. Weise, "Fighting for Their Place: Mexicans and Mexican Americans in the U.S. South, 1910–2008" (PhD diss., Yale University, 2009); and Julie M. Weise, chapter 3 of *Corazón de Dixie: Mexico and Mexicans in the U.S. South since 1910* (Chapel Hill: University of North Carolina Press, 2015). Published sources and publicly available oral history interviews are cited again here. Parts of this chapter were previously published in Steve Striffler and Julie M. Weise, "Arkansas," in *Latino America: A State-by-State Encyclopedia*, ed. Mark Overmyer-Velázquez (Westport, CT: Greenwood Press, 2008); and Julie M. Weise, "Braceros and Jim Crow in Arkansas," in *Que Fronteras? Mexican Braceros and a Re-examination of the Legacy of Migration*, ed. Paul López (Dubuque, IA: Kendall Hunt, 2010).

2. Wayne Allison Grove, "The Economics of Cotton Harvest Mechanization in the United States, 1920–1970" (PhD diss., University of Illinois, 2000). Grove estimates that 251,298 braceros picked cotton in Arkansas between 1953 and 1964. Grove's findings confirm my own estimates from other sources, showing that about 20,000 braceros came into Arkansas annually once the program had ramped up.

3. *Brown v. Board of Education of Topeka,* Kansas, 347 US 483, 74 S. Ct. 686, 98 L. Ed. 873 (1954).

4. Interview with Joe Garcia by John "Pat" Snodgrass, March 29, 2000, the Arkansas Delta in transition, Oral History Collection, Arkansas State University.

5. Mary K. Vaughan, *Cultural Politics in Revolution: Teachers, Peasants, and Schools in Mexico, 1930–1940* (Tucson: University of Arizona Press, 1997).

6. Ana Elizabeth Rosas, "Flexible Families: Bracero Families' Lives across Cultures, Communities, and Countries, 1942–1964" (PhD diss., University of Southern California, 2006).

7. Howard Kester, *Revolt among the Sharecroppers* (New York: Covici Friede Publishers, 1936); Nan Elizabeth Woodruff, *American Congo: The African American Freedom Struggle in the Delta* (Chapel Hill: University of North Carolina Press, 2012).

8. Deborah Cohen, "Caught in the Middle: The Mexican State's Relationship with the United States and Its Own Citizen-Workers, 1942–1954," *Journal of American Ethnic History* 20 (2001).

9. Mae M. Ngai, *Impossible Subjects: Illegal Aliens and the Making of Modern America* (Princeton, NJ: Princeton University Press, 2004). 146.

10. Gamboa observes a similar phenomenon in the case of the Pacific Northwest. Erasmo Gamboa, *Mexican Labor and World War II: Braceros in the Pacific Northwest, 1942–1947* (Austin: University of Texas Press, 1990).

11. Interview with Bernard Lipsey by the author, Memphis, Tennessee, September 22, 2008, Smithsonian Bracero History Project, http://braceroarchive.org (hereafter cited as BHP).

12. Interview with Harrison Locke and Nicole Smith-Neal, Fargo, Arkansas, September 24, 2008, both by the author, BHP.

13. Interview with John Collier by Mireya Loza, September 25, 2008, BHP.

11. A Tenuous Welcome for Latinas/os and Asians: States' Rights Discourse in Late Twentieth-Century Arkansas

1. John Lyon, "Hispanics Have Yet to Make Inroads in Arkansas Politics," *Arkansas News,* January 22, 2012, http://arkansasnews.com/2012/01/22/hispanics-have-yet-to-make-inroads-in-arkansas-politics/ (accessed July 26, 2013).

2. "Univision Insights: Hispanics Show Double Digit Growth in Maryland, Arkansas, Iowa, Indiana and Vermont According to 2010 Census Data," Univision Communications, Inc., February 11, 2011.

3. Lyon, "Hispanics Have Yet to Make Inroads."

4. See, for example, Perla M. Guerrero, "Impacting Arkansas: Vietnamese and Cuban Refugees and Latina/o Immigrants, 1975–2005" (PhD diss., University of Southern California, 2010).

5. David Pryor to Larry J. Cornish, May 13, 1975, box 67, folder 30, "Vietnamese Refugee Program—Unfavorable," David Hampton Pryor Papers, Special Collections Department, University of Arkansas Libraries, Fayetteville, Arkansas (hereafter cited as DHPP).

6. B. E. Aguirre, "Cuban Mass Migration and the Social Construction of Deviants," *Bulletin of Latin American Research* 13, no. 2 (1994): 172.

7. Bill Clinton, letter to Steve Clark, June 17, 1980, box 1, folder "Fort Chaffee Misc.–Freddie 1 of 2," Bill Clinton State Government Project, Unprocessed Papers,

William J. Clinton Presidential Library & Museum, Little Rock, Arkansas (hereafter cited as BCSGP).

8. "Summary of Inquiry of Attorney General Steve Clark," August 27, 1980, box 2, folder 8, "Cuban Refugees/Fort Chaffee–File 19," 1, August 27, 1980, BCSGP.

9. The proposition required people to produce citizenship documents when voting or receiving government and social services and threatened government employers with misdemeanor charges if they provided services to undocumented people.

10. Laura Kellams, "Arizona Alien Law Fuels State Lobbyists," *Arkansas Democrat-Gazette* (Little Rock), January 22, 2005.

11. Laura Kellams, "Senators Research U.S. Law on Aliens," *Arkansas Democrat-Gazette*, January 27, 2005, sec. A.

12. Vicky L. Ruiz, "Nuestra América: Latino History as United States History," *Journal of American History* 93 (2006): 655–72.

13. "Plan Reported to Use Chaffee," *Arkansas Gazette*, April 25, 1975.

14. "Fort Chaffee Just One Possibility as Refugee Camp, Pentagon Says," *Arkansas Gazette*, April 26, 1975.

15. Roy Bode, "Use of Fort Chaffee Confirmed," *Arkansas Gazette*, April 29, 1975.

16. "State Lawmakers Accept Proposal with Qualms," *Arkansas Gazette*, April 29, 1975.

17. "Lawmakers Told Refugees' Impact Will Be Minimal," *Arkansas Gazette*, April 30, 1975.

18. "State Lawmakers Accept Proposal with Qualms"; "Lawmakers Told Refugees' Impact Will Be Minimal"; "Opponents Cite Clause on Troop Use," *Arkansas Gazette*, May 2, 1975.

19. "Lawmakers Told Refugees' Impact Will Be Minimal."

20. Mike Trimble, "Last, Sad Effort Gets Underway in First Welcome," *Arkansas Gazette*, May 3, 1975.

21. Peggy Robertson, "Governor Greets First 71 Refugees," *Arkansas Gazette*, May 3, 1975.

22. "Arkansas: A Temporary Home," *Arkansas Gazette*, May 3, 1975.

23. Trimble, "Last, Sad Effort Gets Underway."

24. The Fort Smith Police Department identified the man as a "professional protester from Hot Springs," a city two hours southeast of Fort Smith; Robertson, "Governor Greets First 71 Refugees."

25. Trimble, "Last, Sad Effort Gets Underway."

26. "Residents Near Chaffee Divided in Reaction to Influx of Vietnamese," *Arkansas Gazette*, May 1, 1975.

27. Ibid.

28. Ibid. The article does not cite which town's mayor made the statement.

29. "Chaffee to Provide Transitory Housing, Bumpers, Pryor Say," *Arkansas Gazette*, April 30, 1975.

30. David Pryor to Larry J. Cornish, May 13, 1975, box 67, folder 30, "Vietnamese Refugee Program—Unfavorable," DHPP.

31. "Officials Uncertain about Raising Limits at Fort Chaffee," *Arkansas Gazette*, May 12, 1975; "Population at Chaffee to Increase," *Arkansas Gazette*, June 19, 1975.

32. "Exhibit A: Refugees Resettled into Society as of December 20, 1975," in a proposal from Reverend Tom Adkinson, associate minister at Lakeside United

Methodist Church, Pine Bluff, February 26, 1976, box 92, folder 19, "Vietnamese/English Education Proposal, 1976," DHPP.

33. Brian Hufker and Gray Cavender, "From Freedom Floatilla to America's Burden: The Social Construction of the Mariel Immigrants," *Sociological Quarterly* 31 (1990): 321–35; John Borneman, "Emigres as Bullets/Immigration as Penetration Perceptions of the Marielitos," *Journal of Popular Culture* 20, no. 3 (1986): 73–92; Susana Peña, "'Obvious Gays' and the State Gaze: Cuban Gay Visibility and U.S. Immigration Policy during the 1980 Mariel Boatlift," *Journal of the History of Sexuality* 16, (2007): 482–514.

34. Silvia Pedraza, "Cuba's Refugees: Manifold Migrations," *Cuba in Transition (ASCE)* 5 (1995): 319.

35. "Problem Population—Gays," *Chaffee—Resettlement, Consolidation*, December 3, 1980, box 2, folder 7, "C/HTF: Office Papers, Nov. 25, 1980–July 29, 1981," 58, Alina Fernandez Papers, Special Collections Department, University of Arkansas Libraries, Fayetteville (hereafter cited as AFP); Wilford J. Forbush, Director, Cuban/Haitian Task Force, "Fort Chaffee Resettlement Plan," Memorandum to Jack Svahn, March 10, 1981, box 1, folder 5, "C/HTF: March 3, 1981–March 31, 1981," 4, AFP; Warren Brown, "Cuban Boatlift Drew Thousands of Homosexuals," *Washington Post*, July 7, 1980; Bob Plunkett, "What Went Wrong at Fort Chaffee: Behind the Cuban Refugee Crisis," *Arkansas Times* (Little Rock), September 1980, 39.

36. Frederick M. Bohen, Director of the Cuban-Haitian Task Force, "Monthly Entrant Report for November," Memorandum to Eugene Eidenberg, December 11, 1980, box 1, folder 2, "C/HTF, Nov 6, 1980-Dec 17, 1980," 13, AFP.

37. Gastón Fernández, "The Freedom Flotilla: A Legitimate Crisis of Cuban Socialism?," *Journal of Interamerican Studies and World Affairs* 24 (1982): 189. Fernández interviewed 225 Cubans, or 1.5 percent of Fort Chaffee's population, with even distribution across 150 barracks.

38. Plunkett, "What Went Wrong at Fort Chaffee," 34–39.

39. Felix Roberto Masud-Piloto, *From Welcomed Exiles to Illegal Immigrants: Cuban Migration to the U.S., 1959–1995* (Lanham, MD: Rowman & Littlefield, 1996).

40. "Better Security for Camp Asked as Refugees Flee," *New York Times*, May 28, 1980.

41. Plunkett, "What Went Wrong at Fort Chaffee," 42–43.

42. Ibid., 34.

43. Ibid., 44.

44. Bill Clinton, quoted in ibid., 44–45.

45. "Chaffee" Timeline memorandum from Bob Lyford and Freddie Nixon to Rob Wiley, October 14, 1980, box 2, folder 2, "Cuban Refugees/Fort Chaffee—Memos & Notes," BCSGP; and "Security at Fort Chaffee for Consolidation," Memorandum from Robert Lyford to Bill Clinton, August 8, 1980, box 2, folder 1, "Cuban Refugees/Fort Chaffee—Memos and Notes," BCSGP.

46. Christian R. Holmes, quoted in Bill Clinton's letter to Steve Clark, September 19, 1980, box 2, folder 9, "Cuban Refugees/Fort Chaffee—File 18," 1, BCSGP.

47. Steve Clark, quoted in the *Lonoke Democrat* and reprinted in "Steve Clark's Opinion on Security at Fort Chaffee," *Arkansas Gazette*, October 20, 1980.

48. Clinton's letter to Clark, September 19, 1980, 2.

49. Ibid.

50. Ibid., 4.

51. "Appendix O: Guidance for State and Local Law Enforcement Agencies," *Joint Security Plan for the Cuban Entrants Processing Center Resettlement Operation,* September 5, 1980, Department of Justice and Department of Defense, box 2, folder 12, "Cuban Refugees/Fort Chaffee–File 15," BCSGP.

52. "Two Decades Later, Mariel Boat Lift Refugees Still Feel Effects of Riot," *Los Angeles Times,* May 5, 2001.

53. The migration also included working-class, native-born Latinas/os, but more research needs to be conducted to determine accurate numbers.

54. Steve Striffler, *Chicken: The Dangerous Transformation of America's Favorite Food* (New Haven, CT: Yale University Press, 2005), 95.

55. Joel Kirkland, "Hispanics Were Issue in Rogers," *Arkansas Democrat-Gazette,* November 6, 1998; Dick Kirschten, "A Melting Pot Chills in Arkansas," *National Journal* 30 (1998): 27–28.

56. "Illegal Immigration a Priority in 3rd District, Hopefuls Say," *Arkansas Democrat-Gazette,* July 27, 2001.

57. Doug Thompson, "Immigration Pushed to Forefront," *Arkansas Democrat-Gazette,* August 5, 2001.

58. Laura Kellams, "Boozman Joins Caucus to Reform Immigration," *Arkansas Democrat-Gazette,* February 11, 2002.

59. Laura Kellams, "Arizona Alien Law Fuels State Lobbyists," *Arkansas Democrat-Gazette,* January 22, 2005.

60. Laura Kellams, "Senators Research U.S. Law on Aliens," *Arkansas Democrat-Gazette,* January 27, 2005.

61. Jake Bleed, "Bill Would Let State Police Enforce Immigration," *Arkansas Democrat-Gazette,* February 5, 2005; quote from US Immigration and Customs Enforcement, "Delegation of Immigration Authority Section 287(g) Immigration and Nationality Act," October 28, 2009, http://www.ice.gov/pi/news/factsheets/section287_g.htm (accessed July 26, 2013).

62. "Delegation of Immigration Authority Section 287(g)." As of late October 2009, Georgia, North Carolina, South Carolina, Tennessee, and Virginia each had two to nine law enforcement agencies participating in the program.

12. Soy el Jefe: How Hispanic Entrepreneurs Are Changing the Economic Landscape of Northeast Arkansas

1. Luis Flores, interview by author, July 19, 2009, Jonesboro, Arkansas.

2. Karin Hill, "Jonesboro Tops 67K in Census," *Jonesboro Sun Online,* http://www.jonesborosun.com/archivedstory.php?ID=46126&Search=census (accessed March 2, 2011).

3. "Another ASU Record: Spring Enrollment Numbers Set Mark for Jonesboro Campus," *Jonesboro Sun Online,* http://www.jonesborosun.com/archivedstory.php?ID=45983&Search=asu (accessed March 2, 2011).

4. Jonesboro is home to three school districts that serve residents within the metropolitan area. Those three districts are Jonesboro Public Schools, Nettleton Public Schools, and the Valley View School District.

5. Anthony Childress, "JSD Moving Forward," *Jonesboro Sun Online*, http://www.jonesborosun.com/archivedstory.php?ID=46107&Search=jsd (accessed March 2, 2011).

6. Anthony Childress, "Nettleton Board Backs Increase in Property Tax," *Jonesboro Sun Online*, http://www.jonesborosun.com/archivedstory.php?ID=46208&Search=education (accessed March 2, 2011). Nettleton proposes to use the funds to build new classrooms and improve technology for faculty and students; see Sherry F. Pruitt, "Valley View looks at March 8 Vote," *Jonesboro Sun Online*, http://www.jonesborosun.com/archivedstory.php?ID=46106&Search=education (accessed March 2, 2011). Valley View wants to use the money to build a $21 million high school to alleviate overcrowding.

7. "Another ASU record."

8. Anthony Childress, "Around the World in Just One Day," *Jonesboro Sun Online,* http://www.jonesborosun.com/archived_story.php?ID=46131 (accessed March 2, 2011).

9. Jeffrey Passel, D'vera Cohn, and Mark Hugo Lopez, "Hispanics Account for More than Half of the Nation's Growth in the Past Decade," March 24, 2011, Pew Hispanic Center, http://www.pewhispanic.org/2011/03/24/hispanics-account-for-more-than-half-of-nations-growth-in-past-decade/ (accessed February 21, 2012).

10. "U.S. Census Bureau American Fact Finder: Race and Hispanic or Latino: 2010—County Subdivision and Place," http://factfinder2.census.gov/faces/tablesevices/jsf/pages/productview.xhtml?pid=DEC_10_PL_GCTPL1.CY10&prodType=table (accessed February 12, 2011).

11. "Profile of General Demographic Characteristics: 2000. Geographic Area: Jonesboro City, Arkansas," http://censtats.census.gov/data/AR/1600535710.pdf (accessed March 2, 2011). The 2000 US Census listed Jonesboro's Hispanic population as 1,297.

12. Flores interview.

13. The Bracero Program grew out of labor shortages in the United States during World War II and the Korean War. Agreements between the United States and Mexico allowed Mexicans to work during short-term stays in the United States. Beginning in 1942, the *braceros* provided labor, mostly for farmers, until the program's end in 1964. For more information about the braceros, visit the Bracero History Archive at http://braceroarchive.org/about.

14. "2 Counties Hispanic Population Skyrockets," *Arkansas Democrat-Gazette* (Little Rock), February 15, 2011.

15. "State's Hot Spot Draw[s] Hispanics: Ethnic Group Grows 12 Times Faster Than Arkansas Population as a Whole," *Arkansas Democrat-Gazette*, August 4, 2006.

16. Pew Hispanic Center, "Demographic Profile of Hispanics in Arkansas, 2009," http://www.pewhispanic.org/states/state/ar/ (accessed March 7, 2012).

17. Luis Madera, interview by author, January 5, 2012, Jonesboro, Arkansas.

18. Madera interview.

19. Melvin Delgado, "Role of Latina-Owned Beauty Parlors in a Latino Community," *Social Work* 42 (September 1997): 447.

20. Thierry Volery, "Ethnic Entrepreneurship: A Theoretical Framework," in *Handbook of Research on Ethnic Minority Entrepreneurship: A Co-evolutionary view on Resource Management*, ed. Léo-Paul Dana (Edward Elgar Publishing, 2007), 37–38.

21. Delgado, "Role of Latina-Owned Beauty Parlors," 448.

22. Ibid.

23. Fred Pearson, interview by author, June 21, 2010, Jonesboro, Arkansas.

24. Larry McElvoy, interview by author, July 10, 2009, Jonesboro, Arkansas.

25. Henry Torres, interview by author, June 2, 2009, Jonesboro, Arkansas.

26. Hispanic Community Services, Incorporated, http://jhcsi.org/english/services/ (accessed February 21, 2012).

27. Mayor Harold Perrin, interview by author, August 7, 2009, Jonesboro, Arkansas.

28. M. Angeles Villarreal, *U.S.-Mexico Economic Relations: Trends, Issues, and Implications* (Congressional Research Service, January 25, 2012), 9, http://fpc.state.gov/documents/organization/183740.pdf (accessed January 25, 2012).

29. Sherry F. Pruitt, "Bakery Offers Hispanic Taste," *Jonesboro Sun*, January 22, 2009, http://www.jonesborosun.com/archivedstory.php?ID=36566&Search=HISPANIC (accessed April 24, 2009).

30. Flores interview.

31. Madera interview.

32. Andres Acosta, interview by author, January 5, 2012, Jonesboro, Arkansas.

33. The Hispanic Community Services, Incorporated, is a nonprofit organization located in Jonesboro and provides many educational, legal, social, and cultural services to the Hispanic community. For more information about the Hispanic Community Services, Inc., visit http://jhcsi.org/english/.

34. Torres interview.

35. Alejandro Lorenzana, interview by author, February 17, 2011, Jonesboro, Arkansas.

36. Ibid.

37. Madera interview.

38. The Business Expo is an annual event sponsored by the Greater Jonesboro Chamber of Commerce where regional profit and nonprofit organizations promote their goods and services. Like most chamber events, the Business Expo provides these organizations a public venue to network with other business and community leaders.

39. Lorenzana interview.

40. Greg Keidan, "Latino Outreach Strategies for Civic Engagement," *National Civic Review* (DOI: 10.1002/ncr.23) (Winter 2008).

CONTRIBUTORS

MELANY BOWMAN, PhD, lived in Costa Rica, Chile, and Colombia for the first twelve years of her life, where she learned Spanish and English simultaneously. Prior to working at Arkansas State University as a Spanish instructor, she taught Spanish for eight years at a private school in the area. She is also active within the Hispanic community in Jonesboro through volunteering and by previously serving as a board member with the Hispanic Community Services Center, Incorporated. Her research interests include the assimilation of Hispanics in Jonesboro and the growth of the Hispanic population in Jonesboro.

JACQUELINE FROELICH is a senior news producer with KUAF National Public Radio in Fayetteville, Arkansas, as well as a correspondent for National Public Radio in Washington, D.C. Her work is broadcast locally on KUAF's daily news hour's "Ozarks at Large," as well as on sister public radio stations across Arkansas. With support from the Arkansas Humanities Council, in 2000 she produced a two-hour public radio documentary titled "Arkansas Ozarks African Americans," the first comprehensive black history of the Arkansas Ozarks. She has also written and published articles on the subject for the *Arkansas Historical Quarterly* and the *Arkansas Democrat-Gazette* newspaper.

PERLA M. GUERRERO is an assistant professor in the Department of American Studies and in the US Latina/o Studies Program at the University of Maryland, College Park. She received her PhD in American studies and ethnicity from the University of Southern California in 2010. Her research and teaching interests lie in comparative race and ethnicity, immigration, space and place, labor, and twentieth-century US history. As an interdisciplinary scholar, her work is informed by historical methods and human geography as they pertain to Latina/o studies, American studies, and the US South. She has been a Latino Smithsonian Postdoctoral Fellow as well as a Goldman Sachs Junior Fellow at the National Museum of American History. She is currently working on her book manuscript, "Latinas/os and Asians Remaking Arkansas: Race, Labor, Place, and Community," which explores how regional history and labor shaped social relations.

KELLY HOUSTON JONES received her BA in history at the University of Arkansas at Little Rock in 2006 and her MA in history at the University of North Texas in 2008. She is currently a PhD candidate at the University of Arkansas, Fayetteville, working on her dissertation, "The Peculiar Institution on the Periphery: Slavery in Arkansas," under the direction of Jeannie Whayne. Her research has been supported by the Diane D. Blair Center for the Study of Southern Politics and Culture at the University of Arkansas, Fayetteville, and the Southern Historical Collection of the University of North Carolina, Chapel Hill.

CHERISSE JONES-BRANCH is associate professor of history at Arkansas State University, Jonesboro, where she teaches courses in US, civil rights, women's, and African American history. She is the author of chapters in *Throwing of the Cloak of Privilege: White Southern Women Activists in the Civil Rights Era*; *Tennessee Women: Their Lives and Times, Volume I*; and *South Carolina Women: Their Lives and Times, Volume III*. Her book *Crossing the Line: Women's Interracial Activism in South Carolina during and after World War II* was recently published, and she is coeditor of the forthcoming *Arkansas Women: Their Lives and Times*.

BARCLAY KEY holds degrees in history and religion from the University of Florida, David Lipscomb University, and the University of North Alabama. He joined the History Department at the University of Arkansas at Little Rock in 2011 as an assistant professor and is currently working on a book about race relations in Churches of Christ.

JOHN A. KIRK is the George W. Donaghey Distinguished Professor of History and department chair at the University of Arkansas at Little Rock. He is author, editor, or coeditor of eight books, including the award-winning *Redefining the Color Line: Black Activism in Little Rock, Arkansas, 1940–1970* and *Martin Luther King, Jr. and the Civil Rights Movement*.

GUY LANCASTER holds a PhD in heritage studies from Arkansas State University and serves as the editor of the online *Encyclopedia of Arkansas History & Culture*, a project of the Butler Center for Arkansas Studies at the Central Arkansas Library System. He is the author of *Racial Cleaning in Arkansas, 1883–1924: Politics, Land, Labor, and Criminality* and has published articles on racial violence in the *Arkansas Historical Quarterly*, *Canadian Journal of History*, *Arkansas Review: A Journal of Delta Studies*, and the *Journal of the Fort Smith Historical Society*, as well as a number of book reviews and encyclopedia articles.

STORY MATKIN-RAWN is an assistant professor of history at the University of Central Arkansas (UCA) and coordinator of UCA's Southern and Arkansas Studies program. She received her PhD in history from the University of Wisconsin–Madison in 2009. Her current work focuses on African American migration to the western South after the Civil War. Her article "'The Great Negro State of the Country': Arkansas's Reconstruction and the Other Great Migration," won the Arkansas Historical Association's Violet B. Gingles Prize for outstanding research manuscript in Arkansas history. She is also at work on a book manuscript titled "We Fight for the Rights of Our Race: Black Arkansan Activism in the Era of Jim Crow." This project traces black Arkansan organizing from the end of Reconstruction to the eve of World War II.

CARL H. MONEYHON is a professor of history at the University of Arkansas at Little Rock, where he has been on the faculty since 1974. He is a specialist in the history of the Civil War and Reconstruction eras. He has published numerous books, including *Arkansas and the New South, 1874–1929* and *The Impact of the Civil War and Reconstruction on Arkansas, 1850–1874: Persistence in the Midst of Ruin*. His articles include "From Slave to Free Labor: The Federal Plantation Experiment in Arkansas" and "Black Politics in Arkansas during the Gilded Age, 1875–1900," both in the *Arkansas Historical Quarterly*.

GRIF STOCKLEY is a graduate of Southwestern University at Memphis and the University of Arkansas, Fayetteville, Law School. He has twice won the Arkansas Historical Association's J. G. Ragsdale Book Award for *Ruled by Race: Black/White Relations in Arkansas from Slavery* to the Present and *Daisy Bates: Civil Rights Crusader from Arkansas*. He is also author of *Blood in Their Eyes: The Elaine Massacres of 1919*. In 2012, he received a lifetime achievement award from the Arkansas Historical Association.

JULIE M. WEISE is an assistant professor of history at the University of Oregon. Trained in both US and Latin American history, she received her PhD from Yale in 2009, where her dissertation won the George Washington Egleston Historical Prize. Research for her first book, *Corazon de Dixie: Mexico and Mexicans in the U.S. South since 1910*, was supported by fellowships from the National Endowment for the Humanities and the School for Advanced Research in Santa Fe, New Mexico. The book includes five historical case studies of largely-forgotten communities: the Mexicans and Mexican Americans who, since 1910, have arrived into landscapes traditionally understood to be black and white in Louisiana, Mississippi, Arkansas, Georgia, and North Carolina. From 2000 to 2002 she worked in the administration of Mexican president Vicente Fox as a speechwriter and researcher for the cabinet-level Office of the President for Mexicans Living Abroad. She has also worked as a translator, paralegal, project manager, and policy researcher at immigration-related agencies in New Haven and Los Angeles.

CALVIN WHITE is an associate professor in the History Department at the University of Arkansas, Fayetteville. His book *The Rise to Respectability: Race, Religion, and the Church of God in Christ* reflects his research interests on the extent to which class, respectability, and the efforts of racial uplift intersected in the development of African Americans' religious traditions and racial identity after emancipation in the Arkansas and Mississippi Deltas. He is the recipient of several national fellowships and has served as a Gilder-Lehrman Fellow at the Schomburg Center for Research in Black Culture in New York.

INDEX

A

Abner, David, Jr., 107
Acosta, Andrés, 159–60
Act 511 (1953), 76
Acts 17:26, 119
Adamson, Norman, 121
Adkins, A. D., 108
African American Episcopal Church, 63
African Methodist Episcopal Church, 21, 31, 35, 42, 67
Agricultural Adjustment Act (AAA), 91
Agricultural Council of Arkansas, 128
agricultural economics, 23–26, 154
Agricultural Extension Service (AES), xiv, 85–95
agricultural protections, 132–34
agricultural schools on wheels, 88–89
Alabama: law enforcement training programs, 150; migration patterns, 34, 36; political terrorism, 38
alcohol purchases, 11–12
Aldridge, Isaac, 44
Aldridge, Thomas, 12
Allen, Judge, 9
Allen, Mr., 135
Alpine, Georgia, 89
Amador, Nick C., 134
American Baptist Publication Society, 104
American Community Survey, 155
American Legion, 74
American Missionary Association, 20
American Party, 22
American Revolution, 103, 104
Amy, Arkansas, 93
Anderson, Charles, 17
Anderson, Mr., 13
Andrews, Reverend, 40
Anthony (slave), 7

anti-black political terrorism, 37–38, 43–44. *See also* racial violence
anti-immigrant campaigns: Mexican workers, xv–xvi, 125–26, 134–38, 142, 151; undocumented immigrants, xvi, 150, 151; Vietnamese immigrants, 144–45
anti-Republican violence, 37, 38
anti-Semitism, 65
Arizona, 150, 151
Arkadelphia, Arkansas, 20, 24
Arkansas Agricultural, Mechanical, and Normal College (Arkansas AM & N), 86, 89, 91, 94
Arkansas Baptist College, 101, 102, 103, 109
Arkansas Baptist State Convention (ABC), xiv, 100, 101, 102, 103
Arkansas Baptist Vanguard, The, 103
Arkansas Council of Home Demonstration Clubs, 89, 94, 95
Arkansas Delta: black population, 99; Bracero Program, xv–xvi, 125–39; racial violence, 50–59; sundown towns, 50–56. *See also* Helena, Arkansas
Arkansas Democrat, 72
Arkansas Department of Education, 80
Arkansas Extension Homemakers Council, 95
Arkansas Gazette: cotton prices, 25; murder reports, 13; newspaper editorials, 21, 23, 79; processing and relocation centers, 143; racial violence reports, 51, 52–53, 54, 55, 61; racist rhetoric, 27–28; William Woodruff, 21, 23, 27–28
Arkansas Mansion, 42

Arkansas Martin Luther King Jr. Commission Nonviolence Youth Summit, 68, 70
Arkansas National Guard, xi
Arkansas Negro Boys Industrial School, xiii–xiv, 71–81
Arkansas Negro State Business League, 105–6
Arkansas Red Cross emergency relief camps, 88
Arkansas River Valley, 39, 40
Arkansas Social Work Conference (1949), 80
Arkansas State Board of Education, 80
Arkansas State Police, 147–48, 150
Arkansas State Press, 74, 76
Arkansas State University (ASU), 154, 158, 160
Arkansas Statute Annotated § 5-401, 142
Arkansas Taxpayer and Citizen Protection Act (2005), 142, 150
Arnold, Malissa, 14
arsonists, 52, 55–56
Arthur, Chester A., 29
Ashley County, Arkansas, 14, 15
Ashmore, Harry, 79
Asian population, xvi, 141, 144–45
Associated Press, 68
Atlanta, Georgia, 34
Atlanta University, 105
autonomy, 11–12, 38–39, 43
Aviles, Alejandro, 155

B

Back Door Policy, 141, 146
Ballard, Rice C., 4, 5, 7, 10–11
Banished: American Ethnic Cleansings (documentary film), 68
Banks, Mary M., 90
Banks, Richard, 62, 63
Bannister (slave), 5
Baptist congregations, xiv, 97, 99–103
Baptist, Edward, 3
Baptist publishing houses, 104–5
bargaining practices, 160
Barling, Arkansas, 142, 144, 147
Barnett, Josephine, 18
Barnhill, A. H., 130, 134

Basin Spring, 63
Bates, Daisy, 74
Bates, L. C., 74, 76
Batesville, Arkansas, 6
Baumann, M. C., 127
Baxter County, Arkansas, 49
Bay, Arkansas, 130
Bayou Bartholomew, 14
Beck, Earl, Jr., 133
Belcher, Andrew, 35
Belgian Congo, 107
Benford, Bob, 26
Benton County, Arkansas, 12, 13, 150
Benton County Sheriff's Office, 150
Benton, Maggie Walker, 10
Berlin, Ira, 3
"Better Rural Living" campaign, 92
Bible Banner, 114, 115
bilingual services, 157–62
billboard messages, 69–70
Bill (slave), 10
Birmingham, Alabama, 121
black Baptist congregations, xiv, 97, 99–103
black clergymen, 97–105, 111–22
black home demonstration agents and clubs, xiv, 85–95
blacklisting, 131–32, 133, 135, 136–37, 139
black-owned businesses, 105–6
black-owned publishing houses, 104–5
Black River, 53
Black Rock, Arkansas, 51, 55, 56, 57
black southern migration, 31–45, 87, 99
black suffrage, 27
black veterans, 107–8
black-white relationships, 21–30, 112–22. *See also* race relations; racial violence; racism
Blake, Henry, 8
Blytheville, Arkansas, 113
boll weevils, 87
Bolton, S. Charles, 6
Bonds, A. B., 80
bondspeople. *See* slave experience
Bonslagel, Connie J., 89
Bookman, Arkansas, 43
Boone County, Arkansas, 49, 66, 69
Boone, Fannie Mae, 89, 91

Boozman, John, 150
Border Patrol, 148
Boston, Massachusetts, 105
Boston University, 156
Bowman, Melany, xvi
Bowser Christian Institute, 118
Bowser, George Phillip, 112–13, 116, 118
Boyd, Richard, 105
Boys' Industrial School at Pine Bluff, 73–74, 78
Bracero Program, xv–xvi, 125–39, 155
Branch Normal School, 72
Bratton, U. S., 108
Braya Carlos, Juán, 130
Brewer, Jan, 151
Briggs, J. B., 54
Brinkley, Arkansas, 55, 101, 137
Brinkley Stave and Heading Company, 55
Brooks-Baxter War (1874), 29, 37
Brown, Betty, 12
Brown, John W., 10
Brown, L. Dean, 143
Brown v. Board of Education of Topeka, Kansas (1954), 117–18, 126
Brunson, R. A., 11
Bryant's Cafe, 136
Buffalo Island, Arkansas, 53, 57
Buffalo Island Drainage District No. 16, 53
Bulkley, Vincent Henry, 40, 41
Bumpers, Dale, 145
Bureau of Refugees, Freedmen, and Abandoned Lands, 20. *See also* Freedmen's Bureau
Burns, Richard, 54
Bush, George W., 142, 150
Business Expo, 162
Bussey, Charles, 75–76

C

Calhoun, Johnnie, 144–45
California: refugee centers, 143; states' rights ideology, 151
Camden, Arkansas, 20, 93
Campbell, Jabez P., 21
Camp Pendleton, California, 143
Camp Pike, Arkansas, 108
canning and food preservation, 87
Cannon, Charles, 119–20
Cano, Angel, 132, 133, 134, 135, 136
Cardiology Associates, 163
Carey, Anthony Gene, 3
Carroll County, Arkansas, 65
Carter, Jimmy, 147, 148
Carver, George Washington, 88
Case, George, 6
Castro, Fidel, 141, 146
Catholic Church, 117, 139
Caver, Robert, 98
Cecil, J. S., 133
Centennial Baptist Church, xiv, 97, 99–100
Center for Investigative Reporting, 68
Central High School (Little Rock), xi, 94, 126, 142
Chamber of Commerce Business Expo, 162
Chambers, Erle, 72
charismatic religious liturgy, 99, 101, 102, 103
Charles (slave), 12
Cherry, Francis Adams, 75, 76
Chicago, Illinois, 54, 107, 130–31, 156
Chicago Tribune, 37
chickens, 149
Chicot County, Arkansas, 4, 7, 10, 13, 42, 92
childcare, 9
child slave labor, 8–9
Christenson, Jeff, 66
Christian Echo, 112, 113, 116–17, 118, 119, 120–21
Christian education, 112–13, 118–19
Christian Methodist Episcopal Church, 111
Christian Recorder, 38, 42
Christmas, Lugenia Bell, 88
Churches of Christ, 111–14, 116–22
Churches of God in Christ, 103
City of Springdale Police Department, 151
Civil Rights Act (1964), 94–95, 138
civil rights inactivism, xiv–xv, 111–22
civil rights movement, 112, 117–22
Civil War, 103, 104

Clark County, Arkansas, 25
Clark, Steve, 142, 148
Clay County, Arkansas, 50, 57
Clayton, Powell, 28–29
clergymen, 97–105, 111–22
Cline, Carolyn, 67
Clinton, Bill, 142, 147–48
Clinton School of Public Service, University of Arkansas, 68
Clover Bend, Arkansas, 51
Cockrill plantation, 9
Coggs, Tandy W., 72–73
Cohen, William, 38
Coker, Joyce, 69
cold-water springs, 63
Collier, John, 137–38
Collins, John M., 35–36, 42
Commercial Appeal, 91
commodity purchases, 11–12
communication networks, 33
community autonomy, 38–39, 43
Compton, T. D., 51
Congress Hotel, 63
Congressional Immigration Reform Caucus, 150
Congressional Research Service, 158
conservers, 101
Consul of Mexico, 129, 131–33, 134, 135, 136, 137
Convention of Colored Citizens, 21, 29
"Cooking for Freedom" talk, 91
Coosa County, Alabama, 5
Cornelius, Elihu, 16
Cornish, Larry J., 145
Costar, Phillip, 6–7
Cotter, Arkansas, 49
cotton agriculture: boll weevils, 87; crop prices, 8, 23–25, 44; forced migrations, 4; general tasks, 8; Jonesboro area, 154; mass migrations, 34, 40; Mexican workers, 125–30, 133, 134, 137, 155; picking time, 10; race relations, 23–25; slave economy, 8, 10–11, 16
Cotton, George H., 65
Cotton, Hugh, 64–65
court cases, 14–15
Craighead County, Arkansas, 155

Crawford County, Arkansas, 12, 13
Crisis, 104
Crittenden County, Arkansas, 41, 91–92
Crooked Creek, 61, 66
Cross County, Arkansas, 53
Cross, John, 63–64
Crowley's Ridge, Arkansas, 53
Cuban-Haitian Task Force (CHTF), 146, 148
Cuban immigrants, xvi, 141–42, 146–49
cultural heritage, 158, 160–62
Curtis, Samuel, 17

D

Dallas Citizen, 38
Dallas County, Arkansas, 6, 9, 10
Daniel, Elizabeth, 14
Daniel, Harriet, 9
Daniel, James, 15
Daniel, Mary, 14
Daniel v. Guy, 14–15
Daniel, William, 14, 15
Davis, Maude B., 92
Davy, Earl, 76
debt, 5, 26
de jure segregation, 138
DeLay, Gunner, 149–50
Delgado, Melvin, 156
Democratic Party: 1868 presidential election, 23, 27, 28; anti-black rhetoric, 28, 29–30; Brooks-Baxter War (1874), 29, 37; political terrorism, 43–44
denominationalism, 102–3, 116–17
Department of Defense, 145
Dermott, Arkansas, 92
Desha County, Arkansas, 6
Detroit, Michigan, 71
DeValls Bluff, Arkansas, 18
Diebold, L. A. "Buddy", Jr., 53–54
Disciples of Christ, 111
discrimination: black soldiers, 18; home demonstration agents, 93–95; Mexican workers, xv, 125–26, 131–32, 134–38; religious groups, 118–22. *See also* segregation; white supremacy
diseases, 40
disfranchisement, xii, 44

disobedience, 13
District of Columbia, 107
diversion of funds controversy, 80–81
domestic slave trade, 4
domestic work, 9
Donaghey, George Washington, 55, 64
Dortch, Charles Green, 6
double consciousness, 122
Driver, W. J., 56
DuBois, W. E. B., 100, 104, 122
Dunn, James H., 14
dynamiters, 53

E

Eaglin Air Force Base, Florida, 143
economic opportunities: freedmen, vii, 20, 32, 39, 41; Hispanic population, xvi–xvii, 153–64
economic self-sufficiency, xii, 18–21, 24, 88, 90, 91, 106
Eddington, Lena H., 91
Edgefield County, South Carolina, 36
educational opportunities: freedmen, 20, 22–23, 26, 28–29, 98; Jonesboro area, 154, 156; racial uplift, 100–101; religious schools, 112–13, 118–19
Edwards, Thomas, 14
Eisenhower, Dwight D., xi
Elaine, Arkansas, 108–9
elderly slaves, 9
El Dorado, Arkansas, 91, 94
Eliza (slave), 14
Elmwood, Arkansas, 10
El Salvador, 153
emancipation process, 17–18. *See also* freedmen
emigration patterns, 31–45, 87, 99
emigration societies, 37, 43
emotional religious liturgy, 99, 101, 102, 103
Encyclopedia of Religion in the South, 79
"Enemies of Righteousness" essay, 119
Engel, K. August, 72
England, Arkansas, 127
enslaved people. *See* slave experience
environmental landscape, 39–40
equal rights and protection, 21, 29, 108
ethnic cleansing, 66

Eureka Springs, Arkansas, 62–64, 65
evangelism, 112–18, 121–22
exodus movements, 31–45, 87, 99
extension services, xiv, 85–95

F

Fancher, Alice Sewell, 62, 63
Fancher, Mattie Rollan, 62, 63
Fargo Agricultural School, 90
farm agent system, 86–93
farm tenancy, 24–26
Faubus, Orval E., xi, 71, 77, 81
Faulkner County, Arkansas, 92
Fayetteville, Arkansas, 11, 13, 65
federal troops, xi
fieldwork, 8–10, 19, 24–26
financial difficulties, 5
Finley, Molly, 4, 8
fire tragedy, xiii–xiv, 71–81
Firm Foundation, 117
First Baptist Church Hispanic Ministries Outreach, 153
First Colored Baptist Mission Church, 98
Fishback, William Meade, 51
fishing practices, 12
Flan (slave), 6
floods, 88
Flores, Luis, 153, 155, 159
Florida: black southern migration, 32, 38; Cuban immigrants, 146; law enforcement training programs, 150; racial violence, 107; refugee centers, 143
Flowers, Monroe, 56
Food for Freedom program, 91
food preservation and production, 87–88, 90–91, 92
forced migrations, 4–5
Ford, Gerald, 143, 144
Forrest City, Arkansas, 35, 52, 91, 94
Fort Chaffee, Arkansas, xvi, 141–48, 151
Fort Smith, Arkansas, xvi, 13, 20, 62, 118, 142, 144, 150
Fortune, T. Thomas, 32
Fourth Avenue (Fort Chaffee), 147
Franklin County, Arkansas, 12
freedmen: economic self-sufficiency, xii,

18–21, 24; educational opportunities, 20, 22–23, 26, 28–29, 98; emancipation process, 17–18; fieldwork, 19, 24–26; ill treatment by whites, 18–19, 25–26; migration patterns, 31–45; military employment, 18; political activism, 21, 29, 31–32, 36–37, 41. *See also* land ownership
Freedmen's Bureau, 20, 24–27, 32, 33–34
freedom struggle, 17–18
Freeze, Jack, 144
Frito-Lay, 154
Froelich, Jacqueline, xiii
Fulbright, J. William, 134
F. W. Tucker and Company, 51

G

Gaines, Lester, 72, 76, 77
Gallego, Agustín, 136
Gallegos, Manuel, 129
Ganier, E. J., 130
García, Joe, 128
Garland, Augustus, 37
Gathings, E. C., 132, 133, 134
Gaxiola, Rubén, 125, 126, 134
gay men and women, 146
Georgia: black southern migration, 42; migration patterns, 32, 33–35, 37, 38; political terrorism, 38
Georgia Emigration Association, 43
Gibbs, Mifflin Wistar, 29, 42–43
Golden Grotto, 157
Gómez, Gina, 162
Gordillo, Ignacio Paz, 130
Gospel Advocate, 117
Gracios Mora, Eduardo, 130
Grant, Isaac, 36
grapevine communication networks, 33
Gray, W. H., 21
Great Depression, 63, 74, 88, 90
Greater Jonesboro Chamber of Commerce, 162–63
Great Passion Play, 65
Greene County, Arkansas, 12, 51–52
Greenwood, Arkansas, 144
Greenwood District (Tulsa, Oklahoma), 62

Grey, William H., 34
Guerrero, Perla M., xvi
Guy, Abby, 14–15
Guy, John, 14

H

Hacket, Nelson, 6
Hahn, Steven, 38
Hallimore, Mike, 65, 66, 68
Hamilton, Cassa L., 89
Hammerschmidt, John Paul, 143–44, 145
Hampton Institute (Virginia), 72, 100
Haraway, C. C., 88–89
Hardin, C. E., 128
Harding College, 121
Harding Spring, 63
hard labor, 8–11
Hardridge, Mary Jane, 6
Harrisburg, Arkansas, 125
Harrison, Arkansas, xiii, 61–62, 64–70
Harrison Chamber of Commerce, 67
Harrison Community Task Force on Race Relations, xiii, 66, 67–70
Harrison Daily Times, 61, 65, 66, 67, 68
Harwick, John A., 6
Healing Fountain, The (Kalklosch), 63
healthcare programs, 93–94
Heard, Elveria, 93
Helena, Arkansas: black population, 20, 99, 105; Elias Camp Morris, xiv, 97, 99; freedmen, 17; Mexican workers, 139; newspaper editorials, 22; race relations, 67, 139; racial violence, 108; slave experience, 7
Hempstead County, Arkansas, 11, 14
Hickory Ridge, Arkansas, 53, 56, 57
Highway 22, 147, 148
Highway 59, 144
Hispanic Celebration, 158, 162
Hispanic Community Services, Incorporated, 158, 160, 162
Hispanic-owned and -operated businesses, xvi, 153–54, 156–64
Hispanic population: anti-immigrant campaigns, xv–xvi, 125–26, 134–38, 142, 150, 151; Bracero Program, xv–xvi, 125–39, 155; Cuban immigrants, xvi, 141–42, 146–49; cultural

heritage, 158, 160–62; economic opportunities, xvi–xvii, 153–64; illegal aliens, xvi, 131, 148–50; in-migrations, 149; international money transfer services, xvi, 158–59; Jonesboro area, 153–63; outreach services, 162–63; poverty levels, 155. *See also* Mexican Americans
Hispanic Relations Task Force, 149
Hoboken, Arkansas, 55
Hogan, Richard Nathaniel, xv, 111–22
Holcomb, George, 65
Holland Cafe, 136
Holland, S. H., 42
Holloway family, 5
Holmes, Christian R., 148
Holt, Jim, 142, 150
home demonstration agents and clubs, xiv, 85–95
homeownership, 36, 149
homesteads, 36, 42–43
Hoop Spur, Arkansas, 108
Hope, John, 105
Hotel Marion, 80
Hot Spring County, Arkansas, 5
Hot Springs, Arkansas, 95, 144
hourly wages, 133
House Bill 1012, 150
housework, 9
Howard, Clara M., 92
Howard, O. O., 32
Hudgens, Molly, 9
Hudson, Jimmy, vii
Hughes, Richard, 117
Hughes, Simon P., 51
Humphries, John, 5
hunting practices, 12, 40
Hutchinson, Jeremy, 150
Hutchinson, Timothy, 150

I

illegal aliens, xvi, 131, 148–50
illnesses, 40
Immanuel, Arkansas, 43
immigrant labor, xv–xvi, 125–39, 155
Immigration Reform and Control Act (1986), 149
Independence County, Arkansas, 5, 6

Independent Lens series (PBS), 68
Indianapolis Freeman, 31
Indian Territory, 6
inferiority, black, 21–23, 26–30, 102
in-migrations, 31–45, 149
Interagency Task Force for Indochinese Refugees (ITFIR), 143
International Magnet School (Jonesboro), 154
international money transfer services, xvi, 158–59
interstate migration, 44–45. *See also* black southern migration

J

Jackson, Mississippi, 94, 121
Jacksonport, Arkansas, 26
Jalisco Guadalajara, Mexico, 156
Jameson, Hannah, 9
Jarrett, Corrie J., 92
Jefferson County, Arkansas, 4, 9, 55
Jenifer, John, 36
Jenny Lind, Arkansas, 146
Jim Crow laws, xii, xv, 44, 86, 99, 106, 115, 137–39
Johnson, D. A., 108
Johnson, James Weldon, 107
Jones, Baker, 4
Jonesboro, Arkansas, xvi, 54, 113, 153–63
Jonesboro Evening Sun, 55
Jonesboro School District, 154
Jonesboro Sun, 154
Jones-Branch, Cherisse, xiv
Jones, Charles Price, 102–3
Jones, Daniel W., 55
Jones, Kelly Houston, xi
Joplin, Missouri, 69
Juan Crown discrimination, xv
juvenile detention centers. *See* Arkansas Negro Boys Industrial School

K

Kalklosch, L. J., 63
Kansas, 32, 37–38, 39
Kansas Industrial and Educational Institute, 89
Kaye, Anthony, 7
Keeble, Marshall, 114, 115

Keiden, Greg, 163
Kelly, Wayne, 65–66
Kenefick, P. M., 132
Kennedy, Claude, 137, 138
Kennedy, John F., 117
Key, Barclay, xv
Kingdom Identity Ministries, 65
King, Martin Luther, Jr., 70
Kissinger, Henry, 144
Kit Karson and Band, 54
Knights Party U.S.A., 65
Knott Hole Cafe, 136
KUAF Public Radio, 65
Ku Klux Klan, 29, 50, 64, 65, 68

L

labor contracts, 24, 26, 125–30, 132, 134–37
labor shortages, xv, 24, 32, 41–42
Lafayette County, Arkansas, 14
Lake Village, Arkansas, 92, 94
Lam Van Thatch, 144
Lancaster, Guy, xiii
Landa, Jose Luís, 129
land-clearing work, 8
landowner behavior, 24–26
land ownership: background information, xii; benefits, 43; black southern migration, 32, 34, 36, 39, 42–44; economic self-sufficiency, 20–21, 24; political activism, 29; racial violence, xiii; tenant farming, 55
Landres, Byron, 132
Langston University, 86
Latino population: anti-immigrant campaigns, xv–xvi, 125–26, 134–38, 142, 150, 151; Bracero Program, xv–xvi, 125–39, 155; Cuban immigrants, xvi, 141–42, 146–49; cultural heritage, 158, 160–62; economic opportunities, xvi–xvii, 153–64; illegal aliens, xvi, 131, 148–50; in-migrations, 149; international money transfer services, xvi, 158–59; Jonesboro area, 153–63; outreach services, 162–63; poverty levels, 155. *See also* Mexican Americans

law enforcement agencies, 147–48, 150–51
Lawrence County, Arkansas, 7, 51, 54
Lawrence County Democrat, 51
League of United Latin American Citizens (LULAC), 155
leased plantations, 19
Lee County Home Demonstration Council, 90
Lepanto, Arkansas, 53, 137
Lever, Asbury F., 85
Lewisville, Arkansas, 25, 26
Liberia, 32, 37–38, 39
Liberia City, Arkansas, 43
Liberia Exodus Arkansas Colony, 37
Lilly, O. R., 108
Lindsay, John A., 7
Lipsey, Bernard, 137
Lithia (slave), 10
Little River, 53
Little Rock and Choctaw railroad, 43
Little Rock, Arkansas: black population, 18, 20; Democratic Party convention, 27; home demonstration agents, 91; market activities, 11; Ministers' Institute, 101; political activism, 21, 29; school desegregation, xi, 94, 126, 142; social work conference, 80
Little Rock Nine, xi, xiv, 94
"Live-at-Home" program, 91–92
livestock, 40
living conditions, 127, 129–31, 132, 134
Locke, Harrison, 137
Loewen, James, 49
long-distance flight, 6
Lonoke, Arkansas, 55
Lonoke County, Arkansas, 55
López, Linda, 159
Lorenzana, Alejandro, 161, 162–63
Los Arcos, 156
Louisiana, 38, 44
Lovell, Jimmie, 115, 116
loyalty, 103
Loza, Juan, 139
Luxora, Arkansas, 135
Lyford, Robert, 147

lynchings, xiii, 58–59, 62, 109
Lyric Theater, 70

M

Macon, Georgia, 34
Macon Telegraph, 32
Madera, Luis, 156, 159, 161–62
Magness, Morgan, 5
Manley, D. J., 44–45
marauders, 52
Marianna, Arkansas, 100, 129, 137
Mariel, Cuba, 141, 146
Marion, Arkansas, 127
Marked Tree, Arkansas, 54, 125, 134–37
Marked Tree City Council, 136
Marked Tree Tribune, 136
Martha (slave), 7
Martin Luther King Jr. Commission Nonviolence Youth Summit, 68, 70
Mary (slave), 9, 13
Mason, Charles Harrison, 102–3
materialism, 36
Matkin-Rawn, Story, xii
Matsukis, Pat, 64
McClellan, John L., 143
McCuistion, Ed, 74–75, 80–81
McCutchen, Joe, 142, 150
McElvoy, Larry, 157
McKinley, William, 107
McKnight, E. D., 128, 133
McMath, Sidney Sanders, 74, 75, 80
Memphis Appeal, 34
Memphis, Tennessee, 4, 7, 91, 127, 131, 134
Menifee, Arkansas, 43
Methvin, Patty, 67, 68
Mexican Americans: anti-immigrant campaigns, xv–xvi, 125–26, 134–38, 142, 151; Bracero Program, xv–xvi, 125–39, 155; international money transfer services, xvi, 158–59; Jonesboro area, 156; population growth, 141
Mexican Embassy, 133
Mexican Foreign Service, 126
Mexican government involvement, 131–33, 138–39

Mexican Independence Day, 129
miasmas, 40
Mid-South Latino Magazine, 161
migration conventions, 34–35, 37
migration patterns, xii, 4–7, 31–45, 87, 99
Military Police, 146–47
Miller, Bernadine, 64
Miller County, Arkansas, 37
Miller Lumber Company, 129–30
Milton, Luville, 71
minimum wages, xvi, 133, 139
Ministers' Institute, 101
Mississippi: black southern migration, 33, 38, 43; home demonstration agents, 91
Mississippi County, Arkansas, 56
Mississippi Delta: black southern migration, 31, 35; Mexican workers, 130, 132
Mississippi flood (1927), 88
Missouri and North Arkansas Railroad, 61
Moberg, Vilhelm, 58
mob violence, 49, 61–62, 65–66, 107–9
Monette, Arkansas, 128
Moneyhon, Carl H., xii
money transfers, xvi, 158–59
Monroe County, Arkansas, 9, 13, 55, 90
Moore, Clarence B., 53
Moore, Emma, 5
Morgan, Gordon, 77
Morrilton, Arkansas, vii
Morris, Elias Camp, xiv–xv, 97–109
Morris, James and Cora, 97–98
mosquitoes, 40
Moss, James, 14
Mourning (slave), 14
Movable Demonstration Schools for Negro Farm Folks, 88–89
Mt. Zion Missionary Baptist Church, 101
Multicultural Dinner and Dance, 158, 162
murders, 13–14
Murray County, Georgia, 97
Muskogee, Oklahoma, 62, 64, 69

N

Nashville Normal Theological Institute, 98, 100
Nashville, Tennessee, 98–99, 105, 112, 113
National Baptist Convention (NBC), xiv, 103–5, 106, 111
National Baptist Publishing House, 105, 109
national black publishing houses, 104–5
National Extension Homemakers Council, 95
National Home Demonstration Agents' Association (NHDAA), 94, 95
National Negro Business League, 105
National Republican Convention, 107
negative reputation of Arkansas, 35–36
Negro Boys Industrial School, xiii–xiv, 71–81
Negro National Home Demonstration Agents Association (NNHDAA), 94, 95
Negro Slavery in Arkansas (Taylor), 3
Negro Spring, 63
Negro supremacy, 27–28
Negro, The (pamphlet), 28
Negro Uprising, 108
Neiman Marcus, 160
Nestlé, 154
Nettleton School District, 154
New Deal programs, 91, 132–33
New England Baptists, 103
New Hearts Church, 66
New Orleans, Louisiana, 4, 5, 7, 129
newspaper editorials, 22–23, 27, 31–32, 38–39, 41–42, 79
New York Age, 31, 32
New York Times, 38–39, 51, 108
Nice-Pak, 154
nightriding, 49–50, 53, 56
Nix, Jerry, 33
non-Hispanic businesses, 157–58, 161
non-Hispanic customers, 159–60
Nordex, 154
North Arkansas Community College, 68
North Carolina, 34, 43, 44
North Carolina Emigration Association, 43
northeast Arkansas, xvi
Nuss, Jeannie, 68
nutritional improvement, 91, 94
Nutt farm, 12

O

O'Donnell Bend, Arkansas, 56
offensive billboards, 69–70
Oklahoma: black southern migration, 31, 32, 44; racial violence, 62; school desegregation, 117
Oklahoma City, Oklahoma, 113–14
Omey, Mr., 12
Oregon, 133
Ortiz Lutieros, Jesús, 136
Osceola, Arkansas, 56, 57, 58, 59, 90, 135
Ouachita County Rural Development Advisory Board, 93
Ouachita Mountains, 40, 49
out-migration, 31–45, 87, 99
Overton, Claude, 127
Ozark Mountains, 40, 49, 56, 58. *See also* Harrison, Arkansas

P

Painter, Nell Irvin, 38
Panadería El Buen Gusto (The Good Taste Bakery), 159
Pantograph, 23
Paragould, Arkansas, 49, 51–53, 56, 57, 58
Paragould Cotton Compress, 52
Parkin, Arkansas, 138
Parkin Farmers' Association, 133
patriotism, 103–4
Payless Rent-to-Own Cars, 157
Payless Rent-to-Own Furniture and Appliances, 157
Payne, Harriet McFarlin, 9
PBS, 68
Pearson, Fred, 157
penal work farms. *See* Arkansas Negro Boys Industrial School
Pentagon, 143
Perrin, Harold, 154, 158
Peters, Frazier, 71
Peter (slave), 16
Pew Hispanic Center, 155
Phillips County, Arkansas: background

information, 99; Elias Camp Morris, 100, 106; land-clearing work, 8; Mexican workers, 129; political activism, 21; racial violence, 108. *See also* Helena, Arkansas
Phillips, Helen, 99
Phillips, Sylvanus, 99
Phoenix Cotton Oil Company, 55
phone cards, xvi, 159
picking time, 10
Pike, Albert, 22
Pilgrim's Chapel, 63
Pine Bluff, Arkansas: Arkansas Agricultural, Mechanical, and Normal College (Arkansas AM & N), 86, 89, 91, 94; black education, 27; black population, 20, 57; home demonstration agents, 88, 90; Mexican workers, 127; Negro Boys Industrial School, xiii–xiv, 71–81; racial violence, 55
plantation agriculture, 8, 9–11, 19, 24–26, 87, 127
Poinsett County, Arkansas, 53, 54, 57, 91, 93
Poinsett Lumber and Manufacturing Company, 54
political activism, 21, 29, 31–32, 36–37, 41, 94, 106–7
political conditions, 40–41, 78–79. *See also* Arkansas Negro Boys Industrial School
political terrorism, 37–38, 43–44
Polly (slave), 14
Pond, William, 5
poor living conditions, 127
Post, 154
post-Reconstruction era, xii
poultry industry, 149
Powell, Leo, 133–34
Powell, William, 12
Powhattan, Arkansas, 7
preachers, 65–66, 97–105, 111–22. *See also* black clergymen
processing and relocation centers, 141–48, 151
property ownership. *See* land ownership
Proposition 200 (Arizona), 150, 151

Protect Arkansas Now, 142, 150
Pryor, David H., 141, 144, 145
public lands, 43
publishing houses, 104–5
Pulaski County, Arkansas, 11–12, 73, 77
Pulaski County Grand Jury, 77–78
Pulaski County State Fair, 88

Q
Quakers, 20

R
race reconciliation task force, 66–70
race relations: Eureka Springs, Arkansas, 63–64; farm tenancy, 24–25; Harrison, Arkansas, xiii, 65–70; home demonstration agents, 91; Mexican workers, 134–39; religious affiliations, 118–22; Sid McMath, 74; Winthrop Rockefeller, vii. *See also* Hispanic population
race riots, 49, 61–62, 65–66, 107–9
racial cleansing, 50–58, 66
racial segregation. *See* segregation
racial status, 14–15
racial uplift, 92, 97, 100–103, 105–6, 107, 109
racial violence: Arkansas Delta, 50–59; background information, xiii; black southern migration, 35, 37–38, 41, 43–44; economic factors, 23; Harrison, xiii, 61–62, 64–66; land ownership, xiii; Oklahoma, 62; Pine Bluff, 55, 57; Red Summer of 1919, 107–9; state government, 29; vigilantism, xiii, 49–59. *See also* Arkansas Negro Boys Industrial School
racism: anti-immigrant campaigns, 142, 144–45, 150, 151; background information, xii, xiii–xiv; black inferiority, 21–23, 26–30, 102; Bracero Program, 125–39; historical context, 79–80; racial ideas, 17, 21–23, 26–30; religious values, 79; states' rights ideology, 142–43, 150–51; Union forces, 18
Ragsdale, Layne, 67–68

railroad development, 42–43, 50, 56, 61
Ramírez López, Angel, 130
rape, 108–9
Rawlings, John, 74–75
Ray, Gloria, xiv, 94
Ray, Harvey C., xiv, 86–87, 94
Ray, Julia Miller, 94
Ray, Mary McCrary, xiv, 86–87
Reconstruction, 33, 98, 105
Red Cross, 88
Red Summer of 1919, 107–9
refined religious liturgy, 98–99, 100, 101
reform schools. *See* Arkansas Negro Boys Industrial School
refugee centers, 141–48, 151
religious affiliations, 111–22.
    See also Baptist congregations
religious publishing houses, 104–5
religious schools, 112–13, 118–19
Republican Party, 28–29, 34, 37, 106–7
retail services, 156–58
revival meetings, 113–15
Reynolds, Bob, 66
rice cultivation, 154
Riceland Foods, 154
Richards, Eliza, 62
Richardson, Cora, 62
Richmond, Virginia, 6
Ridge, Sarah, 12
Ritter, E., 134–35, 136
Robb, Thom, 65, 68
Rockefeller, Winthrop Paul, vii
Rock Garden restaurant, 135
Rogers, Arkansas, 149–50
Rogers, John Henry, 62
Rogers, Mark, 56
Rogers Police Department, 150
Roger Williams University, 98, 100
Roosevelt, Theodore, 107
Rose, Nancy, 13
Rose, William, 9, 13
Rosewood, Florida, 107
Ruiz, Vicky, 143
runaway slaves, 6–7
rural black communities, 85–95
rural uplift program, 88, 90, 92, 95

S

Sam (Holloway family slave), 5
Sam (Lindsay family slave), 7
Sampier, John, 149
San Antonio Light, 64
sanctification doctrine, 101–2
Santiago, Miguel, 132
Sauceda, Jacinto, 131
school desegregation, xi, xiv, 94, 117–19, 126, 142
School of Social Work, Boston University, 156
Scott, C. E., 127
Scribners, 39
Scull family, 6
Searcy, Arkansas, 5
second middle passage, 4, 6
segregation: Charles Cannon, 119–20; Christian colleges, 116, 118–19; Democratic Party, 44; Elias Camp Morris, 100, 106; Eureka Springs, Arkansas, 63; Foy Wallace, 114–15; Harrison, Arkansas, 61; home demonstration agents, xiv, 85, 86, 94, 95; laws and customs, 78; Mexican workers, 125–26; religious affiliations, 100, 117–22; Richard Nathaniel Hogan, 112, 116; school desegregation, xi, 94, 117–19, 126, 142; white supremacy, 78, 79
self-determination, 104, 106
self-employment opportunities, 156–57, 159–64
separate-but-equal practice, 138
sexual assaults, 108–9
sharecropping, 24–26, 55, 99, 106, 108, 109
Shivers, Clothilde M., 93–94
shotgun houses, 54
Silver Point, Tennessee, 112
Simpson, Giles, 56
sin-free living, 101–2
Singer Manufacturing Company, 54
Singleton, Benjamin (Pap), 99
Sisson, James, 39
slave experience: autonomous conditions, 11–12; court cases, 14–15; disobedience, 13–14; emancipation

process, 17–18; freedom efforts,
14; market activities, 11–12;
master-slave interactions, 3–16;
migration and movement patterns,
4–7; research background, 3;
resistance efforts, xi–xii, 10–11;
social situations, 15; weapons, 12;
work routines and expectations,
8–11
slave patrols, 15
Smith, Alecta Caledonia Melvina
(Aunt Vine), 69
Smith, Gerald L. K., 65
Smith, Hoke, 85
Smith, J. L., 13
Smith-Lever Act (1914), 85–86
social conditions, 40–41, 78–79. *See also*
Arkansas Negro Boys Industrial
School
social discrimination. *See* discrimination
social equality, 108, 115–16, 126
social networks, 156–57, 162
social separatism, 38–39
Social Work Conference (1949), 80
Solís Aguilera, Gabino, 127, 128
Sosa, José Dionisio, 130
Soto Amaya, Pablo, 128
South Carolina: black southern
migration, 32, 34, 36, 42;
political terrorism, 38
Southern Homestead Act (1866), 36
southern interstate migration, 44–45.
See also black southern migration
Southern Tenant Farmer's Union,
131, 132
Southwestern Christian Advocate, 41
Spanish American War, 104
Spanish-speaking population. *See*
Hispanic population
Spann, J. C., 56
spiritual revival meetings, 113–15
Sprague, John W., 24
Springdale, Arkansas, 142, 150, 151
Springfield Lumber Company, 54
Springfield, Missouri, 62
Stancill Hotel, 52
Stanford, Anthony, 37
Stanton, Edwin M., 18

Starkey-Dixon Cemetery, 109
State Board of Education, 80
State Bureau of Immigration, 34
State Council of Home Demonstration
Clubs, 89, 92–93, 95
State Emigration Society, 34
State Police, 147–48, 150
states' rights ideology, 142–43, 150–51
St. Bernard's Hospital, 153
Stenson, Alabama, 98
Stenson Institute, 98
St. Francis, Arkansas, 50, 56
St. Francis County, Arkansas, 52, 88
St. Francis River, 50, 53
Stinnett, Charley, 64, 69
Stinnett, Lettie, 64
Stockley, Grif, xiii
Striffler, Steve, 149
strikes, 129–30, 147
Stubblefield, Royce, 128
subsistence farming, 40
suffrage, black, 27
sundown counties, 57
sundown towns: Arkansas Delta, 50–56;
background information, xiii, 49–50;
defining characteristics, 56–58
Swafford, Jesse, 56
Swanson, 154

T

Taylor, Anthony, 25
Taylor, Marshal, 41–42
Taylor, Orville W., 3, 7, 16
Taylor, S. S., 74
Tejanos, 127, 129, 131, 134, 136
tenant farming, 55
Tennessee: black southern migration, 36,
37; home demonstration agents, 91
Tenth Amendment (U.S. Constitution),
148
Texarkana, Arkansas, 94
Texas: black southern migration, 31, 32,
34, 43, 44; Mexican workers, 127,
131, 133; racial violence, 107; school
desegregation, 117
theological institutes, 98–99
Third Congressional District, 143–44,
150

Thomas, Lorenzo, 18
Thomas P. Ray (steamboat), 6
Toler, Lula, 88
Tollette, Arkansas, 43
Torres, Henry, 158, 160
truancy, 6–7
Trulock, James Hines, 4
Trumann, Arkansas, 54, 56, 57, 136
Tulsa, Oklahoma, 62
Turner, Henry McNeal, 8, 31–32, 33, 35, 41
Tuskegee Institute, 89, 100
Two Tone Productions, 68

U

undocumented immigrants, xvi, 131, 148–50
Unilever, 154
Union African Methodist Episcopal Church, 61, 67
Union forces, 17–19
unionization efforts, 108
Union Labor Party, 44
Unity Arts Celebration, 70
University of Arkansas at Fayetteville, 71, 86
University of Arkansas law and medical schools, 117
University of Minnesota at Minneapolis, 91
US Census, 155
US Department of Agriculture (USDA) Cooperative Extension Service, 85, 90–91
US Department of Defense, 145
US Department of Labor, 134, 135, 136
US Employment Services (USES), 133, 136
US Farm Placement Service, 135
US Immigration and Customs Enforcement training program, 150–51
US Supreme Court decisions, 117–18, 126, 138

V

vagrancy laws, 105
Valley View School District, 154
Van Buren, Arkansas, 12
Vázquez Martínez, Cristóbal, 128
veterans, black, 107–8
Vietnamese immigrants, xvi, 141, 144–45, 151
vigilantism, white, xiii, 49–55
Villarreal, Pedro, Jr., 127
Vines, C. A., 93
violence, racial: Arkansas Delta, 50–59; background information, xiii; black southern migration, 35, 37–38, 41, 43–44; economic factors, 23; Harrison, xiii, 61–62, 64–66; land ownership, xiii; Oklahoma, 62; Pine Bluff, 55, 57; Red Summer of 1919, 107–9; state government, 29; vigilantism, xiii, 49–59. *See also* Arkansas Negro Boys Industrial School
vocational training programs, 73–74, 75, 77
voting rights, 27

W

Waddle, Bill, 50
wages: black southern migration, 32, 33, 34, 35, 36; dishonest landowners, 26; labor shortages, 32, 33, 34, 41; Mexican workers, xvi, 128–35, 139; minimum wages, xvi, 133, 139; racial factors, 23; unionization efforts, 108
Wagram Plantation, 4
Walden University, 112
Walgreens, 157
Walker, William "Sonny", vii
Wallace, Alfred, 6
Wallace, Foy, 114–16
Wallace, John, 12
Walmart, 157, 160
Walnut Ridge, Arkansas, 54–55, 56, 57, 58
Walters, S. M., 34
warning notices, 51–52, 54–56
washday, 9
Washington, Booker T., 88, 92, 105
Washington County, Arkansas, 141, 151
Washington County Republican Women, 149–50

Washington County Sheriff's Office, 151
Washington, D.C., 107
weapons, 12
weather delays, 10
Weathers, Walter, 114
Weise, Julie M., xv
Western Clarion, 22
Western District Federal Court, 62
Western Tuskegee Institute, 89
Whayne, Jeannie M., 55
white boys' reform school, 73–74, 78
White, Calvin, xiv
whitecapping, 49–53, 58–59
White County, Arkansas, 33
white home demonstration agents, 89, 93, 94
whiteness, 14–15
white racism. *See* racism
white religious denominations, 111–22
White River, 53
white separatists, 65, 68
white supremacy, 78–81, 86, 126
white vigilantism, xiii, 49–55
Wike's Drive Inn, 125, 135
Wikipedia, 68
Wilborn family, 8
Wilborn, "Uncle Dock," 8

wildlife, 40
Williamson, Joel, 32
Wilson, Pete, 151
Womack, John, 149
Women's Discovery Center, 163
women, slave, 8, 9, 10
Woodruff County, Arkansas, 92
Woodruff, William, 21–22, 23, 27–28
Woodward, Jennie Lou, 88–89
word-of-mouth communication networks, 33
work-avoidance efforts, 10–11
working conditions, 127–28, 130, 132, 134
work routines and expectations, 8–11
work stoppages, 129–30
World War I, 87
World War II, 90–91
Wrightsville, Arkansas, xiii, 72–81
Wyse, Charles, 52

Y

Yellville, Arkansas, 64, 69
Young brothers, 130

Z

Zigler, Charles, 41
Zinc, Arkansas, 65